MW01491958

AN
INTRODUCTION
TO THE
U.S. CONGRESS

AN INTRODUCTION TO THE U.S. CONGRESS

CHARLES B. CUSHMAN JR.

M.E.Sharpe
Armonk, New York
London, England

Copyright © 2006 by M.E. Sharpe, Inc.

All rights reserved. No part of this book may be reproduced in any form
without written permission from the publisher, M.E. Sharpe, Inc.,
80 Business Park Drive, Armonk, New York 10504.

Library of Congress Cataloging-in-Publication Data

Cushman, Charles Bancroft.
 An introduction to the U.S. Congress / Charles Bancroft Cushman, Jr.
  p. cm.
 Includes bibliographical references and index.
 ISBN 0-7656-1506-1 (cloth : alk. paper) — ISBN 0-7656-1507-X (pbk. : alk. paper)
 1. United States. Congress. I. Title.

JK1021.C87 2006
328.73—dc22   2005025785

Printed in the United States of America

The paper used in this publication meets the minimum requirements of
American National Standard for Information Sciences
Permanence of Paper for Printed Library Materials,
ANSI Z 39.48-1984.

∞

BM (c) 10   9   8   7   6   5   4   3   2   1
BM (p) 10   9   8   7   6   5   4   3   2   1

For Tommie W. Bates

O God—give him back, give him back to us! . . .
Please give us back our Owen Meany . . .
—John Irving, A Prayer for Owen Meany

Contents

Tables and Figures

Tables

Figures

Acknowledgments

An amazing array of wonderful people helped me figure out what I wanted to say about Congress and how to say it in a logical way. Five groups stand out.

First, several former employers got me started on the quest to understand Congress. At the U.S. Military Academy, Col. Jay Parker of the Department of Social Sciences and Brig. Gen. Daniel Kaufman, dean of the Academic Board, were instrumental in getting me to graduate school to prepare for a teaching assignment at West Point. They steered me to American politics and supported me as I worked on my dissertation. My professors at the University of North Carolina at Chapel Hill excited me about the complexities of congressional politics. Terry Sullivan is a giant for his support and guidance as my adviser. Deil Wright, David Lowery, Eric Mlyn, and Steve Leonard all taught me well. Rep. David Price, of North Carolina's Fourth Congressional District, was a wonderful boss and a tremendous public servant; his wisdom helped me make full use of the inside knowledge I got as one of his legislative assistants in the 105th Congress. Billy Moore, Jean-Louise Beard, Darek Newby, and Mark Harkins of his staff added immensely to the joy of life on the Hill.

Second, my fellows at the Graduate School of Political Management at The George Washington University put up with incessant ramblings about this project for fifteen months. Their good humor, and good advice, made this a much better book. Special thanks to our dean, Chris Arterton, for his support and steady hand at the helm of our school, and to Dennis Johnson, Steve Billet, Rick Virgin, Todd Berkoff, Melissa Donner, and David Marshall for their advice and enthusiasm in discussing sections of the book with me.

Third, I owe special thanks to the Government Affairs Institute at Georgetown University. Since 2001 I have been lecturing in their Congressional Operations Seminars, and that series of talks evolved into this book. Thanks to Ken Gold, John Haskell, Susan Lagon, Worth Hester, Howard Stevens, Jim Hershman, and Valerie Heitshusen for their feedback.

Fourth, I cannot calculate how much I have learned from my students in the master's program in legislative affairs since my start at The George Washington University in 1998. I love their enthusiasm for graduate school, especially since most of them are full-time working professionals.

Finally, my friends and family have put up with obsessive research and writing for a long time. My parents have been great in pushing me to get this written. Steven Stichter earned much treasure in heaven for his careful and most excellent editing of early drafts of much of the book; his hand greatly improved what follows. My partner Christopher Gregg is a prince for enduring all the late nights of writing, mad discussions of seventeenth-century English politics, and bizarre arcana of committee jurisdictions. Thanks for being amazing!

Plaudits to the crack staff at M.E. Sharpe for their work. Editor Niels Aaboe was Job-like in his strength and patience with a first-time author, and his assistant, Amanda Allensworth, was great. Thanks to Laurie Lieb for her great copyediting. Thanks also to editorial director Patricia Kolb and project editor Henrietta Toth for launching this book. You rock! Thanks also to the anonymous reviewers, whose questions and advice sharpened the argument I present here.

I cannot express my thanks strongly enough to all of these great folks. Their support made this project possible, and they made it better. The good stuff here is due to their help; I am solely responsible for any errors or confusion that remains.

AN
INTRODUCTION
TO THE
U.S. CONGRESS

1 • Introduction

In republican government, the legislative authority necessarily predominates. The remedy for this inconveniency is to divide the legislature into different branches; and to render them, by different modes of election and different principles of action, as little connected with each other as the nature of their common functions and their common dependence on the society will admit.
—Federalist No. 51[1]

Why is Congress such a complicated institution? What does Congress do, and how does it do it? Will it be able to meet the policy challenges of the next few decades?

Ever since beginning my study of Congress in 1992 at the University of North Carolina at Chapel Hill, I have been trying to figure out good answers to those three questions. After my graduate studies, during which I examined the role of congressional leaders in setting defense policy, I went to work in professional politics for several years, a sort of practical postdoctoral fellowship in real-world congressional politics. I worked on a congressional campaign during the 1996 election and spent two years working for Rep. David Price (D-NC) as a legislative assistant, working on a variety of issues in the fast-paced environment of a Capitol Hill office—still seeking answers to those three questions. The campaign and the staff work made the central importance of serving constituents come alive for me and helped me to see the powers and limitations of political science as a means of explaining our complicated political system in the United States. Following my time on the Hill, I worked as a lobbyist and as a consultant in Washington for several years and saw firsthand how Congress sits at the center of the decision-making network. Congress is the mechanism that connects politics and policy in Washington, DC, and Congress provides the forum for discussing all the important issues in the national government. Since 2001 I have been working on understanding how Congress brings policy and politics together at The George Washington University's Graduate School of Political Management, teaching about Congress and continuing my research on the legislature's role in national politics.

This short text on Congress is what I have learned so far. This book is an overview of the House and Senate, their history, organization, and powers. But I have a strong bias toward practicality. This text gains insight from the leading theoretical debates in political science today, but it does not stop there. This book also assesses the real-world successes and failures of Congress in doing its job and considers whether Congress might do better.

But do not expect this book to explain the entire national policymaking system or to discuss state or local policymaking. In this introductory chapter, we will review the national policymaking system, and we will meet the many players who work with Congress to make important policy choices, but we will not explore the rest of the system, or the other players, in detail: those are the subjects of libraries full of interesting and excellent books. This one is about Congress. Any survey of politics in the United States quickly makes it clear that a great deal of American politics does not happen on Capitol Hill or in Washington. But that is not the focus of this story: Congress is.

Congress and Public Policymaking

Here is my story about Congress. The Framers built a flexible, adaptable system of government that was designed so that each part limited the power of the other parts: the states limit the national government, and vice versa; and in Washington, Congress, the president, and the courts share power. In the next section I will offer an overview of how this system makes public policy, but the star of this story—and of the Framers' system of government—is Congress.

Congress is the centerpiece of the whole constitutional design. Congress makes the major decisions in the national government designed by the Founders. In the Framers' system, Congress has two roles (representation and lawmaking) that frequently conflict, and two chambers that are designed to react differently to political challenges. The Framers wanted the two chambers to check each other, as well as the other branches. So the House and the Senate take two completely different approaches to balancing their twin roles of lawmaking and representation. The two bodies combine their constituent members, committees, and parties in two different patterns that reflect the Framers' different designs for House and Senate. In the House, the balance tips toward representation, giving us a majoritarian body, controlled by its majority party, that works hard to stay close to the political views of its constituents. The Senate manages to represent the states and make national policy reasonably well in a more egalitarian style that gives individual senators a great deal of power to shape legislation in the Senate. But Congress has a severe limitation: it cannot implement its own policies.

The executive branch and the courts execute the policy decisions made by Congress. So how does Congress enforce its decisions? There was no large executive branch planned in the Constitution, so the Framers did not give Congress an extensive toolbox to use in managing the actions of the other branches. While Congress does wrestle with how to shape the activities of the federal court system, its main energies have usually gone to influencing the executive branch, so that is what we will concentrate on in this story. Congress has derived three main powers from the Constitution to influence the executive branch—the powers of oversight, appropriations, and organization. These are good but fairly blunt instruments, which do not always work well to force agencies to comply with Congress's desires. Congress has evolved since the founding to reflect the desires of the Framers fairly well, and Congress uses the three powers reasonably well to enforce its decisions. But the way Congress has organized itself to use the powers is complicated, and that fragmentation, along with partisanship and parochialism, does limit the effectiveness of the Framers' system.

Public Policymaking in Washington

Before we see what the Framers were thinking when they wrote the Constitution, let us examine the American public policymaking system and get a sense of what makes up the system: What does it take to make public policy? Who decides what to work on? What sort of issues does the system address? Who plays a role, and what does each actor do?

The public policy literature is extensive and detailed—and there are several competing theories of how the system works. Each theory focuses on a specific question, and none of them effectively covers the full range and complexity of public policymaking in the United States. Researchers use models to simplify the complex world they study—otherwise it would be nearly impossible to make sense of what goes on in Washington. All of us use models to make it through our own lives—simplifying assumptions that allow us to concentrate on the important things happening around us and make good decisions about our own actions. Public policy in the United States is the product of an amazingly complex set of actions, taken by an enormous number of players, much of which occurs nearly simultaneously—some simplification is mandatory! The American Political Science Association has endorsed the study of politics from many angles, using many complementary approaches; the same advice applies when we look at public policy.[2] In the spirit of gaining understanding by casting our net broadly, here are a few of the main approaches and their answers to the questions asked above.

The oldest and simplest approach to understanding American public policy is to break the process into its several steps, from identification of a policy problem through specification of criteria for evaluation, generation of alternative solutions, and selection of the alternative to implementation and evaluation. While most policy debates do flow through these steps, they do not always occur in sequence, some steps may disappear in certain cases, and a set group of participants does not usually take part throughout the life of a policy debate.[3] But three steps seem to generate great interest, and they all involve Congress: setting the agenda (deciding which issues demand attention); selecting the policy option to pursue, which is Congress's main responsibility in public policy; and evaluating the policy once implemented, which takes up much of Congress's time (as we will see in part II of this book).

Several key public policy studies have expanded the "policy stages" model by exploring specific steps in more depth; the most important and most interesting of these studies deal with agenda-setting. Agenda-setting seeks to explain how an issue rises in importance to the level at which the White House and Congress agree to spend some of their limited time and political capital to solve the perceived problem. One of the most intriguing efforts to understand agenda-setting is the "multiple streams" theory advanced most forcefully by John Kingdon.[4] In this conception of how Washington's policy agenda is set, three streams flow through the Washington policy community simultaneously: a problems stream, which consists of the many potential issues Congress could spend time trying to resolve; a policies stream, which contains possible solutions advanced by one of the players in the system; and a politics stream, which consists of political events and efforts to focus the attention of the system on one problem or another. When the three streams come together—when politics allows Congress the chance to connect a policy solution to a problem—a window of opportunity opens, allowing the players to craft a solution. Three key features drive Kingdon's complex, chaotic view of policymaking. First, many of the policy actors hold "problematic preferences," which means that they either do not fully understand what they want to accomplish or they have not clearly expressed their policy goals. Second, policymaking occurs with "fluid participation," with players entering and leaving the discussions as they proceed, and with many players performing unspecified, changing roles in the process; this instability makes it difficult to track who is doing what—especially since the pattern changes for every issue, as well! Third, policymakers choose among "uncertain technologies," which means that they are not sure that their proposed solutions will actually solve the problems they are trying to resolve. With such a complicated and uncertain environment, Kingdon argues, there is not a clearly defined, easy to follow "process" that addresses public policy; rather, the various actors in Washington struggle somewhat blindly to connect reasonable solutions to some problems, with limited success.

Other researchers have concentrated on understanding how policy actors can successfully navigate the complexity Kingdon describes. One framework explains how advocates for a policy work together in a coalition to raise awareness of their issue and build enough support to get their proposals through Congress. Recognizing that many policy issues are complex, and that they can take as long as a decade or more to reach the stage where Congress can vote on a bill, Paul Sabatier has focused his research efforts on understanding how all of the actors in a policy domain might come together to solve a problem. Rather than relying on a narrow focus on government actors, his "advocacy coalitions" model seeks to identify all the players inside and outside government who can take part in a policy debate. Given that many issues require substantial technical expertise, outside groups like think tanks, university researchers, advocacy organizations, and industry technicians and researchers all have a role to play in formulating both the problem and the possible solutions to that problem. Finally, Sabatier also recognizes that policy debates are not purely scientific or rational discussions of how best to solve a problem; instead, many issues generate emotional responses, which play into how the actors think about policy solutions.[5]

Other researchers have extended the idea of policy domains, noting that policymaking in the United States is not exclusively the job of Washington or of government. Some decisions fall to Congress or to state legislatures, with their particular style of politics that favors compromise and collegiality. Other players make other decisions in our system, too. Presidents, governors, and city managers or mayors make chief executive decisions, which follow a more hierarchical pattern than legislative politics. Courts make many decisions, with their particular style dependent upon the adversarial process used in trial settings. Government agencies make many decisions, as well, using their standard operating procedures, rules, and traditions; bureaucratic politics is unlike the decision-making formats used by the other branches of the government. Business leaders in the United States make many important decisions that have significant impacts on policy, and the politics of the boardroom does not follow the patterns of the political actors. Finally, public opinion, family discussions, and constituents all play vital roles in the American political system, shaping how the other actors all make their decisions. Of course, many challenging policy issues require decisions—some independent and some arrived at jointly—from several players together. Although our focus in this book is the part that Congress plays, the "policy domains" approach is useful in reminding us that a great deal of other important decision making takes place all over the nation, without much congressional input—and that many of these other decisions can have an impact on what Congress seeks to do.[6]

All the preceding approaches treat policymakers as rational to some degree. That is, the actors seek to advance their interests, which they conceive of in personal or individual terms. Some form of rationality has been part of American politics, and the study of American politics, since the founding—what else is the Constitution but an attempt to balance the interests of competing political players?[7] Since the 1950s, American political scientists have attempted to craft a more rigorous method to explain the rational basis of political actions, using techniques and language drawn from economics.[8] The "rational choice" approach, which underpins much of the research already described above, has clearly produced a great deal of interesting work on the question of how political players make decisions. But it is only one approach among many, and other researchers have sought to explore issues that rational choice does not elucidate. How do values play into politics? How does the political system balance among competing values—or among different interpretations of the same value? Unlike economics, where interests can be treated as outside the purview of the theory, in politics interests and values are part of the story. In fact, politics is at heart the process a community uses to identify its values and interests and to come to some agreement about common purpose. Rationality plays a key role in much of the discussion about politics, but it does not help when we are studying the values side of politics. The values-based approach seeks to understand how communities grapple with disagreements over values and what values mean to the community.

The precision and specificity that make rational choice a powerful tool for studying politics are missing from the values-based approach to public policy, which takes for granted that uncertainty and ambiguity are part of politics. While all Americans may feel comfortable agreeing to the shared values of liberty, equity, justice, and efficiency, for instance, once we leave the abstract and start to define what these terms mean to each citizen, we discover that each term means many things. In this approach, public policymaking is society's attempt to wrestle with the competing meanings of these ideals and come to some general understanding that can guide decision makers. Values-based public policy research looks at the social basis of political thinking and seeks to determine how the community shapes political behaviors. In this approach to public policy research, the focus is on ideas, not interests.[9]

This is admittedly a short overview of what public policymaking is all about, and I hope you noticed that it is a little unclear—I never defined public policy in a specific way, for instance. That is deliberate! Ambiguity and uncertainty are part of the process of making public policy decisions, and we should grow comfortable with that fact. And we should recognize that the best way to understand public policymaking in the United States is to draw on the insights of each of the approaches mentioned above. Each has strengths and weaknesses, and each explains some aspects of the process better than the others; together, though, the various schools of thought combine to offer a comprehensive explanation of the various facets of public policy.

Even with all this confusion about what the policy process is, we can still identify five key players that participate in policymaking, especially in the Congress-centered national politics of Washington.[10] Note that each of these players is a simplified version of a much messier reality. First is the president, including the actual person in the Oval Office and the offices and staff that directly support the White House. The second player is Congress, especially the leaders in their role as spokespeople for the institution. The third player is the bureaucracy—the civil servants who staff the agencies, not the political appointees (they are part of the presidency, since they are appointed by, and are loyal to, the president). Of course, each federal agency is organized in a specific way, dependent upon the mission(s) assigned to that agency, and in some agencies, multiple operating directorates or divisions may not share the same set of goals. For instance, the army, navy, and air force all belong in the Department of Defense, but each has its own traditions, organizations, and methods of accomplishing the department's mission—and they frequently find themselves arguing over policy choices because of their differences. The fourth set of players is the congressional committees that have jurisdiction over a particular issue area. The last player is the private sector, including all the unofficial, nongovernmental actors, such as political parties, interest groups, corporations, think tanks, the media, and citizens.[11]

Nonofficial players in Washington make up a huge segment of political activity in the capital. Some 40,000 lobbyists and advocates toil away on their issues of interest, seeking to influence congressional action. Who are they? Some are professional lobbyists, whose firms manage government relations on behalf of a broad array of clients interested in some piece of legislation before Congress, like the famous firms of Akin, Gump and Patton Boggs. Others are corporate representatives, hired by their firm to work on issues of importance to the business; nearly every important company in the United States has an office in Washington. Other lobbyists represent an industry or a group of like-minded clients in a business association, such as the U.S. Chamber of Commerce. Still others bring together the interests of all the businesses in a single industry, such as the Motion Picture Association of America or the National Defense Industry Association. Public-interest groups, such as the Sierra Club, the National Rifle Association, and the American Israel Public Affairs Committee, also lobby Congress, seeking to advance their causes. Public-interest groups run across the ideological spectrum, working on issues as diverse as environmental stewardship, reproductive rights, the teaching of evolution, and awareness of many illnesses. And labor unions also spend a great deal of money and energy working on issues of importance to working families, adding to their lobbying work in Washington a ferocious ability to organize voters during election campaigns. Lobbyists tend to get bad press, but they perform a helpful function in public policymaking that would be hard to replace: they generate many of the ideas that make their way through the policy process, and they provide legislators and their staffs with information on the myriad issues they work on. In Washington good information is among the most valuable assets, and lobbyists' willingness to share that information helps Congress learn more about policy issues. Honesty is the most important characteristic a lobbyist can have— good, accurate information helps lobbyists open doors, so only bad lobbyists try to manipulate the information they share.[12]

In the past thirty years, think tanks have spawned all over Washington, and they play an important role in the policymaking process, too. More than a hundred research institutes work in Washington today, from small, ideological think tanks to large, more centrist organizations with hundreds of staff and researchers. What do think tanks do? Some focus on specific issues, like the foreign policy focus of the Center for Strategic and International Studies, or the narrower focus of the Washington Institute for Near East Policy. Some, such as the Heritage Foundation or the Progressive Policy Institute, advance ideological positions on a range of issues. Think tanks produce research on their topics of interest and provide their findings to policymakers in Congress and the executive branch in the hopes of influencing policy outcomes. While it is nearly impossible to track the effectiveness of think tank policy lobbying, evidence does suggest that the long-term relationships that can form between think tank personnel and civil servants in the bureaucracy do seem to provide the best avenue for think tanks to use in seeking influence over policy. Legislators answer to too many other influences, and their staffs tend to turn over quickly, making long relationships difficult. Think tanks, like lobbyists, provide new ideas and new arguments for old ideas, adding to the policy debate available to Congress.[13]

Another key nonofficial player in politics and policymaking is the media. The media hold a unique position, though—they perform some official roles for government, making them half-in and half-out. The semiofficial status of the media comes from their role in communicating ideas and positions from one government entity to another, as for instance when the media televise a presidential speech or Rose Garden press conference, allowing the president to signal his intentions to Congress without having to meet with any legislators directly. Government uses the press as well to communicate to the public; in fact, the government supports the media heavily in this effort, with its public affairs offices, press secretaries, and official spokespeople.[14] Without the access to government activities provided by these offices, the media could have a difficult keeping track of policy debates in Washington. And media offices provide two benefits to their agencies as well: they allow for easy dissemination of agency positions on proposals, and they free the rest of the agency to concentrate on executing their mission rather than talking to the press.[15] Nowhere in government is proper management of the relationship with the press more important than in the White House. The presidency is an office of quite limited constitutional powers,[16] especially in the legislative arena,[17] so the White House needs a disciplined press operation to help shape news coverage and manage the policy agenda in Washington.[18] So the media's task is bridging the gap between the official actors, and between them and the public.

The final nonofficial player is the public: how do citizens participate in public policy? We can trace three inputs that shape policy in key ways. First, of course, is that citizens vote: they pick the legislators who serve in Congress. They look to legislators' (and other candidates') positions on issues and how they have acted in the past.[19] Citizens also participate in policy debates by communicating with their representatives: representatives and senators keep close tabs on the number and tone of the letters, phone calls, and e-mails that come into their offices on Capitol Hill. Finally, public opinion also shapes legislators' views of policy issues. Congress takes all three forms of input into account whenever it makes a decision. Citizens' participation thus helps to shape policy outcomes. But participation is not evenly distributed across the population of the United States. People at the upper end of the socioeconomic scale (those with higher incomes and better education) tend to participate more actively than others, so Congress pays more attention to the issues that they care about.[20] Legislators do not ignore the citizens who do not participate in politics, but they pay much more attention to the active participants, even if they are few in number.[21]

Policy Types

In addition to studying the key players we have just identified, many public policy researchers have observed patterns in how the players interact across broad groups of similar policies. From among these several approaches to the topic, one excellent review of policymaking from the public policy literature identifies six types of national policy[22] that fall into two broad categories: domestic policies, which are called distributive, regulatory, and redistributive, and defense and foreign policies, called strategic, structural, and crisis. This framework looks at the patterns of relationships among the key players in Washington rather than focusing on specific issues (such as farm policy or health care). In each case, Congress works with a variety of other players, and these players are excellent sources of ideas—not only of alternatives for solving problems, but also for identifying problems from the start. Congress makes use of all these other actors as sources of new thinking on recurring problems; when we explore Congress as a legislative body in part I and Congress's tools for enforcing its legislative will in part II, remember that the other players often provide Congress with much of the argument it will debate as it makes decisions.

Congress spends much of its time working on domestic policy. Voters generally care more about domestic policy than foreign and defense issues, so Congress follows suit. The three domestic policy types involve the bulk of Congress's committees in one way or another. Distributive policies concern federal support for private activities that are thought to be good for the country, but that might not happen without some government aid. Federal aid can take the form of a direct payment or it a tax incentive to promote a stated policy goal. Examples include farm subsidy programs, research grants, and mortgage interest tax credits.[23] Regulatory policy, the second domestic policy category, establishes standards for specified private activities. The intent of these policies is to protect the public from harmful actions or to advance good public policy outcomes. Business and labor standards, and air and water pollution statutes, are all regulatory policies.[24] Finally, redistributive policies seek to move resources from one group to another through government policy, frequently through tax incentives or credits. Although redistribution can move in any direction, it usually means moving resources to disadvantaged groups or communities. Examples include the progressive tax code, which charges higher rates at the upper end of the income scale; the earned income tax credit for low-income taxpayers; federal housing regulations, which prohibit discrimination; federal job training programs; and food aid programs.[25]

The other three policy types cover the foreign and defense policy decisions facing the federal government. First is strategic policy, which lays out the goals of U.S. national security policy. It includes important decisions such as foreign policy and diplomatic initiatives, overseas basing plans, nuclear deterrence policy, and the proper balance among army, navy, and air force units.[26] Structural policy closely follows strategic decision making concerning decisions about what forces, weapons, and other resources the United States needs to achieve its strategic goals. Structural policies include weapons procurement and organization of military forces.[27] The annual defense authorization bill contains the bulk of U.S. structural policy, including the procurement of new weapons. The third defense policy, crisis policy, is about responding to international emergencies.[28] The defining note of crisis policy "is the perception of an immediate threat to US national interests, usually one involving the use or potential use of force."[29]

Policy Patterns

Looking across all the policy types, we can see that policymaking and oversight fall into four patterns that describe how the five policy players interact: top-down, where Congressional leaders and/or the White House dictate policy; cooperative, where leaders and committees work together to set policy; committee-driven, where the committees make the key decisions; and nonparticipatory, where the White House (and sometimes congressional leaders) make decisions without committee involvement at all. Each of the policy types has a well-developed pattern of relationships among the five policy players, and each involves Congress to varying degrees.

Strategic policy follows the top-down pattern (see Figure 1.1). The president and close advisers play the major role in setting strategic policy. Congressional leaders can have strong influence on the strategic direction of the country. The unofficial actors involved in strategic policy debates also play a role, although they are not as important as the elected leaders. Congressional committees and the defense agencies play a limited role in setting strategic policy.[30] While Congress may complain about this, Congress is not particularly good at strategic thinking.[31] Another limitation to Congressional oversight in this area is that the network of participants is not stable: while the president and congressional leaders take part in strategic policy discussions, the large group of unofficial participants (defense policy think tanks, interest groups, and the defense industry) shifts over time, so it hard to develop a stable group of players.[32]

Redistributive and protective regulatory policies involve the main actors in cooperative patterns (see Figure 1.2). The main actors in these two policy types are the leaders (the president and advisers, and the congressional leadership) and the unofficial actors, especially the main advocacy organizations and trade associations representing the regulated industries.[33] Cooperative policymaking starts out like the top-down pattern, but the congressional committees involved with these policy types play a larger role. In redistributive policy, committees participate, but their role is weakened by ideological and political controversy surrounding most redistributive policies. These policies, which aim to shift resources from the haves to the have-nots, excite both supporters and opponents whenever a program modification is called for. Because disputes on these policies are so power-

Figure 1.1   **Top-Down Policy**

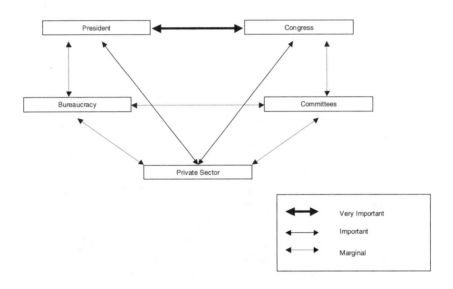

Source: Adapted from Ripley and Franklin, 1991.

ful and so partisan, congressional leaders tend not to delegate all the decision making to the oversight committees. In fact, the broad outlines of such programs are usually set by congressional leaders and the president, with the committees left to oversee the implementation of those decisions.[34] In the case of protective regulatory policies, congressional committees and the federal regulatory agencies have much more of a role in setting policy, which increases the committees' ability to do good oversight.[35] The federal government has taken on the task of producing regulatory policy aimed at many commercial activities, increasing since its early forays into this type of policy in the late nineteenth century. As in distributive policies, congressional leaders and the president set broad goals or guidelines, leaving the details to the agencies and committees with the necessary jurisdiction.[36] The relationship between the oversight committees, regulatory agencies, and the industries affected (and the consumer and environmental advocates that also participate in the policy process for regulatory issues) is generally stable, with the committees and the agencies delegating the bulk of the responsibility to produce the regulations, in line with leadership guidelines.[37] In both these cases, the president and the congressional leadership make the major decisions in coordination with the chief interested parties

Figure 1.2 **Cooperative Policy**

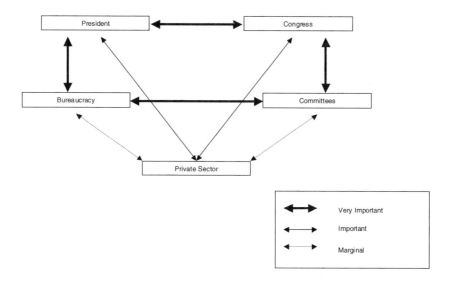

Source: Adapted from Ripley and Franklin, 1991.

outside government, and the committees find themselves with less leverage to do good oversight as a result.

Distributive and structural policies exhibit a committee-driven pattern of relationships among the five actors: the committees play the main role in setting policy, and their oversight capacity is high because of their command of the issues (see Figure 1.3). Many researchers refer to the power of "subgovernments" in setting key policies; it is these two policy types that give rise to the phenomenon because of the key players that make most of the decisions.[38] Committees and subcommittees, federal agencies, and interested unofficial players work together in close cooperation, with the other players less involved.[39] On the domestic side, distributive policy plays into the parochial preferences of most legislators (distributive policy is the nice way to say pork barrel politics). In distributive policy, the committees, the agencies involved, and the unofficial actors interested in the policy outcomes tend to share a (broad) common view of their issue, making policy formulation stable and compromise-driven. The committees manage most of the decision making on distributive policies.[40] In defense policy, a similar pattern emerges in the creation of structural policy.[41] The armed services committees are intimately involved in structural policy decisions, far more so than the oversight committees in other issue areas. Their staffs have

Figure 1.3   **Committee-Driven Policy**

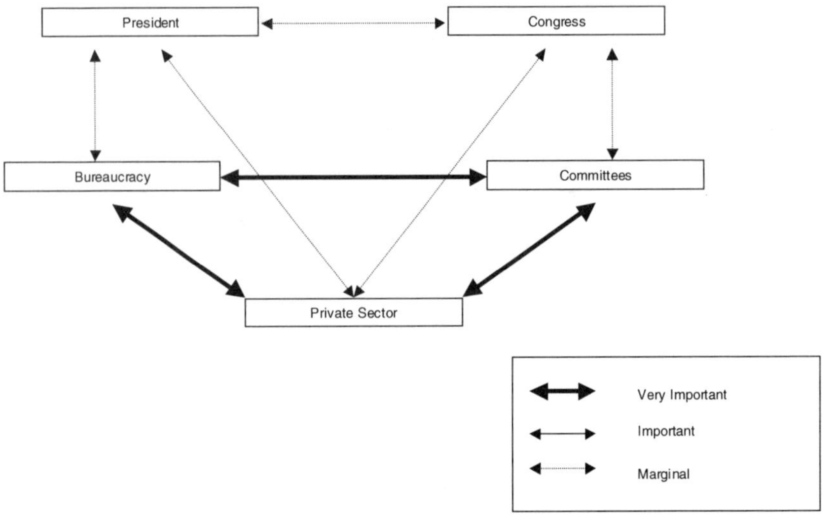

Source: Adapted from Ripley and Franklin, 1991.

expertise in program evaluation and an understanding of the Defense Department's organization that rivals the Pentagon's own understanding, and that makes these two committees very effective at policy and oversight.[42]

Crisis policy is the final, nonparticipatory category.[43] The president makes crisis decisions with a small number of senior advisers. Given the speed required to respond to crises, and their unexpectedness, there is no stable set of participants, and congressional action is too slow to allow Congress to take an active role in responding to the situation (see Figure 1.4). Oversight of crisis policy usually happens long after the fact, with the hope that any lessons learned will be useful in a future crisis.[44] Neither committees nor congressional leaders play much of a role in responding to crises. For example, in 1984 President Ronald Reagan did not inform Speaker of the House Thomas P. "Tip" O'Neill (D-MA) of the invasion of Grenada until the attack had already started.[45] President George H.W. Bush invaded Panama in December 1989 without congressional input and ordered the army's Eighty-second Airborne Division to deploy to Saudi Arabia in August 1990 (before the Persian Gulf War) with no congressional discussion.[46] The president dominates crisis policy, both because of constitutional authority to take on foreign policy challenges and because of the institutional advantages of a unitary

Figure 1.4 **Nonparticipatory Policy**

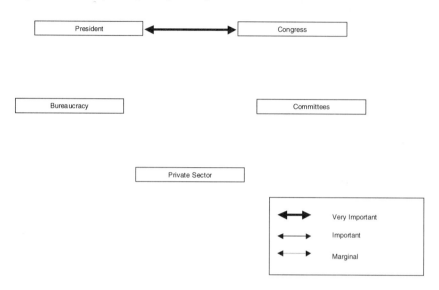

Source: Adapted from Ripley and Franklin, 1991.

actor over the fractious debate required to get anything accomplished in Congress. Congressional leaders also recognize the "rally 'round the flag" effect, which makes it politically attractive to defer to presidential decisions during crises.[47] Despite having only minimal capability to respond to crises, Congress has been sensitive to the potential for the White House to overstep the traditional boundaries of acceptable action in some circumstances.

The most ambitious congressional effort to limit White House overreach in crisis response was the passage of the war powers resolution. In the wake of serious questions about the management of the Vietnam War, Congress passed the war powers resolution in 1973 (over the veto of President Richard Nixon) in order to establish a standard procedure that would allow Congress some role in crisis response. Under the resolution, the president must report to Congress within forty-eight hours whenever he commits U.S. forces into a combat situation; Congress then has sixty days to approve the action, or the forces must withdraw.[48] Despite Congress's intent to find a role for itself in crisis policy, there is little evidence that the resolution succeeded in this task. While Presidents Gerald Ford and Jimmy Carter did not make extensive commitments of U.S. forces, U.S. military actions occurred regularly under Presidents Reagan, George H.W. Bush, and Bill Clinton without any notification or congressional input until well after

Figure 1.5 **Summary of Policy Patterns**

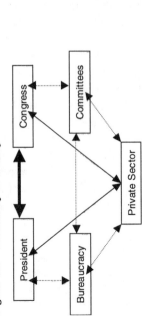

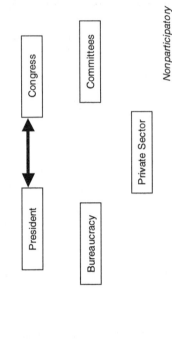

Source: Adapted from Ripley and Franklin, 1991.

the operations had begun.[49] The war powers resolution has not worked successfully either to provide Congress with a role in crisis policy or to limit the president's power to commit military forces in emergency situations.[50]

Not all committees are equally capable of successful oversight. The types of policy that the committees oversee can make it harder or easier for a committee to advance its goals through oversight. Some committees work with issues that allow them tremendous impact on policy, while others have a tougher time performing oversight because their issue areas do not give Congress much of a role in settling policy (Figure 1.5 shows the four patterns described in this section). Crisis policy is nonparticipatory—committees have no way to participate until long after the emergency is over. Top-down policy areas do not give committees much freedom to make policy or to oversee it. Cooperative policy areas allow committees to work with congressional leaders and the White House to make and oversee policy. And committee-dominated policy areas leave most of the key decisions in committee hands, which make oversight in those areas far more powerful.

How to Read This Book

The rest of this book will introduce you to the Congress as it operates today—to its politics, structures, procedures, and leaders. This book is an introduction to Congress, not an exhaustive study of the institution. So the book includes two resources for further learning. Each chapter ends with a list of interesting Web sites that expand on what the chapter covers. At the end of the book is a selected bibliography that collects the major sources mentioned in the footnotes throughout the book.

Armed with this premise of the complexity of public policymaking and some idea of the centrality of Congress to the process, we can explore what Congress does and how it does it. Before we examine Congress today, though, we need to see where the institution came from and how it has evolved since the First Congress opened for business in 1789. Much research today, of course, concentrates on recent political activity, but how can we evaluate Congress if we do not know what it was designed to do? It may look inefficient, slow, and not too forward-looking to us today—but what if that is what the Framers wanted? If that is so, then Congress does what it is supposed to do! Even if you prefer to focus on today or the future, chapter 2 is important to the story, because it sets the stage for us by showing what the Founders were trying to do. In the last round of American history testing done by the National Assessment of Educational Progress in 2001, 57 percent of the tested high school seniors scored below the basic level on the test.[51] The political thought that supports the Constitution is the Framers' legacy, our heritage of liberty. We need to know it, not just as students of politics, but also as American citizens. So read it before you go on to the meat of the book. Chapter 2 introduces the Framers and their times. The Framers' fear of tyranny came from English history and their own experiences with King George III. They thought like Englishmen and their Constitution reflects an English answer to the challenges of self-government. The chapter closes with a review of American political development since 1789, with attention to developments in the House and Senate as they changed over time.

Part I explores the two chambers, the House of the people and the Senate of the states. These chapters examine the nature of politics in each chamber, noting the role of the parties, committees, leaders, and individual members in each chamber. These chapters point out that the members of Congress have twin responsibilities: representation (of their constituents) and lawmaking (for the nation). But the Framers designed the chambers to balance these two often conflicting roles in different ways. Chapter 3 describes the House of Representatives, showing how the principle of majority rule has evolved into the modern, majority-party-dominated House. Chapter 4 does the same for the Senate, tracing how its underlying principle of equality developed into the individualistic chamber of today. By the end of the first section of the book, you should understand the different political natures of the House and the Senate and see why it is so difficult for the two chambers to cooperate.

The second section of the book concerns Congress and its interaction with the rest of the federal government. Congress does look to the courts for action, but the bulk of its energy goes to monitoring the federal agencies, rather than the courts, so we will focus on the Congress-agencies relationship. Once Congress enacts a law declaring national policy on some issue, it must enforce that decision somehow, although Congress cannot actually "do" anything: it must rely on the executive branch to effect its decisions. Congress uses three powers to keep the agencies in line. Chapter 5 describes the oversight power and how House and Senate committees use it to shape agency policies. Chapter 6 details the appropriation power and how Congress uses the budget to influence bureaucracies. Chapter 7 explains the organizing power, the most powerful of Congress's tools, and shows why it is the least used of the three powers.

The third section of the book looks to the future. The federal government confronts an array of domestic and foreign challenges that promise to drive Congress's agenda for many years. What will Congress decide, and how will Congress use its three powers to make its policies work? Chapter 8 offers a case study of how Congress uses its powers to address major public policy challenges. After the terrorist attacks of September 11, 2001, Congress worked to improve the way the federal government protects the

United States, culminating in November 2002 with the passage of a bill creating the Department of Homeland Security. This chapter will examine the history of this effort and assess how effective Congress's use of its powers has been. Chapter 9 concludes our discussion of Congress, closing with some thoughts on how Congress might make itself a more effective representative *and* legislative body.

Web Resources

Akin Gump: One of the top five lobbying operations in Washington (www.akingump.com).

Patton Boggs: One of the top five lobbying firms in Washington (www.pattonboggs.com/Home.aspx).

Center for Strategic and International Studies (CSIS): One of the largest defense and foreign policy research institutes in Washington (www.csis.org/).

Heritage Foundation: The leading conservative think tank (www.heritage.org).

Progressive Policy Institute: The think tank of the Democratic Leadership Council, the "New Democrats" (www.ppionline.org/).

Washington Institute for Near East Policy: This think tank studies U.S. policy in the Middle East (www.washingtoninstitute.org/).

American Israel Public Affairs Committee (AIPAC): The most effective foreign policy interest group in Washington, AIPAC lobbies for a strong U.S.-Israel relationship (www.aipac.org/).

Motion Picture Association of America: Represents the movie industry in Washington, in addition to rating films before they are released (www.mpaa.org/).

National Defense Industry Association: This trade group represents the interests of defense contractors (www.ndia.org/).

National Rifle Association: Lobbies the government in support of gun owner rights (www.nra.org/).

Sierra Club: One of the premier environmental organizations in the nation (www.sierraclub.org/).

U.S. Chamber of Commerce: The Chamber is the leading business lobby in the nation (www.uschamber.com/default).

2 • Origins and Evolution of the Congressional System

Ambition must be made to counteract ambition. The interest of the man must be connected with the constitutional rights of the place. It may be a reflection on human nature, that such devices should be necessary to control the abuses of government. But what is government itself, but the greatest of all reflections on human nature? If men were angels, no government would be necessary. If angels were to govern men, neither external nor internal controls on government would be necessary. In framing a government which is to be administered by men over men, the great difficulty lies in this: you must first enable the government to control the governed; and in the next place oblige it to control itself. A dependence on the people is, no doubt, the primary control on the government; but experience has taught mankind the necessity of auxiliary precautions.
—Federalist No. 51[1]

It is all Oliver Cromwell's fault.

Cromwell's ghost[2] has been said to have been in the room throughout the writing of the Constitution in Philadelphia in 1787, and the presence of his ghost reminded the Framers that human nature (greed and desire for power) made self-government difficult. As Alexander Hamilton wrote in the *Federalist,* "men are ambitious, vindictive, and rapacious."[3] The Framers feared human ambition and knew that they would need to devise a government that could keep these darker human traits in check.

Why Oliver Cromwell, a man who had been dead for almost 130 years when the Framers crafted their document?

For English people on both sides of the Atlantic—in the British Isles and in the colonies on the eastern coast of North America—Cromwell was the dominant figure of the most important political event of the preceding century: the English Civil War (1642–1648). The political and psychological lessons of the Civil War reverberated throughout the English-speaking world for generations after the war ended. The issues raised by the Civil War were not resolved in England without another fight, the Glorious Revolution of 1688–1690, and nearly fifty years of political discussion and reorganization; in the colonies, those same issues continued to float around in political debates until the American Revolution began in 1775.

For many of the colonial leaders in the thirteen American colonies, the years before the Revolution were something of a Civil War flashback, thus bringing Cromwell back into sharp focus. King George III seemed to be acting in a high-handed manner as his predecessor, Charles I, had in the years before the Civil War.

The political fallout of the tumultuous seventeenth century in England profoundly shaped English views on power and government, on both sides of the Atlantic. The century saw the Stuart succession (1603), the English Civil War, the Commonwealth (1649–1660), and the Glorious Revolution. Throughout the seventeenth century, English people, already quite mobile at home, expanded their movement to the New World, as regular waves of new colonists left England to find work in the colonies, bringing with them news of the struggles and new political ideas from home. This movement from England to the colonies continued right up to the eve of the Revolution.[4] And the Framers thought of themselves as English, and acted like Englishmen, right up to the fateful moment in July 1776 when the Continental Congress declared independence. When it came time to write a new constitution for the United States of America, the Framers devised their new federal system based on the lessons of English politics, as they had lived those lessons in the New World.

What were the two lessons of the period from the Civil War through the Glorious Revolution that shaped how the Framers' generation thought about government? The first lesson was the political result of the Civil War and the Glorious Revolution: a theory of self-government—one consented to by the citizenry, a limited government of checks and balances. This became the underpinning of both English and later American thinking about politics, giving the Framers their central ideas about how to frame the Constitution they devised in 1787.

But it was the second lesson that meant more to Englishmen everywhere. The 1600s showed them the dark side of human nature and made them nervous about the ability of a free people to govern itself. The story of Oliver Cromwell's rise to power, from gentleman farmer to member of Parliament to soldier to Parliament's commanding general to Lord Protector of the Commonwealth (in fact, he was military dictator of the country), loomed large in the minds of Englishmen on both sides of the Atlantic. His example would be a major argument in favor of limited government for the next two centuries.

Thus, the ideas that inspired the Founders as they drafted the Constitution were old ideas, which came to the Founders through their English history. The basic concepts came from the English Civil War. These concepts were further articulated and explained by England's first political party, the Whigs, during the Glorious Revolution. From the time of the Restoration in 1660, the Whigs expanded the Civil War argument about the corruption of government by the Stuart monarchs, and their pamphlets, which were known in the colonies as well as in England, were the basis of early American political thought. Even after government reforms in London made much of the Whig argument irrelevant there, Whig fears about corruption remained an important part of American political thinking. Colonists were primed by their understanding of politics to see corruption and tyranny in the slightest governmental flap. It took only a few missteps by King George III and his supporters in Parliament to convince the colonists that they were experiencing a Cromwellian flashback and bring on the American Revolution.

The Framers had historical precedent for their fear of power. A brief history of English politics in the century before the American Revolution helps to show what made the Framers devise our complicated system of government.

Civil War and Revolution: Britain and Tyranny

The English Civil War grew out of a conflict between two different governing philosophies. On one side, the king believed in unrestricted right to rule by personal decree, because of his "divine right" to reign.[5] On the other, Parliament sought to restrain the king's power and to preserve the traditional liberties of the English people, in whose name it governed. Because these two sides could not compromise, this philosophical difference could not be resolved without war.

The story started well enough. When James VI of Scotland came to London in 1603 to assume the English throne after the death of Elizabeth I, he brought with him foreign, Scottish ideas about the king's role in running the state.[6] James found a new situation in London.

Since Magna Carta in 1215 had given the nobility a role in ruling England, the English people had been engaged in a four-centuries-long experiment in expanding the circle of people who participated in governing. English society consisted of three estates—royalty, nobility, and the people—and all three had a role to play in English government.[7]

The king, now James I of England, recognized the differences between his two kingdoms and managed to rule both effectively in the style the subjects of both expected. Unlike his Scottish subjects, who accepted the idea of a king's personal rule, James I's English subjects thought of Parliament—

king, Lords, and Commons, meeting together to make law—as the legiti-mate government of England.[8] So James worked within this framework. Charles I acceded to the throne in 1625. Like his father (and like most Euro-peans at the time), Charles believed that kings were chosen by God to reign,[9] that he served as God's "immediate Lieutenant and Viceregent," adding that "Princes are not bound to give accompt of their actions but to God alone."[10]

Unfortunately, his conception of the "divine right" led him to attempt to rule without Parliament. After an unhappy effort to work with a series of fractious Parliaments, in 1630 Charles dismissed the Parliament he had called to help pay for religious wars he hoped to continue on the Continent. He would not seek another one until financial disarray and rebellion in Scotland demanded new taxes in 1641.

Eleven years of "personal rule" caused a deep rift between the king and Parliament. Having shown little respect for the Parliaments he had called and dismissed, Charles could not expect a friendly reception from the new one, either. Charles I's philosophy of personal rule under divine right now led to a slow hardening of two camps in the government, each with its own theory of proper English government.[11]

The king continued to believe in divine right and continued to feel that this meant no person or body could limit his authority.[12] It was with this attitude that Charles called for a new Parliament in 1641. Charles asked the new Parliament for new revenues, which it would not consider until the king agreed to apologize for his high-handedness of the past eleven years.

He would not. Dissatisfaction turned to disbelief after Charles dismissed the Parliament of 1641 almost as soon as it sat. The leaders in the House of Commons began to articulate a new understanding of their role in the gov-ernment of England.[13] Distancing themselves from divine right, Leaders in the Commons started to ground legitimate government in the consent of the governed.[14] The Leveller leader Richard Overton plainly saw Parliament as the chosen arm of the people, writing to the House of Commons in 1646:

> For effecting whereof, we possessed you with the same Power that was in our selves, to have done it our selves without you, if we had thought it convenient. . . . Wee are your Principalls, and you our Agents; it is a Truth which you cannot but acknowledge.[15]

As the elected branch of the English government, the House of Commons began to see that it was the truest voice of the people. And as the king and his supporters in the House of Lords continued to press for unrestricted royal prerogatives, the Commons slowly began to oppose the king more force-fully, until the two sides could no longer discuss a solution to the impasse.

In 1642, the king raised his standard against the rebellious Parliament, which responded by drafting its own army, in order to bring the king around to performing his role in the proper, limited, English way.

Most of the fighting was over by late 1646,[16] ending with Charles imprisoned and the Parliamentary army victorious. Parliament was by this time simply the House of Commons, as the Lords had ceased to meet shortly after the fighting began. Parliamentary leaders, seeking to bring the country back to normalcy as soon as possible, made moves to disband the larger part of their army, now that it was no longer needed in order to save expenses.[17] The army refused to be decommissioned.[18] Many regiments had not been paid in months, and demanded their back pay before they would return home; they knew that they were more likely to see their back pay if they stayed together.

Cromwell and the senior army leaders met with representatives of the soldiers, called Agitators, to discuss how to resolve the standoff with Parliament.[19] In a series of wide-ranging debates held at Putney, the leaders and the Agitators explored not only the demands of the army concerning its back pay, but also the nature of government by a free people.[20]

The Agitators were influenced by a group of writers, derisively called "Levellers" by their opponents who sought a more equitable Parliament. Their foes thought they were seeking to make everyone literally equal—in wealth, power, and status—thus "leveling" society.[21] Actually, the Levellers hoped to create a more equitable political structure—a political leveling—so all English citizens could live their lives according to the dictates of their consciences, free of government intrusion.[22]

The Levellers introduced a series of concepts into English political philosophy that would become key to the evolution of British government—and to how the colonists in the New World came to understand self-government—in the decades that followed the Civil War.[23] The Levellers began their critique of government with a call to all leaders to observe the rule of law. Their chief argument with the king was his refusal to abide by the traditions of the common law. The Levellers also demanded the publication of a Bill of Rights, so the government and the people would know what the rulers could and could not do.[24]

But once the king was imprisoned, the Levellers turned their attention to Parliament—for it, too, trampled on the rights of the people. They argued that the army had become the most representative body in England, since Parliament, by now seated for almost eight years, had been so reduced by departures that it no longer reflected the will of the people.[25] Not that it was ever truly representative, they also argued: too few Englishmen had the franchise, and the boroughs that chose members for Parliament no longer reflected the population of the country. So the Levellers called on Parliament to adopt a new constitution for England and then disband so a new, more representative Parliament could be elected to rule the country.

The basic Leveller proposal, called *An Agreement of the People,* would redistrict the boroughs based on current population, expand the franchise to all free-born males, and allow Parliaments to last no longer than three years. It also established a Bill of Rights to protect the liberties of the people. The experience of the Civil War, only recently concluded, showed the Levellers the need to break with tradition and write the constitution down, in a permanent form:

> Its chiefly because for these things wee first ingaged gainst the King, He would not permit the peoples Representatives to provide for the Nations safety, by disposing of the Militia, and otherwayes, according to their Trust, but raised a Warre against them, and we ingaged for the defence of that power, and right of the people, in their Representatives. Therefore these things in the Agreement, the people are to claime as their native right, and price of their bloud, which you are obliged absolutely to procure for them.
>
> And these being the foundations of freedom, its necessary, that they should be setled inalterably, which can be by no meanes, but this Agreement with the people.[26]

Parliament never took up the Leveller proposals, but it did take action to resolve its argument with the king. Since the end of the fighting, the king had been negotiating with Parliament over the terms of his return to the throne. At this point, nearly all political leaders in England expected the Civil War to end with a return to the traditional form of government—king, Lords, and Commons—as soon as a mutually acceptable agreement could be formulated.[27] Parliament wanted the king to agree to specific limits on his power, but the king, despite his loss in the Civil War, refused to change his ways. He hoped that he could outlast his opponents in Parliament and return to power without being forced to accept limits on his authority. Parliament was riven by factions, and the king proceeded with his negotiations slowly, hoping that the factions would turn on one another—in the chaos that would follow, the king saw an opportunity to return to the throne and restore order and his personal rule.[28]

Unfortunately for him, Oliver Cromwell saw through his designs, recognizing that the king "had amply proved himself to be an impossible person with whom to negotiate. No settlement to which he was a party could have been expected to last, even if it had ever been achieved in the first place."[29] So Cromwell decided to end the standoff between the crown and Parliament by removing the king from power permanently. Acting on Cromwell's urging in late 1648, Parliament accused the king of treason for having made war against his own people.[30] After the Lords reluctantly followed the lead of the Commons, a court was established, and in January 1649, the king was tried, convicted, and executed.[31] His sons had already fled London to preserve the succession, leaving England without a king.

In May 1649, the House of Commons declared the monarchy illegal and disbanded the House of Lords. Once enacted, these laws forced the House of Commons to take up the reins of government alone, and it did so with limited success. Parliament formulated a new constitution, but order was still not fully restored, for many Englishmen were not ready to accept the revolutionary concept of a republic—they had not fought the Civil War to replace the king, but to reform the monarchy. With the Commons struggling to manage the new republic, Cromwell stepped into the breach.[32]

Oliver Cromwell had been sent to Ireland in August 1649 to command the English army sent there to put down a rebellion. Parliament feared that Charles II, who had been proclaimed king in Scotland after his father's death, might go to Ireland to rally the people there to his cause. Parliament wanted the Irish rebellion ended quickly, before Charles II could make more trouble in Ireland. Cromwell fulfilled Parliament's desires as commander in Ireland. When he returned to London, flush with another victory, he realized that England was in crisis.

With his fame and his command of the army as his power base, Cromwell took charge of the situation, leading the Commons to create another new constitution for the Commonwealth, and then he swept the remnants of the Long Parliament from office in 1653, seating a new House of Commons. It in turn granted him executive authority to rule the Commonwealth of England, under the title of Lord Protector, an ancient office whose prior inhabitants had held power temporarily, as leaders of regency councils. The temporary nature of the title appealed to all political players, including Cromwell, who had refused Parliament's offer of the crown and now accepted the Protectorate instead.[33]

The challenge of government had long bedeviled England. In the wake of the king's execution and Cromwell's takeover of power, an English writer sought to make sense of the tumultuous times. In 1651, Thomas Hobbes produced one of the earliest political theory texts in English, *Leviathan*. Whereas the Levellers and others during this period were what we would call activists, engaged in the formulation and execution of policy, Hobbes was not trying to participate in the debates in the Commons. His goal was to make a clear argument in defense of strong government. Hobbes reasoned through the process whereby people came together to form commonwealths, or communities, and how these commonwealths governed themselves. After showing that the state of nature left much to be desired, in that people's lives were "solitary, poor, nasty, brutish, and short,"[34] Hobbes explained how people gave up some liberty to a single leader or to an assembly of men, so that they could all work together for mutual support. It is this communal leader that embodies commonwealth, according to Hobbes, and whose role it is to rule:

> And in him consisteth of the essence of the Commonwealth; which, to define it, is one person, of whose acts a great multitude, by mutual covenants one with another, have made themselves every one the author, to the end he may use the strength and means of them all, as he shall think expedient, for their peace and common defense.[35]

Hobbes's strong penchant for order and for a powerful governor makes sense, given that he wrote his book at the end of the Civil War, a violent and dangerous time. Hobbes was so strongly in favor of order that *Leviathan* accepted the current government and called on English subjects to comply with their government's orders. This call to support existing governments gave comfort to Cromwell and his supporters and also outlined an argument for Cromwell that came to be known as "de factoism" for its willingness to overlook the unsavory origins of Cromwell's reign.[36]

Cromwell's constitution of 1653 would be short-lived. Following his death in 1658, his son Richard assumed the title of Lord Protector, but he did not have the heart for the job. Working without the strong support of the army, he could not command respect as his father had, and the political situation deteriorated quickly. Less than a year after taking over, Richard Cromwell resigned the Protectorate, and the constitution of 1653 was abrogated.[37] The surviving members of the Long Parliament reassembled one last time and agreed on the terms to offer Charles II in order to restore the monarchy and rebuild the traditional English government of king, Lords, and Commons. In 1660 Charles II returned to London, and the Restoration began.

Oliver Cromwell left a double legacy behind. On a positive note, Cromwell's military genius allowed Parliament to win the Civil War and ensure the preservation of representative government in England. On the negative side, however, Cromwell's willingness to take, and use, power and his career as military dictator made it clear that human nature was deeply suspect. His example would be the case study for English-speaking people everywhere about the danger of power and the challenges of self-government.

The lessons of Cromwell would shape the perceptions of his successors for more than a century. The thirty years following the Restoration worked out many of the lessons of the Civil War and helped lead to the establishment of the modern British monarchy, within a constitutional arrangement that limited the crown's powers and moved the House of Commons to the center of the English government.

The Restoration started reasonably well, with Charles determined to assume the throne peaceably and with the support of the people. His supporters moved forcefully in the House of Commons and the newly restored House of Lords to sweep away most of the reforms and innovations of the Commonwealth period.[38] But too much had changed to allow a return to a divine-right monarchy, and Charles II had to become accustomed to working with his Parliaments to get things done.

When Charles II died in 1685, his younger brother, James, the Duke of York, took the throne. His brief reign was troubled from the start. As king and head of the Church of England, James agreed to rule England according to its existing laws, including the preservation of the Church of England. As long as James worked within these rules, his reign was reasonably successful. Unfortunately for him and for England, James was a faithful Catholic, and he wanted to reform English government. His subjects could live with neither of these traits, and James slowly came into conflict with his bishops and his Parliament.[39] James II's problems came to a head in November 1688, when the Dutch prince William of Orange, the husband of the king's daughter Mary, landed in England with his army, at the invitation of seven prominent politicians nervous about their Catholic king.[40] William was intent on protecting England's Protestants from a feared Catholic takeover. On December 11, 1688, James fled London in the midst of this crisis. Parliament declared the throne vacant and offered the crown to William and Mary. They accepted the offer and assumed control of the government. After a few smaller battles with James's forces, King William III defeated James in Ireland in 1689 at the Battle of the Boyne, ending James II's efforts to regain the throne.[41]

The political effects of the Glorious Revolution of 1688–1690 brought the House of Commons to the fore and began the process of creating a true constitutional monarchy in England. William II had not been required to accept limits on his power before he took the throne, but at his coronation ceremony, a Declaration of Rights was read. He said after hearing the Declaration, "[A]s I had no other intention in coming hither than to preserve your religion, laws and liberties, so you may be sure that I shall endeavor to support them."[42]

William III and Mary II ushered in the beginning of the modern monarchy, limited in scope and restricted by a return to the traditional English constitution, based on the common law and cooperation between the king, Lords, and Commons. But this was not a complete return to the old balance; after the Civil War, the Commonwealth, and the Glorious Revolution, the House of Commons had become more influential than either crown or the Lords.

A key feature of English politics was introduced after the Restoration: the first recognizable political party, the Whigs, formed in about 1679 to oppose the possible succession of James II to the throne, on account of his Catholicism.[43] After the Glorious Revolution, the Whigs[44] were known for their generally antiroyalist leanings and their preference for a strong Parliament. They sought to influence public opinion through aggressive pamphleteering. Just as the Levellers and other groups had during the Civil War period, Whig politicians and their supporters published numerous tracts laying out their political philosophy, their opposition to corrupt governmental practices, and their proposals for reforming the government. In language borrowed from the Levellers, they returned to the ideas of popular sovereignty, limited government, and the need for checks and balances.

Like the reformers in the Civil War period, the Whigs who helped to bring on the Glorious Revolution were not scholars, but active participants in politics. John Locke would produce the most developed explanation of how government should work in his *Two Treatises of Government,* first published in 1690, but possibly written as early as ten years before.[45] Locke's vision of human nature and the need for government is not nearly as grim as Hobbes's views; Locke reflects the calmer situation after the Restoration. Even the Glorious Revolution was tame in comparison to the Civil War; it was shorter and involved fewer battles and many fewer soldiers. Locke argued that people agreed to enter into commonwealths, and established governments, by compact. A person would agree to join such a community for a simple reason:

> [H]e seeks out, and is willing to joyn in Society with others who already united, or have a mind to unite for the mutual *Preservation* of their Lives, Liberties and Estates, which I call by the general Name, *Property.*
>
> The great and *chief end* therefore, of Mens uniting into Commonwealths, and putting themselves under Government, *is the Preservation of their Property.*[46]

Locke and the Whigs argued strongly for the idea of limited government by consent. Their work extended the ideas of the Levellers from the Civil War into a more complete system of thought about how a free people should govern itself. Having learned the lessons of Cromwell, the Whigs looked for incipient tyranny everywhere. In the decades following the Glorious Revolution, Whigs would fight to maintain the traditional balance between king, Lords, and Commons, criticizing royal efforts (mostly successful) to influence the Commons and thereby corrupt the system of checks and balances upon which English government depended. In the colonies, these ferocious Whig critiques of royal and Parliamentary corruption would find a willing audience.

Revolution in America: A Cromwell Flashback

Though an ocean away from the tumult in England, the inhabitants of the colonies paid close attention to the political crises back home. With Puritans founding New England colonies[47] and Cavaliers expanding the settlements in Virginia, English settlers brought their English politics with them to the New World. The colonists also received mail, newspapers, and books from England with every ship that came from home. The stream of news from England not only kept the colonists up to date on the events in London, but also introduced new political ideas as they developed back home. Whig politics—and Whig attitudes—were chief among the political ideas that came to the colonies in the later 1600s and early 1700s.[48]

Whig fixation on political corruption played well in the colonies. So many of the settlers had left England for political reasons that they would be sympathetic to charges of corruption in the government. Although the popularity of the Whig arguments began to ebb in England by about 1730, colonial writers and politicians continued to use those critical Whig ideas as the basis for their own thoughts on self-government.[49] This may help to explain why the colonial leaders were able to move from arguing with Parliament and the king over a tax dispute to revolution so quickly in the years after the French and Indian War (1754–1763).[50] Primed by their knowledge of Whig political thought, they easily saw the taint of corruption in nearly any pronouncement from London.

Political disputes between the colonial governments and London began to heat up during the French and Indian War. For the first time, British regular troops were assigned to the colonies to fight French forces based in Quebec. As was traditional at that time, soldiers lived in private homes rather than in barracks. Homeowners were responsible for housing and feeding the soldiers out of their own pockets. The colonists had not had to deal with a garrison in their midst before this, and it caused serious tension between the colonies and London.[51]

Following the war, George III, who had come to the throne in 1760, asked Parliament for a series of new taxes to pay off the war debts. Because the war had started in the colonies and because England had spent so much to protect them from French forces in Canada, Parliament passed several new taxes on the colonies themselves, as a way of spreading the costs across all those who benefited from the successful war. The two most noticeable and most hated taxes were on paper and tea. The paper tax was quite intrusive: nothing escaped the grasp of this tax, which covered stationery, newsprint, and paper for documents.[52]

Colonial leaders were incensed. They were not allowed to vote for representatives to sit in Parliament, so how could they be taxed like this, without their consent? Leaders in London pointed out that Parliament spoke for the whole of the English people, and since the colonies were British, Parliament spoke for them as well. But the colonies would have none of it. Colonial experience made it difficult to accept the idea of "virtual representation." Colonial practice led the political leaders to revert to an older, medieval concept of direct representation. Their own legislatures, being close to the people, functioned in that manner: citizens expected their representatives to speak for their interests, and they could see their representatives working for them. Decisions handed down by Parliament in London frequently caused problems in the colonies: the government in London rarely had access to timely information about conditions across the Atlantic, so its bills made trouble for the colonial governments that had to enforce them.[53] Further, the colonists could not accept that Parliament truly represented them, let alone the English people at home. Virtual representation, they argued, did not even work in England, where new cities like Manchester returned no members of Parliament![54] If Parliament could not represent all of England effectively, then it could not hope to speak for the colonies. Therefore, since they had no direct voice in Parliament, colonial leaders saw no reason to accept what they saw as illegal taxes. They refused to pay them and forced Parliament and the king to rescind most of the taxes.[55]

But George III still insisted on his and Parliament's right to tax the colonies, setting the stage for a final confrontation. His tax collectors and the royal governors of the colonies attempted to force the citizens to comply with the remaining taxes. But the citizens of the colonies refused all efforts. The situation deteriorated until British forces in Massachusetts were ordered to confiscate militia arms and restore peace in the colony. The colonial militia opposed this move in April 1775, leading to the battles of Lexington and Concord and the beginning of the American Revolutionary War.

Colonial leaders, trained in English history and attuned by their Whig pamphlets to fear tyranny in every governmental action, saw a disturbing pattern in the tax disputes after the French and Indian War. They could see in George III's actions the beginnings of the same path that had led to the tyranny of Charles I and Cromwell, and they would not stand for it. To preserve their rights as Englishmen, they had to fight against this rising tyranny from London. When Parliament, supporting the king, sought to force compliance with the new taxes, the colonists' worst fears were realized: as the Whigs had after the Glorious Revolution, the colonists saw corruption at the root of the English government. They had no choice but to declare independence and create a new nation.

Following their victory at Yorktown in 1781 and the end of the war with the Peace of Paris in 1784, the leaders of the new United States of America found themselves in trouble. The government they had constructed during the war, under the Articles of Confederation, could not successfully lead the new nation in time of peace. War had unified the leaders and the nation, so the balky Articles, which required unanimous votes on all laws set before the Continental Congress, could be made to work. But the singleness of purpose found in war disappeared once peace began. By 1787, it was clear that the Articles of Confederation had failed as a system of government for the new nation. So a convention was called to revise the Articles.

The Constitutional Settlement

When the members of the convention gathered in Philadelphia in 1787, only some of them were thinking about revising the Articles.[56] Many of the members of the convention, including its leaders, realized that the Articles would have to be replaced with a new, more effective system of government. This new government, they believed, needed to meet the twin challenges of government in the New World: the new government would need sufficient energy to enable the country to make use of the resources it could access across the continent of North America, but such a government had to be built in a way that would prevent the slide into corruption and tyranny that England had experienced in the century before the American Revolution.

The key concept to understanding the Founders is their fear of tyranny. While many of the Framers were familiar with French political philosophy, such as the essays of Montesquieu and Rousseau, and tried to address their concerns about government, the Framers' main inspiration was English history and English government.[57] The Framers knew their English history well, and they were determined to construct a government that could prevent tyranny.[58] Seeing the seed of Cromwell in George III and fearing a future, American Cromwell,[59] the Framers wanted to build a government that could successfully prevent the establishment of tyranny. One of the anti-Federalists, "Brutus," reminded his readers during the debates over ratification of the twin legacy of Oliver Cromwell: "the same army, that in Britain, vindicated the liberties of that people from the encroachments and despotism of a tyrant king, assisted Cromwell, their General, in wresting from the people, that liberty they had so dearly earned."[60] Faced with this deep fear, the Framers decided to create a complicated government, not an efficient government. They sought to spread power all around the government, rather than collecting it in one place. They thus sought to use the powers of each part of the government to limit the other sections of the government; as Hamilton or Madison wrote in *Federalist* No. 51, "ambition must be made to counteract ambition."[61]

The first innovation that the Framers introduced was the concept of federalism, or a system of government on several levels. At the national level, there was to be a central government, which would manage the foreign affairs of the new nation. The thirteen state governments would continue to manage local matters as they had since the establishment of each of the original colonies.[62] The Framers also limited the power of the central government by leaving the militia in the hands of the states, so the states would have a military force to counterbalance the army and the navy of the new nation.

At the national level, the Framers sought to spread power across three branches. They shared with their English cousins a respect for the idea of consent, and they also shared their belief in a "mixed constitution" that relied on the strengths of the many parts of the government to counter those of the other parts. They sought to re-create the balance that they knew from English history, but they could not simply import the British idea of king, Lords, and Commons.[63] Since they did not want a king or hereditary nobility, they replicated the triple system of shared powers in three separate branches: legislative, executive, and judiciary. In order to make each of these branches limit the power of the other branches, the Framers designed a constitutional process that would require each of the branches to cooperate with the others in order to govern the nation. While the legislative branch would debate and pass laws, they could not take effect until the president, the chief executive, signed them, and they must pass constitutional muster, governed by the courts. In other words, the Framers went beyond crafting a government with separation of powers; they "created a system of separated institutions *sharing* powers"—and "sometimes competing for"[64] control over the powers of government.

Based on their English heritage, the Framers saw the legislative branch as the key to this new federal government. As the elected voice of the people, Congress would be the most likely branch to amass too much power, if English history was any guide:

> In republican government, the legislative authority necessarily predominates. The remedy for this inconveniency is to divide the legislature into different branches; and to render them, by different modes of election and different principles of action, as little connected with each other as the nature of their common functions and their common dependence on the society will admit.[65]

The "Great Compromise" at the constitutional convention involved the nature of the Congress. The Great Compromise did double duty: it met the political needs of moment, enabling large and small states together to ratify the new Constitution, and it also met the philosophical need to complicate the system of government and make tyranny harder to achieve. The House of Representatives served the needs of the large states, since it was based on population and the concept of majority rule. The Senate, on the other hand, protected the interests of the small states, since it would give each state an equal voice in the national government.[66] In addition to meeting the needs of the large and small states, this Great Compromise also met the Founders' need to combat tyranny.

The Framers sought to limit the reach of their new Congress. They built two conflicts into Congress that would limit its power. First, the Framers gave the members of Congress two jobs, making laws for the nation and representing the interests of their constituents, which frequently place different demands on individual legislators, forcing the members to balance constituents' and national interests. Second, the Framers designed Congress as a bicameral legislature, with two chambers that reflected two different takes on politics. They required any law to pass both of these different chambers in identical form before it could go to the president. By building two chambers that responded to political inputs differently and forcing them to cooperate to make law, the Framers hoped to restrain Congress and limit its power.

In the case of the House, the Framers built a chamber that focused on the representative role—they wanted to ensure that the people's voice was heard in the national government. The principle governing the structure and operation of the House would be majority rule. Thus, the seats in the House would be apportioned among the states according to population, and the states with more of the nation's citizens would have a louder voice in Congress than the smaller states. The Framers sought to make the members of the House hew closely to the desires of their constituents. By calling for the creation of small districts and by requiring frequent elections of the whole membership of the House, the Founders thought they could guarantee that the members of the House would stay very close to the people who chose them. Whatever the political whims of the moment might be, the House would reflect them with passion.

The Senate met the needs of the smaller states. The Framers designed the Senate to reflect the principle of equality—after all, each of the states had taken an equal risk in declaring independence, and each had an equal stake in the success of the new government. So each state would have two senators, giving all the states an equal voice in the affairs of the Senate. In addition, the Framers wanted the Senate to react differently than the House to political problems. Unlike the House, senators would serve long terms, and only one-third of them would face election[67] at a time. Long terms and staggered elections would insulate the Senate from day-to-day politics, allowing the chamber to reflect more on issues. The Framers hoped that this would allow the Senate, unlike the House, to consider the national interest as it made laws.

So the Framers met the need for ratification by addressing the concerns of both large and small states with their Great Compromise. They also hoped that their Congress would be self-limiting, with a partisan, populist House close to the people and a deliberative Senate looking to the national interest. Their creation has evolved and added some innovations since the First Congress met in 1789, but the intentions of the Framers still shape Congress today.

Evolution of Government Since the Constitution

How did the Founders' federal government, small and distant, evolve into the large set of institutions we know today? We can trace the slow evolution of Congress and the rest of the federal government through five time periods. Many historians have developed their own set of periods, designed to highlight certain key factors in the development of the nation; the one in use here focuses on changes in political organization, governmental structure, and congressional activities throughout U.S. history.[68] We will trace the evolution of Congress and the federal government through five periods: 1789–1830s, when the national government slowly established itself, began to institutionalize Congress, and dealt with the rise of political parties in the 1830s; 1830–1890, which saw the golden age of partisan politics in the United States and also witnessed the first stage of growing a large federal government after the Civil War; 1890–1947, which saw the building of most of the federal bureaucracy during the Progressive Era, the Great Depression, and the start of the Cold War; 1947–1991, the Cold War; and finally 1991 to the present, in which Congress has struggled with new challenges for which it is largely unprepared.

In the first period of our national history, Washington was small and focused on a few major issues of national importance, particularly how to retire the Revolutionary War debt and trade with Europe. Since state and local governments provided what citizens wanted, Washington had little to do to meet the needs of the people, other than deliver mail.[69] In 1787, the scale of life was much smaller than it is today. Most citizens lived out their lives in an area around their homes, no larger than the distance they could walk in a day, about twenty miles.

The House of Representatives was the important chamber of Congress and the central political operator in the national government. The Senate rarely took initiative on legislation, seeing its role as concurring (or disagreeing) with House legislation. Although many charismatic presidents served the nation in the early years (notably Thomas Jefferson and Andrew Jackson), they were not the imposing political figures that modern presidents can be (with the exception of George Washington, the political titan of his age).[70] Early presidents oversaw a small federal government with only a tiny retinue of personal staff to help them.

The most important feature of the early years of the Republic is the lack of national political parties. Although there were factions or regional political organizations in the United States almost from the beginning, our familiar two-party system did not fully form until the 1830s and was not fully mature until the eve of the Civil War. Parties in the first period were tied to political figures and to regional concerns.[71] The Framers did not anticipate the rise and power of political parties in the United States, but they knew Congress would have to respond to competing groups of citizens. The Framers could already see something like national parties forming in their own time, which James Madison called "factions" in his *Federalist* No. 10. Madison hoped that the new, complex national government would make use of factions and, in the mixing of their various views, be able to find the national interest.[72] The Framers made up two broad factions: Federalists who supported the new Constitution, and anti-Federalists who opposed it. Federalists supported a strong central government that was vigorous in pursuit of the national interest, while Democratic-Republicans continued to fear a powerful national government, preferring that the states be more important.[73]

So in this early period, Washington was a remote place to most Americans, and the House of Representatives was the engine of most political discussion and action. President Thomas Jefferson, for example, used his friend and political ally James Madison in the House to push his agenda, rather than attempting to do so from the White House. In the early period, the House operated with temporary committees until about 1816, when it began to establish standing committees to deal with recurring issues, such as military and naval affairs, foreign policy, and revenue questions. The House's leaders were informal, and the Speaker in this early time acted like a parliamentary officer, overseeing debate and imposing order, rather than directing the actions of the chamber.[74]

The Senate's early years were not busy by today's standards. The Senate took no legislative action on any bills until the House had passed them and sent them to the Senate for consideration. Like the House, the Senate used ad hoc committees to deal with important bills through about 1820; by the mid-1820s, the Senate's standing committees had also been established, but they deferred to the whole Senate, which made its major decisions on the floor.

By the 1830s change swept the American political landscape. The original issues of importance faded and were replaced by sectional issues, including how to expand the nation across the continent and how to deal with slavery. In addition, organized national political parties arose, changing national politics permanently. Parties shaped political debate, recruited candidates, and used their organized power to control the federal government. In this period, the national government ran on patronage, and every office was a political gift to supporters. The House began to shift toward a more partisan style of politics, and the Speaker became an important party leader. In the years after the Civil War (1861–1865), the federal government also began to take on more domestic chores, requiring the establishment of federal agencies, such as the establishment of the Justice Department in 1872 to enforce the Thirteenth and Fourteenth Amendments.[75]

A two-party system has been the heart of U.S. political competition since the presidency of Andrew Jackson (1829–1837). And this reality of party politics also shaped the House of Representatives, which came to be dominated by the majority party in the nineteenth century, as was all of Washington: when a new president came into office, the whole executive branch disappeared, replaced by partisan supporters of the new administration.[76] In this period, the Speaker evolved into the majority party leader of the House, and the majority party began to exert control over the actions of the chamber, taking control of the committee system and shaping the floor procedures that allow the majority to dominate the House.

The Senate in this period began its slow evolution from policy backwater to equal partner in legislation. Through the Civil War, the Senate conducted most of its work and made all its key decisions on the floor; although the formal committee system was in place, the committees did not move to the forefront of legislative action until after 1865. The Senate did not initiate any legislation until after the Civil War, preferring to wait for the House to approve a bill before acting on it.[77] Although the parties played a role in Senate politics, the individual senators were few enough and important enough that they could vote against party consensus if it made sense to them to do so. Furthermore, regional differences, as important in the Senate as party membership, tended to shape senators' views more than partisanship did. And despite the strong partisanship in nineteenth-century Washington, there was no party leadership in the Senate.

The third period of governmental evolution began around 1890 and lasted through the start of the Cold War in 1947. The Progressive Era (1890–1910) saw the creation of many agencies to oversee consumer protection, food safety, and workplace regulation. In this period, partisanship came to dominate politics. The strong partisanship of the early 1800s, though, led to a backlash during the Progressive Era, when reformers sought to limit partisanship, creating the civil service to guarantee a more professional executive branch.[78] The majority party in the House dominated the proceedings of the chamber, but in this period the majority party started exercising its power through the committee system, which was led by experienced, career legislators. The Speaker of the House retained his leadership role, but after 1910, the Speaker began to act more as a broker among the powerful committee chairs rather than as the unquestioned ruler of the chamber that he had been from the 1830s to the 1890s.[79] The Senate began to take a more active role in politics, as well, with some states looking to the public for their choice of senators (a constitutional amendment allowed direct election of senators). And as the federal executive branch began to grow, the president also began to take on a larger role in policymaking, which has allowed the president to emerge as the key agenda setter for Washington today. The Budget Act of 1921 gave the president an official role in legislation for the first time. With the later addition of the agencies and programs designed to combat the Depression (Social Security and employment agencies) and the Cold War (the Defense Department and the Central Intelligence Agency), the president now resides atop an enormous, multitalented bureaucracy.

The House continued to entrench rule by the majority party, with the Speaker's power diminished and spread out, first to the committee chairs (through the 1920s) and later to subcommittee chairs and the party caucuses in the 1970s. The leadership that evolved out of this time was centralized and very powerful.[80] The Speaker of the House had previously run the House with nearly dictatorial power, which critics referred to as "czar rule."[81] In 1910, however, the modern House can be said to have begun—a chamber dominated by committee (and later, subcommittee) chairs, working in concert with the majority party's leaders, the Speaker and the Majority Leader, to manage the affairs of the House.[83] In a fight with Speaker Joseph Cannon (R-IL) over his right to control floor debates, minority Democrats allied with a small group of reform-minded Republicans to limit Cannon's powers. House rules were modified after the fight with Cannon, introducing the period when committees took more power. Seniority rules protected the committee chairs from replacement by the Speaker, who also lost the ability to appoint every member of the key committees.

In this period the Senate became a full partner in legislation with the House. After the passage of the Seventeenth Amendment in 1913 allowed for direct election of senators, the chamber started to mimic the House in its initiation of new bills. By 1925 both Democrats and Republicans in the Senate had developed party organizations and selected party leaders to push their agendas.[83] Strong GOP government in the 1920s gave way to a Democratic majority during the New Deal years, during which the Senate's committee system and parties consolidated and became institutionalized. Following a Congress-wide reform in the Legislative Reorganization Act of 1946, the Senate took on the form that it has had since, with a few changes.

The Cold War period was next (1947–1991). Congress finished building the large executive branch we know today with the establishment of the Defense Department, the Central Intelligence Agency, and the National Security Council in 1947. These agencies, designed to manage the strategy of containment, served well throughout the Cold War, which demanded centralized coordination of global U.S. and allied military, intelligence, and diplomatic operations. With the creation of Medicare in the 1960s, the network of large programs and large agencies we still have today was essentially complete. The Cold War also had an effect on the relationship between the White House and Congress: the decades-long threat of the USSR and its satellites demanded focused leadership in Washington, strengthening the presidency in its legislative and policy battles with Congress.

The 1960s ushered in a decade of House reforms that further expanded the ability of individual members to participate in decision making, with the result that the Speaker's role evolved into chief bargainer for the House, working with committee and subcommittee leaders, party caucuses, and interested members to pass legislation.[84] In addition to securing additional power and staff resources for subcommittee and committee chairs, the reforms also empowered the Democratic Caucus and Republican Conference to assign members to committees. This period of reform ended a relatively quiet, less contentious political era.[85] House reforms echoed the political turmoil and change of the 1960s and 1970s, including the resurgence of strong partisanship. As the Republicans began to shift toward a more conservative and ideological viewpoint, the liberal side of the Democratic Party became more prominent, mainly because many conservative southern Democrats shifted the balance by leaving the party. This period also saw the emergence of a new, candidate-centered politics. Radio and television advertising made it possible for candidates to connect with voters directly. Prior to the mass media age, candidates had needed the party's precinct-by-precinct organization to reach voters. With less dependence on party leaders, candidates could set their own course during the campaign and continue to do so once in office. This freedom came at a price: while TV campaigning freed candidates from party control, it cost a lot of money. Members of the House devoted many hours to raising money to finance reelection, which came to dominate members' lives as much as their duties on the Hill do. The end result was a more participatory House, with a less powerful Speaker and committee chairs, but more powerful subcommittee chairs and reinvigorated party organizations.

The Senate in the 1950s and 1960s was the conservative bastion in Washington, refusing to move on civil rights and voting legislation. Individual senators have always been less responsive to their party leaders than their House peers; the rise of the mass media gave already independent senators another tool to carve their own political futures, without party help. Conservative southern Democrats, who held many of the key committee chairmanships, limited Senate action and reforms by refusing to work on such legislation without strong White House involvement. And the Senate also began to battle successive administrations over foreign policy issues. From the Vietnam War through Watergate and the intelligence scandals of the 1970s, to the "Star Wars" missile defense and the Contras in Nicaragua in the 1980s, the Senate limited the ability of Presidents Johnson, Nixon, Ford, Carter, Reagan, Bush, and Clinton to operate freely. Operationally, the Senate evolved further under its majority and minority leaders, with the majority leadership introducing the use of the unanimous consent agreement to manage floor action, a technique still used today.

Since 1991, politics in Washington has been in a new phase, one still without a clear focus. The end of the Cold War meant the end of nearly fifty years of foreign policy consensus. No new vision has emerged yet to replace the powerful idea of containment, with the result that Congress and Presidents G.H.W. Bush, Bill Clinton, and G.W. Bush have struggled to devise a new, broad agreement on U.S. foreign policy.

Politics has also changed since 1991. Following the Republican takeover of the House in the 1994 elections, the trend toward a distributed leadership slowed down, with Speaker Newt Gingrich (R-GA) centralizing GOP power under his control. For example, the rules adopted for the 104th Congress (1995–1997) imposed term limits of six years on committee and subcommittee chairs as a way to keep them loyal to the Speaker, who would have an opportunity to reward them with another committee post, or refuse one, depending on their performance.

In the Senate, the GOP takeover in 1994 did not have as significant an impact; the Senate had changed hands recently, and its weaker leadership positions and more independent membership meant that little structural change occurred. And with narrow margins to work with anyway, Senate GOP leaders faced stiff challenges to manage the Senate forcefully. Both Trent Lott (R-MS) and Bill Frist (R-TN) found it difficult to advance their party's agenda as they contended with independent-minded Republican senators like John McCain (R-AZ) and the New England group of Lincoln Chafee (R-RI), Olympia Snowe (R-ME), Susan Collins (R-ME), and, until he became an independent in 2001, Jim Jeffords (VT)—and as they confronted a unified Democratic minority only a few votes smaller than the GOP majority.

From its inception in 1789 to today, the Senate has evolved to reflect the independence of each senator; its committee chairs and party leaders have limited capabilities to dictate outcomes in the chamber. The House developed a stronger party role after the national two-party system emerged in the 1830s, and this has evolved since the late 1800s into the majority party institution we know today. House party leadership has expanded since 1910 beyond the Speaker and now includes committee and subcommittee chairs as well as party conference and caucus officers.

Summary

The Framers created a new federal government for the United States out of their own heritage and their own experiences. They saw the need for energy in government, and they knew that the weak, nearly paralyzed government of the Articles of Confederation could no longer work. They also feared tyranny, so they created a complicated government, whose various parts had to cooperate to get anything done. The combination—fear of tyranny and the need for energy—gave the Framers the impetus to devise a new government that drew heavily on English tradition, but that reflected the desire of Americans to create a government that would allow maximum liberty for its citizens, and would make an American Cromwell almost impossible. In this, it seems they may have succeeded too well—in ensuring no tyranny by a dictator, they may have built a machine that allows a sort of tyranny by inaction in its stead.

Web Resources

House of Commons, UK (www.parliament.uk/about_commons/about_commons.cfm).
House of Lords, UK (www.parliament.uk/about_lords/about_lords.cfm).
Hansard: This is the official record of debate in the Houses of Commons and Lords (www.parliament.uk/hansard/hansard.cfm).
Prime Minister's Office, London: The prime minister runs the British government in addition to leading the House of Commons. The prime minister sets the agenda for the government (www.number-10.gov.uk/output/Page1.asp).
The House of Windsor: This is the official Web site of the royal family. It includes historical information as well as the activities of the monarch (www.royal.gov.uk/output/Page1.asp).
The Oliver Cromwell Association: Dedicated to the study of Cromwell and the seventeenth century (www.olivercromwell.org/).

The Federalist Papers: Collected by the Library of Congress, in searchable format (http://thomas.loc.gov/home/histdox/fedpapers.html).

The Anti-Federalists: This interesting site from the University of Groningen, Nether-lands, collects several of the anti-Federalist writings (http://grid.let.rug.nl/~usa/D/ 1776–1800/federalist/antixx.htm).

Library of Congress: Established in 1800, the Library of Congress holds not only the extensive library collections of Congress, but also the Congressional Research Service and the THOMAS legislative information system (www.loc.gov/homepage/ lchp.html).

The Congressional Record: Like Parliament's *Hansard,* the *Congressional Record* reports the official transcripts of floor action in both the House and Senate (http:// thomas.loc.gov/home/r109query.html).

I • Competing Roles

Lawmaker and Representative

Members of Congress have two main functions in the national government—as policymakers and representatives—and those two roles sometimes conflict. Chapters 3 and 4 examine the House and Senate, respectively. Each chapter outlines the Framers' intent for the chamber, how it is organized, how the parties and committees operate in it, and what sort of leadership is needed in it.

The two chambers have evolved over time into two very distinct bodies for a reason: their modes of representation make them act very differently. In each chapter, the key idea is how the different institutions of House and Senate shape the way their members deal with the conflict between their twin responsibilities as lawmakers and policymakers.

The Framers were afraid of tyranny, so they designed a complicated national government for the United States. They made Congress the center of the government, then made it complex to limit its potential for mischief. They designed the House of Representatives and the Senate to find different answers to the challenge of lawmaking and representation. Each chamber has a different principle of representation, a different scale, and a different time frame.

The House runs on majority rule. The principle pf majoritarianism drives the House, as do its large-scale and rapid electoral cycles. All of these features were designed to keep the House and its members close to the political pulse of the people. Chapter 3 shows how these features have led to a House that is "all representation, all the time."

Equality drives the Senate. The Senate's equal voice for each state in the Union is reflected in its rules, which protect the minority party and give it a role in governing. The Senate is also smaller and slower than the House, which fosters a sense of collegiality that is still strong despite the increasing partisanship in Washington. As chapter 4 shows, the Senate can balance local representation with national policymaking better than the House can.

These two chapters show that the Founders sought to make the Congress self-limiting, in that House and Senate politics are so different from each other that it is hard for tyranny to seep in, because the two chambers fight with each other more than they cooperate—even when a single party controls both of the chambers.

3 • Speaking for the People

The Majoritarian House

As it is essential to liberty that the government in general should have a common interest with the people, so it is particularly essential that the branch of it under consideration should have an immediate dependence on, and an intimate sympathy with, the people. Frequent elections are unquestionably the only policy by which this dependence and sympathy can be effectually secured.
—Federalist No. 52[1]

House majority leader Rep. Tom DeLay R-TX and Speaker of the House Dennis Hastert R-IL were not happy. Despite every effort to channel the bill to unfriendly committees to kill it, the Bipartisan Campaign Reform Act of 2001, called Shays-Meehan for its two main sponsors,[2] just would not die. Despite a negative recommendation from the House Administration Committee, the bill's supporters had still wanted a floor vote. They did not like the rule proposed for managing the bill's floor action, so they defeated it. And now a majority of the House, 218 members, had signed a discharge petition to force the bill to the floor for a final vote. The leaders had worked for four years to kill Shays-Meehan, but the bill had too much bipartisan support. Over their objections, the bill came to the floor for House debate on February 13, 2002, and the chamber passed the bill 240–189 at two in the morning on February 14. Shays-Meehan was on the way to the Senate.[3]

The difficult history of the campaign finance bill reflects several truths about the House of Representatives. Its leaders are strong and the rules of the House usually allow them to get their way. Committees do most of the legislative work, preparing bills for the House to pass. But if a determined majority of the House chooses, it may force the leaders to deal with a bill they do not support. The House is a majoritarian institution: the majority party usually rules there, but sometimes the majority's leaders can be sidestepped. This passionate chamber was designed by the Framers to reflect popular opinion and to allow the majority to be heard. In this chapter, we will explore how the House operates today and how it allows the majority to be heard. We begin by reviewing the Framers' intent for the House. Then we will consider how political scientists study Congress and what they have identified as the key parts of the House. From there we can examine how the House is organized and what the individual members, the party leaders and the parties, and the committees do for the House. Then we will look at the House in action—how the majority party manages bills through the chamber, from introduction to passage during floor debates. The chapter ends by evaluating today's House against the ideas of the Founders.

The Logic of the House: Representation Over Legislation

The Framers intended the House to serve as the voice of the people in the Federal government. They wanted the members to reflect the interests of their constituents, so the Founders built a House that would stay close to the voters. They created small districts that would make it possible for members to know and understand the needs of their constituencies, and ensured close contact between the members and their voters by requiring elections every two years. By designing the House in this manner, the Framers sought to balance the two roles of the House in a specific way: they shifted the balance away from the lawmaking role and toward the representative role.[4]

The Founders designed the House to favor representation over lawmaking: they wanted House members to think first of their own districts and to reflect the districts' interests in the national government. The Framers wanted the House to be a majoritarian institution, and they made sure this would happen by addressing three issues. The House is devoted to the principle of majority rule; it is large, so its members all end up with small districts; and it faces the voters frequently. The idea of majority rule underlies all of the House's activities. States receive representation in the House proportional to their population, so states with the majority of the citizens also have most of the seats in the House. The House extended this idea into its own organization by looking to the majority party for leadership of the chamber; as parties evolved in the United States, this habit became even more pronounced, so that today the House reflects the will of the majority party very effectively. The Framers establish a large House to match the scale of the nation they imagined would grow from the original thirteen states, with the prospect of further expansion as the nation grew in both population and number of states. A large House means that the individual districts of each member can be small, encouraging the members to form close ties with their districts get to know the whole range of its industry, agriculture, and population. Although congressional districts have grown substantially since 1789, they are still small enough that members can learn everything that goes on in their home districts. The Framers sought to ensure that this close connection between member and constituents would stay strong, no matter how long a member served in Washington, by requiring frequent elections. The two-year cycle means that every decision a legislator makes will be fresh in the constituents' minds when the next election occurs—and a wise member knows this. Members therefore work hard to understand the political views of their voters and to reflect them forcefully in Congress. Frequent elections also expose the whole House to the potential for large turnover in an election: since every seat is up every two years, a major political change such as a scandal in the ruling party or the election of a popular new president can cause a corresponding shift in the House.

What have the Founders wrought? The House they created is passionate, partisan, and responsive to the political winds. In terms of the balance between representation and legislation, the House is "all representation, all the time." The modern House is concerned almost entirely with the role of representation. The House creates, debates, and passes bills that are designed to advance the interests of the members of the House particularly, the members of the majority party, rather than to meet the general interests of the nation except, of course, as defined by the majority party. The House uses its members' desire to get reelected as a good to get them to take on all the difficult work needed to accomplish things in the House—especially the committee work that creates most of the legislation done by the House.[5]

The House has been the subject of intense research by political scientists since the discipline emerged in the late 1800s.[6] From the beginning, political scientists have tried to simplify their research efforts by creating models that focus on the really important pieces of the complicated puzzle of the House. The earliest efforts targeted the structure and the rules: if we could define the committee system and the floor rules of the House precisely enough, we would understand Congress. The institutionalist approach helped us to see how the official actors and the formal structures shaped House action. By the 1950s, some researchers expanded the study of Congress to include the actions of groups in politics and how individuals developed political opinions and made decisions. Incorporating ideas from sociology and psychology, the behavioralists showed how parties, interest groups, and other unofficial actors took part in congressional action. In the late 1950s and through the 1970s, a new wave of research began to use economics models to study politics. Rational choice researchers focused on the actions of individuals and how they satisfied their interests through political action. Using rigorous assumptions and intense mathematical modeling, this approach relies heavily on deductive reasoning to get to the bottom of politics. The 1980s saw two new approaches emerge. The neoinstitutionalists make use of the interesting work from each of the preceding schools. This approach sees that none of the earlier approaches can explain all of politics, so it favors combining the best of each; and now some researchers employ the insights and methods of complexity theory to explore Congress.[7] Research continues using all of these methods, and, taken together, the scholarship tells us that to understand Congress, we need to know how individual members think, how committees act, and how parties and leaders act— and we need to know how each of these players interacts with all the others.

Researchers use several methods to study the important features of the House. Empirical research is the focus of this story: that is, real-world evidence that theories help to explain. Some studies rely on statistical analyses of large sets of data drawn from congressional documents such as bills, committee reports, and the *Congressional Record* itself.[8] Others focus on legislative history,[9] surveys, and polls to track how the House wrestles with ideas.[10] When data are scarce, or when the House does something rarely, we can use the case study method to explore specific instances; it is extremely difficult to generalize from case studies, but they can illuminate how the House does its work if done thoroughly.[11] Some political scientists concentrate on theoretical approaches, and others stress normative political science suggesting what Congress ought to be doing rather than what the institution actually does[12]; this story about the House will not draw too much on these types of research because our focus is empirical.

Organizing the House

The House is not a single operation: it is a loose conglomeration of 440 individual offices,[13] plus the offices of the committees and subcommittees, plus the minority and majority leadership offices, plus the administrative and support offices that operate the House chamber, its space in the Capitol, and its three main office buildings. In addition to the administrative offices, the House relies heavily on its committee system, which manages the flow of legislation. Given the range of issues and number of bills that the Congress considers in any session, it would be impossible to do everything on the floor, so the House has come to depend on the committee system for issue expertise, for information about policy options, and to signal the rest of the House how to respond to bills. The House started using committees almost immediately, establishing its first permanent committee, Ways and Means, in 1802. Each member maintains a personal staff to manage constituent service and legislative work. And in addition to these formal components of the House, many unofficial groups also take part in the business of the House. These caucuses allow like-minded members to work together to pursue particular issues, or to highlight important concerns that neither party may articulate, or to work on policies that do not fall neatly under the jurisdiction of a single committee. The Congressional Black Caucus and the "Blue Dog" conservative southern Democrats are two of the most well-known caucuses.[14]

There are three important components of the House to explore—the individual lawmakers themselves, the party organizations and their leaders, and the committees. We will start with the members—who they are, how they got to Washington, and what they do while they are in the House. Then we will examine how they work together to get things done in committees and in parties.

Members of the House

The three primary reasons that people run for seats in the House are to represent the interests of their voters, to make good policy, and to seek power and prestige in the chamber.[15] The first decision any future member must make is to run for a seat in the first place. While many people are angered by certain political events or motivated by a specific issue to participate in politics, it is a much bigger step to run for office to change Washington. Candidates decide to run for Congress when they calculate that they have a chance to win a race.[16] Usually a candidate begins the process a year or more before the election, by seeking out donors and supporters. In a primary with several candidates, the participants need to introduce themselves to the electorate and distinguish themselves from the other candidates. Name recognition for many of these candidates will be very low, as many of them will be making their first foray into public life with their congressional campaign. Without the backing of important party leaders in the district and the endorsements of supporting groups, candidates in a contested primary face a steep battle for votes and campaign funding. Running for Congress is expensive, and once they win office, members of Congress will have to keep raising money for reelection campaigns—a constant worry for most of them. Some even maintain a campaign office all the time to manage this work.[17]

From the start of their first campaigns to the end of their careers in Congress, members of the House keep close to the views of their constituents. Once in Washington, members devote enormous energy to serving their constituents: if they do not do this well, they run the risk of losing their next election. Representatives must respond to any letters, calls, or e-mails their constituents send them, including many requests for help from citizens who are having trouble with a federal agency. Besides dealing with their constituents' needs, members of the House also face legislative duties: they have to keep up with bills under debate on the floor, and they must serve on several committees. Members are allowed to hire up to sixteen full-time staffers to help with these tasks. These employees serve at the pleasure of the member and have no civil service protections. If they displease their boss—or if the member loses the next election—they are out of a job.

Most congressional offices operate district offices and a Washington office. A senior staffer usually oversees the member's district office or offices. The staffers hired to work in the district offices focus on casework. They meet with individual citizens and work with them to resolve problems with federal agencies, such as confusing forms, missing Social Security checks, and collecting all benefits available to veterans. While most studies of Congress examine legislation in detail, district office casework does more for many legislators' reelection campaigns than any legislative success—it is easier for constituents to see the results of casework, and it has a more direct effect than any committee hearings.[18]

The Washington office concentrates on the representative's legislative work. It surprises many visitors to the House to see the relative youth of the typical Washington staffers. The backbone of congressional operations is the long-term employees who make a career of working for the House, but most House staffers work for a few years only before heading into other jobs in Washington—usually outside of government, where their skills and experience earn higher salaries. Members do not receive large allowances for their staffs, so for the past thirty years or so, they have offered relatively low salaries to the large number of energetic young people who seek jobs on the Hill, in exchange for the unsurpassed on-the-job training these jobs provide.[19] Despite the youth of most staffers, they are responsible for much of the work that happens in Congress. The House is a busy place, with hundreds of meetings, committee hearings, and floor debates happening daily whenever the House is in session. Members' offices keep track of these activities for their bosses. The typical office staff consists of a chief of staff, or administrative assistant, who manages the office, and a number of legislative assistants, who track the activities of the House's committees and kept the member apprised of bills coming to the floor for debate. Another key player in every member's office is the press secretary, who stays in close contact with media outlets in the district, keeping them informed of the member's work for the district. With so much of the House's work taking place in Washington, the members need a strong connection to their constituents, and the media offer the best opportunity to maintain a presence back home. Most offices also have a scheduler, who keeps track of daily appointments, meetings, hearings, and other scheduled events, and a receptionist, who manages the flow of visitors into the office.[20]

Besides helping the members to remain connected closely to the constituents back home, these staffers also help the members with their committee work.

Figure 3.1   **A Day in the Life of a Representative**

7:15 – 8:00 AM	Breakfast meeting with issue caucus, Longworth Building
8:30 – 9:30 AM	Meeting with committee chair and policy expert, Rayburn Building
9:30 AM – 7:00 PM	Floor action, three bills, recorded votes expected
10:00 AM – 12:00 PM	Subcommittee mark-up, authorization issues, subcommittee room, Cannon Building
10:30 AM – 1:00 PM	Full committee meeting, committee room, Rayburn Building
12:00 – 1:00 PM	Leader's luncheon, Capitol
1:00 – 1:30 PM	Meeting with constituent
1:30 – 2:00 PM	Meeting with constituent
2:00 – 2:30 PM	Meeting with constituent
3:00 – 4:00 PM	Meeting with constituent and representative from national advocacy organization
5:00 – 6:00 PM	Issue caucus meeting, Capitol
7:00 – 9:00 PM	Four receptions, various locations on Capitol Hill

Each member of the House serves on a number of committees, assigned to them by their party organization. Since the House does its legislative work through the committees, members strive to gain assignment to committees that will allow them to serve their districts well and that will help their own electoral chances. Members from rural districts, for example, might try for a seat on the Committee on Agriculture, as the best way they can serve their constituents' needs.[21]

Members of the House are busy people. When Congress is in session, legislators in the House run from meeting to meeting, usually starting with a breakfast meeting and continuing through the evening. In addition to meetings with constituents and interest groups in their own offices, members attend committee hearings and working sessions, and they must go to the floor regularly whenever bills come up for votes. Figure 3.1 lists a typical day in Washington for a member of the House.[22]

Members of the House run to serve their constituents, to make good policy, and to find a niche in the chamber so they can contribute. And they have to raise money all the while, so they can prepare for reelection. They have their own staffs to help with their work, but even so, legislators are busy people. They look to their party leaders to help them achieve their policy goals and get reelected.

Parties and Leaders in the House

The House is a majority-party institution, which means that the majority party must govern, as well as pursue its own specific goals. Several models have been offered to explain how the majority party maintains control over the chamber, from an analogy to a sports team[23] although it would have to be a team managed by player-coaches, since the House leaders are not as powerful as a football team's head coach, to the most compelling recent effort, which models the parties in the House as cartels. In this view, parties use the committees to control the shape of bills, and the majority party acts as a sort of procedural coalition that maintains power in the House by controlling the outcomes of floor debates.[24] The majority party's leaders work for their party to manage this system, but they are also the leaders of the House, and they must preserve the powers of the institution. As party leaders, they work to ensure that their members get reelected and preserve their majority status. After service to their constituents, party affiliation is the most important concern for most House members. Majority or minority status dictates how successfully the members can advance their policy goals. Since the contemporary House is a majority-party institution, the policy goals of the majority party members carry a great deal of weight.

"Majority" and "minority" are not merely labels used for convenience. Studies of voting behavior in the House indicate that there is a strong difference between Republicans and Democrats, a difference that persists over time. If we imagine an issue space and attempt to graph the specific issue preferences of all House members across that space, we would see a clear pattern emerge: while there is a little overlap, most of the Democrats fall closer to one end of the space the liberal end, we call that, and most of the Republicans fall closer to the other end of the issue space the conservative position. Figure 3.2 depicts this bimodal distribution for the 105th Congress.[25] These "spatial voting" studies disagree on whether the single liberal-conservative dimension is enough to explain voting patterns, but even those researchers who advocate other dimensions such as southern versus northern, or racial issues, or big government versus small government recognize that the party labels reflect a real difference in opinion between the representatives in the two parties.[26] Table 3.1 lists the House majority parties in every Congress since 1950.[27] And that difference plays out in relations with the executive branch as well. Since George W. Bush won the White House in 2001, the House's leaders have endorsed the president's agenda. The House balked at some of his controversial reelection campaign proposals, such as an amnesty for illegal immigrants, but in general, Republican House leaders have supported the Bush White House.[28]

The House has two sets of leaders, one for the majority party which also runs the House itself, and one for the minority party. The House majority leadership teams starts with the Speaker, who serves as the voice of the House in discussions with the other parts of the federal government. The Framers took the idea for the Speaker from their heritage as Britons: the House of

Figure 3.2   **Liberal/Conservative Split, 105th Congress**

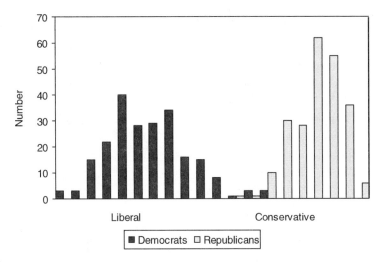

Commons has a Speaker, who represents the Commons in dealings with the Lords and the Crown. The Speaker also maintains discipline in the chamber and enforces the rules of debate in the commons. The British Speaker is guided by the desires of the Commons, as the English Civil War–era Speaker William Lenthall put it to Charles I: "May it please Your Majesty, I have neither eyes to see, nor tongue to speak in this place, but as the House is pleased to direct me, whose servant I am here, and I humbly beg Your Majesty's pardon that I cannot give any other answer than this to what Your Majesty is pleased to demand of me."[29] The Speaker of the House of Representatives is the formal leader of the chamber, as well as leader of the majority party. The Speaker is the majority party's strategic leader, responsible for setting the party's agenda in the House.

The day-to-day activities on the House floor fall to the House majority leader, who schedules floor debate on bills and ensures that the committees are crafting bills in keeping with the plans of the majority party. The House majority whip is third in command, with the responsibility to use the whip organizations of regional managers, who help motivate the members from a geographical region to maintain voting discipline in the party, so it can make full use of its majority status.

The House's minority party leaders have no institutional role similar to the agenda management and floor scheduling duties of the majority leaders. With no role in running the House, the minority leaders are free to concentrate their energies on meeting party needs. And they do! Minority leaders have two tasks. They rally their party members to oppose majority party

Table 3.1

Majority Party, U.S. House, 1950–2005

Congress	Years	Majority
82nd	1951–1953	Democrats
83rd	1953–1955	Republicans
84th	1955–1957	Democrats
85th	1957–1959	Democrats
86th	1959–1961	Democrats
87th	1961–1963	Democrats
88th	1963–1965	Democrats
89th	1965–1967	Democrats
90th	1967–1969	Democrats
91st	1969–1971	Democrats
92nd	1971–1973	Democrats
93rd	1973–1975	Democrats
94th	1975–1977	Democrats
95th	1977–1979	Democrats
96th	1979–1981	Democrats
97th	1981–1983	Democrats
98th	1983–1985	Democrats
99th	1985–1987	Democrats
100th	1987–1989	Democrats
101st	1989–1991	Democrats
102nd	1991–1993	Democrats
103rd	1993–1995	Democrats
104th	1995–1997	Republicans
105th	1997–1999	Republicans
106th	1999–2001	Republicans
107th	2001–2003	Republicans
108th	2003–2005	Republicans
109th	2005–2007	Republicans

Source: Adapted from Clerk of the House, *Party Division, 1989 to Present.*

policies, pointing out the flaws in their proposals and offering alternatives for consideration.[30] Minority leaders also work hard to identify good challengers to recruit to run for House seats in future elections, so they can help earn their party the majority and thus control of the House. The minority leaders are free to be "bomb throwers" and to make life as miserable as possible for the majority leadership. The House minority leader organizes the party's messages on bills coming up for debate and coordinates with the majority leadership when major bills come to the floor, or when some dispute arises. Minority whips maintain party discipline, using a similar system of deputies and regional whips to keep the House's minority Representatives together during votes. The minority whip is responsible for advising party members what bills are scheduled to come to the floor, how the Rules Committee is planning on structuring the debate and the vote, and the political consequences of each bill.

Each party supports its leaders with an organization that helps define the agenda and generate support for the leaders. On the Republican side, the GOP conference chair oversees majority planning and policy development for the Republicans in the House, who organize themselves into a conference. The chair leads internal party debates, formulates and presents alternatives, and crafts the political messages that the party's members will need to explain their activities in Washington. The GOP conference also helps by approving committee assignments for all Republican representatives. Party leaders also must help their members get reelected, and they must find good candidates to run in open races. This task falls to the National Republican Congressional Committee, chaired by Rep. Thomas Reynolds of New York in the 109th Congress, which spent $185.7 million in the 2004 election to get more GOP lawmakers into the House.[31]

The Democrats organize themselves into the Democratic caucus, and their steering committees help the leaders with message formulation, legislative proposals, and committee assignments for all the Democrats serving in the House. The Democratic Congressional Campaign Committee, managed by a House Democrat Rep. Rahm Emmanuel of Illinois in the 109th Congress, spent $92.8 million in the 2004 elections.[32]

Committees

The committee system is vital to the workflow, policy expertise, and management of the House. While party leaders set the agenda for the House, the committees do its real work. The House membership is too large to allow for significant work to be done on the floor—a debate with 435 participants can spin out of control and take too much time. The committee system evolved as early as 1810 in recognition that the House floor was too unruly a place to resolve major policy issues.[32] A group of members sitting on a committee could develop the expertise in an issue area necessary to craft legislative responses to problems. Committees could also resolve partisan disputes before bills went to the floor, thus minimizing the time needed by the House to meet in a single group to make decisions. Committee chairs grew to their modern degree of power after the 1910 rebellion against Speaker Cannon. By giving them autonomy—the power to organize their own committee staffs and to manage the legislative work of their committees—the House sought a counterweight to a powerful Speaker with tightly centralized control over the House. Since then, Speakers have had to work with the committee chairs to get bills passed, which has democratized the House by spreading power over a larger number of members. Power sharing further expanded to the subcommittee chairs in the post-Watergate reforms in 1974, along with an end to the rigid adherence to the seniority rule.[33]

The House manages its work using two types of committees: legislative committees, with responsibility to produce bills in an issue area, and nonlegislative committees, that do not write legislation.[34] The Ethics Committee is an example of a nonlegislative committee; it does not produce legislation but it performs an administrative service for the House, namely oversight of the House's internal ethics rules. Among the legislative committees, there are two groups of committees, as well: the money committees, with responsibility for some aspect of the federal budget raising money, setting budget goals, or making spending decisions, and policy oversight committees, which monitor the actions of the federal executive branch and make policy recommendations for the House. Money committees do have oversight responsibility, and oversight committees do authorize spending, but we will see in chapters 5 to 7 that the two groups of committees help Congress enforce its decisions in different ways.

Rule 10 of the House Rules sets the jurisdictions of the House's twenty standing permanent committees, three joint committees, and its one select special committee. Figure 3.3 lists the House committees in the 109th Congress. A committee's jurisdiction is the range of issue areas that fall under the committee's legislative responsibility. Committee jurisdictions have been fairly stable in general terms because powerful committees protect their turf jealously and expand it whenever new issues arise.[35] Committees use many other strategies for enhancing their power in the House, such as writing themselves into laws, holding numerous hearings, and building a history of working on an issue.[36] Each of the committees writes its own rules for how it will conduct meetings and take votes on bills. Using a formula agreed upon by the majority and minority, based on the party split in the House, each party assigns members to the committees and subcommittees. The chairs and ranking minority members of each committee and subcommittee wield tremendous power. The chairs decide how to organize the professional staff of the committees, and they alone set the agenda for their committees or subcommittees. On most committees, the chair and the ranking minority member each get funding from the House to set up staff, with the majority receiving the preponderance of the funds since it has to craft legislation. Each committee has a suite of offices somewhere on the House side of the Capitol complex. These offices house the professional staff, in separate majority and minority workspaces. Committees also have hearing rooms where they conduct their work. Committee staff personnel research issues, carry out investigations for the committee, and craft legislation to be considered by the

Figure 3.3 **House Committees of the 109th Congress**

Legislative/Oversight	Legislative/Money	Nonlegislative
Agriculture	Appropriations	House Administration
Armed Services	Budget	Standards of Official
Conduct		
Education and Workforce	Ways and Means	Economic Joint
Energy and Commerce	Taxation Joint	Printing Joint
Financial Services		
Government Reform		
Homeland Security		
International Relations		
Judiciary		
Resources		
Rules		
Science		
Small Business		
Transportation and Infrastructure		
Veterans' Affairs		
Intelligence Permanent Select		

Source: U.S. House of Representatives.

committee. Some committee staffers are assigned to help specific members manage their committee work. Many staffs also make use of fellows provided by executive branch agencies or by outside organizations, such as the National Science Foundation or the American Political Science Association, whose members work in Congress for a few months to a year in order to learn the inside story of how Congress does its work.[37]

Every member of Congress serves on committees, and each legislator spends much of the time in Washington on committee work. Each of these types of committees plays a different role in how the House executes its lawmaking responsibility, as we will see in the next section.

Majority Rule in the House

What the House does is pass bills. As one half of the national legislature, the House announces its policy decisions to the rest of the federal government and to the people by passing bills. The majoritarian House usually passes bills that have the support of a majority of the members *of the majority party* of the chamber. The House's rules, structures, and processes are all designed to help the majority party maintain discipline—not just over the various members of the House, but also over the power distributed to the various committees of the House, and over the numerous bills it examines every Congress—5,758 bills in the 107th and 5,359 in the 108th Congress, for example.[38]

Box 3.1

Congress and College I

Brother, Can You Spare a Dime?

Does Congress do anything that affects your daily life? The answer is yes if you are attending college using federal student loans.

Growth in available funds for federal loan programs was slight for 2006. The House proposal for spending on all education programs was approved at $56.7 billion, an increase of just $118 million over the previous year's level. House committee action also sought to close a loophole in federal loan programs that guaranteed a high rate of return to participating banks, which costs about $1 billion a year. The small increase in federal education spending and limits to future profits might squeeze federal loan availability for students.

Every time you have to go to the student financial aid office, and every time you send in a payment on your student loans once you graduate, think of the House of Representatives. . . .

Sources: Committee on Appropriations, "Full Committee Reports FY06 Labor, HHS, Education Appropriations Bill," Press Release, U.S. House, 109th Cong., 1st sess., June 17, 2005; "The Loophole's Loophole," *Washington Post,* July 18, 2005.

In order to allow the majority party to work its will effectively, the House has evolved a power structure designed to distribute legislatives tasks and, by extension, legislative power over the whole House, so the House can deal with all the bills that it generates every year. In this system, the committees play the decisive role. While House leaders craft the agenda, arrange the floor schedule, and control the rule-making process for dealing with debate on each bill when it comes to the floor, without the committees, the House would not be able to pass any bills. Again, in keeping with the House's majority-rule approach to representation, the majority party controls the levers of power over the legislative process, with the minority able to offer only token resistance without breakaway support from disaffected majority party members.

Any member of Congress and all of the legislative committees can produce bills. Once a bill is accepted, it is assigned a number such as HR 234, "To amend chapter 81 of title 5, United States Code, to authorize the use of clinical social workers to conduct evaluations to determine work-related emotional and mental illnesses," introduced in the 109th Congress and the

Speaker refers the bill to the appropriate committee or committees for review. If the committee likes the bill, one of its subcommittees will work on the bill, and pass it, so the full committee can examine it. Once a committee approves a bill, it reports the bill back to the whole House. If the leaders decide to support the bill, it goes to the floor for action, either on a fast-track process called suspension of the rules if it is noncontroversial or on the regular track. The Rules Committee prepares a resolution for each regular bill that defines how the House will debate the bill. The House then debates the rule, and if it accepts the rule, it then debates the bill. Bills earning a majority of votes on the floor can go to the Senate for its consideration.

The number 218 is what matters in the House: that is the number of votes the majority needs to pass a bill on the House floor. Everything the committees and leaders do aims at convincing 218 of the individual members to vote for a bill when it comes to the floor. To see how the House gets to 218, we will study the majority party leaders, the committees, and floor action in the House.

House Leadership and Legislation

The House is not very hierarchical: its leaders are leading their peers who also won seats in Congress and have their own power bases. Leaders run a weak party system with limited ability to discipline individual legislators; they also have to compete with the committee system, which does most of the legislative work in the House and therefore has a great deal of power.[39] The other members of the majority party look to their leaders to "[mobilize] others toward a goal shared by leader and followers."[40] House leaders manage tasks on three levels: institutional concerns, which preserve the powers of the House relative to the Senate and the executive branch; programmatic issues, which advance the majority party's policies and protect its majority status at election time; and tactical concerns, which focus on passing bills connected with the majority party's larger concerns.[41] House action on policy comes in the form of bills, and leaders must always remember that "lawmaking is the central and defining task of a democratic legislature."[42] The House leaders' role is to make it possible for the majority party to pass the agenda it wants. In pursuit of this responsibility, they are responsible for managing the flow of bills through the House, from their initial introduction through committee action to deliberation on the floor and on to passage and referral to the Senate.

Before they can pass bills, leaders must help their fellow majority party members develop their policy agenda. Starting in the 1960s, both parties started using their caucus/conference policy or steering committee to manage this important task. Working with the chair of the policy/steering committee, majority leaders help plot out the major legislative tasks for each Congress shortly after the elections. The leaders include their whole party team in this process so everybody in the majority party supports the program they develop. The leaders know the distribution of views in their party and the House as shown in Figure 3.2, and the leaders use this information in their party meetings, so they can feel comfortable that they are crafting policies that will attract the maximum amount of support. Reforms in the House since 1974 have brought the committees under some control by the leaders and by the majority party caucus/conference, as well. These reforms include conference votes for committee chairs; the ability to send a bill to several committees, that can dilute a single committee's influence; floor procedures that allow for many amendments; leadership input on conference committees with the Senate to finalize bills; and spending caps in the budget rules, which limit the freedom of other committees to set their own budgets.[43]

Party leaders have limited ways to force their members to stay in line. They can remove individuals from committee slots or give less support to them at reelection time, but committee removals happen very rarely, usually after a major transgression, such as James Traficant's D-OH conviction for financial irregularities in 2002, after which the Democratic leaders removed him from his committee assignments. The House expelled him shortly thereafter.[44]

When the GOP took over the House majority in 1995, it added another mechanism to rein in committee chairs—a three-term limit on serving as chair. And the leaders can always remove a chair. Ethics Committee officially called the Committee on Standards of Official Conduct chair Joel Hefley R-CO and Veterans' Affairs chair Christopher Smith R-NJ were both replaced after the 2004 elections because they did not follow party guidelines: Hefley's committee admonished majority leader Tom DeLay R-TX three times in 2004 for ethics lapses, and Smith's committee authorized veterans' spending far higher than party leaders had specified.[45]

Leaders devote much of their energy, though, to getting bills passed. As soon as a legislator introduces a bill, the leaders can help or hinder the bill by referring it to a sympathetic or skeptical committee. Leaders can also send the bill to several committees if it deals with issues that cross the House's jurisdictional boundaries. Once a committee has approved a bill and reported it to the House, the leaders decide if they want to go forward with the bill. The Speaker and the majority leader decide the floor schedule, and that is a powerful tool: if they decide against a bill, it dies unless 218 legislators agree to force them, using a "discharge petition" that forces the bill onto the floor calendar. And leaders do not always follow the rules in getting bills ready for the floor. For instance, during the first few months of the 104th Congress, Speaker Newt Gingrich did not send all ten of the bills supporting the goals of the 1994 congressonal election campaign's Contract With America to committees for action; Gingrich and his team drafted many of the bills themselves and bypassed the committees completely, sending the bills right to the floor; they also wrote other bills and pressured the committees to pass them with little or no debate, and no amendments.[46]

What can leaders do to get bills passed? They have three tactics for gaining the votes they need to pass a bill: they can persuade people to support their proposal, they can modify it to expand their supporting coalition, or they can use procedural maneuvers to increase their chances of victory. Leaders use persuasion to convince majority members to support a bill as written. Both parties have expanded the policy formulation role of their caucuses in the past thirty years to develop stronger support for their programs; if the members help to develop the plans, they are more likely to support bills when they come to the floor for action.[47] Leaders agree to modification of a bill when they cannot muster enough support to ensure victory; leaders can allow amendments on the floor, or they can push a committee to incorporate changes to entice more supporters to back the bill.[48] Finally, leaders can use procedure to protect their members from electoral problems by hiding controversial votes. For instance, leaders frequently combine several spending bills at the end of the fiscal year into large omnibus bills, containing many separate provisions: lawmakers can vote for the whole package and use the helpful items in the giant bill as cover for any difficult choices they also made. Another instance of procedural maneuvering is the base closing commission devised by Richard Armey R-TX in 1988, which allowed the Pentagon to close unwanted military bases without interference from congressional members desperate to protect bases in their home districts. After an independent commission reviews recommendations for base closings, it forwards the whole list of targeted bases to the president, who sends it to Congress if he supports it. Congress must vote to approve the whole list or nothing—and without the ability to carve out a few bases, Congress had the political cover needed to close bases in the name of improved national security and financial responsibility.[49]

Leaders have to bring many working parts of the chamber together to get bills passed—they have to account for party, committee, and personal ties, and they have to deal with independent legislators who each have their own constituencies. Facing the constraints of fragmented power across the committees, weak parties, and independent lawmakers, leaders use persuasion, modification, and procedure to coax together a winning coalition behind a bill. Before we can see what happens to bills on the House floor, though, we must trace their paths through the committee system. All the leaders do is set the conditions for a bill's success; it is left to the committee chairs to manage a bill's fate from the time they first get the bill in committee to the time it reaches the floor.

Committee Action

House committees perform two important functions for the chamber and for the majority party. First, they provide individual legislators with opportunities to advance their own electoral interests. According to the "distributive" view of committees, they exist to distribute goods and services to districts around the country, and policymaking is just the aggregation of benefits by the various committees.[50] And while legislators do in fact seek out committee assignments that can help their districts and their own reelection chances, committees do far more than that for the House. The committee structure also helps the House handle its workload by spreading the policy work out among the committees. The "informational" approach notes that the committees also develop policy expertise to manage oversight and legislation.[51] Individual legislators' needs lead them to specialize in policy areas, and their expertise ends up helping the House.[52] The House then looks to the committees to produce appropriate bills for passage; even if the committee tends to be out of step with the majority views, its work can still be a decent signal to the rest of the House members. And only committees with narrow jurisdictions run the risk of developing such a bias.[53]

Although the House relies on the committees to carry the weight of legislative work, House leaders and other members can influence committee action on bills. Leaders can adjust a bill so it goes to a friendly committee, or they can meet with committee leaders to impress their wishes upon the committee. Leaders can also create task forces to deal with specific bills, as happened frequently while Newt Gingrich was Speaker.[54] Legislators not serving on a committee frequently write letters to committee leaders making specific legislative requests, and legislators who have special expertise on an issue frequently testify before an oversight committee to press for action. Outside actors, including the White House and interest groups, also try to influence committee deliberations.[55] Committees do not work in a vacuum, in other words: as they do their legislative work, they must respond to the desires of the majority party, the chamber as a whole, and outside groups.[56] If the committees stray too far from the issue positions of the median majority member, they can expect difficulty on the floor and scrutiny of future bills.

Committees do most of the basic work of researching and writing the bills that go to the House floor for action. Every bill introduced in the House goes to the committee with jurisdiction over the bill's main issue, and the committee's chair has complete control over the bill's fate—the chair can decide to work on the bill by referring it to a subcommittee, or take no action, killing the bill. Subcommittee staff and members will study the bill and hold hearings if they need to learn more about the issue. They usually call witnesses from the executive branch, in order to hear the testimony of those who would enforce the bill if it became law. They also hear from interest groups, scholars, and other experts on the issue. If they decide to pursue the bill, the subcommittee meets to consider the bill and any amendments needed to align the bill with subcommittee preferences. Since rules changes in 1973, the subcommittees have had a key role in working on bills; they now have control over their staff and their agendas, freeing them from domination by the committee chairs.[57] If a majority of the subcommittee supports the bill, it goes to the full committee, where the committee chair leads a discussion on the bill. The committee will consider both the bill and any needed amendments, and if it passes again, the committee sends the bill to the full House for action. The committee prepares a report to accompany the bill, explaining the purpose of the bill and the work done by the committee on the bill. If the House leaders agree to bring the bill to the floor, the committee chair and ranking member will manage the floor debate on passage of their bill.

Before a bill goes to the floor, though, it passes through the Rules Committee, the gatekeeper to the House floor. Because of the complexity and difficulty of using the House rules to debate a bill on the floor, the House crafts special rules for each bill as it comes out of committee. Loyal majority party members who fully support the leadership dominate the Rules Committee, which produces rules for bills that meet the leaders' goals. Rules designed for bills announce the time limit for debate on the bill, any special requirements about waiving specific House rules or preventing "points of order" that could derail the debate, and what amendments, if any, will be allowed during debate on the bill. Acceptable bills tend to go to the floor under restrictive, or "closed," rules, which prevent amendments making the floor vote an up or down vote only. The Rules Committee issues "modified closed" rules for bills that generally meet the leaders' expectations. This type of rule specifies the amendments that can be debated on the floor. In some cases, the leaders either have no clear opinion on the shape of a bill or desire to see what will happen to a bill in floor debate; these bills go to the floor under "open" rules merely set the time limit for debate, with no restrictions on amendments that might be offered.

Floor Action in the House

Floor action is the last step in the complicated dance of approving bills. For most of the twentieth century, scholars paid very little attention to floor action, since the committees or the party leaders were usually thought to be far more important influences on the shape of bills coming out of the House. Since the reforms of 1974, the floor has become more active and has had more impact on the shape of House bills. In addition to increasing the power of subcommittee chairs and increasing the role of the party conference/caucus in policy formulation and committee assignments, the 1974 reforms also increased opportunities to use the floor to shape bills.[58]

As we have seen, most bills in the House go through a committee or several before they are ready for consideration on the floor. Leaders sometimes use less regular paths for some bills. No matter how it comes to the floor, though, the leaders put any bill that goes to the full House for passage on one of two schedules for action. Noncontroversial bills can pass without too much trouble, so they do not go through the Rules Committee. Most Mondays and Tuesdays, the House considers such noncontroversial bills on the Suspension Calendar. Generally, minority and majority leaders agree which bills should go on the Suspension Calendar. The House discusses these bills using an expedited process called suspension of the rules: each bill gets ninety minutes of debate, it cannot be amended, and the House must pass it with a two-thirds majority of those voting.[59]

Bills that require more debate go on the Union Calendar, and they require a special rule from the Rules Committee, discussed in the previous section, before they can go to the floor. Floor action on these bills occurs in two steps: first the House accepts the rule for the debate on the bill; then the House debates the bill itself. The House considers both the rule and the bill first in a committee that consists of the entire House membership, and that committee recommends passage to the House, which then votes on final passage of the bill.

Why add a step to an already involved process? Votes in the House are binding, and a failed vote requires House leaders to wait before they can reintroduce the bill. Using a procedure from the British House of Commons, the Continental Congress adopted the idea of the Committee of the Whole House, which consists of the entire body; early House leaders continued the tradition. The Committee of the Whole allows the House to consider a bill without making a final judgment; House members can debate a bill, consider amendments, and discuss the possibility of sending the bill back to committee for further work, all without a binding vote. Visitors to the House chamber or C-SPAN watchers can tell when the House is in the Committee of the Whole by two key distinctions: the Speaker does not preside over the Committee of the Whole, and whenever it is meeting, the ceremonial mace is removed from its pedestal to the right of the Speaker's chair. The Committee of the Whole needs a hundred members for a working quorum rather than 218 in the House, and all amendments are debated under a five-minute limit, rather than the one-hour limit in the House. The Committee of the Whole debates the proposed rule for a bill for one hour before voting on it; if it accepts the rule, the Committee then debates the bill under the provisions of the rule.[60]

Each rule specifies the time for debate, the amendments that are allowed, and any special instructions that may be needed for the bill. If the rule is closed, no amendments are allowed, and the bill must be approved or defeated as it came out of committee. Complicated tax and revenue bills from the House Ways and Means Committee frequently come to the floor under closed rules. Restricted rules allow certain amendments, specified in the rule, with no other amendments allowed. House leaders like this type of rule when they want a bill to pass as its originating committee created it. Open rules allow any amendment in correct legislative form to be offered during debate. Leaders allow this kind of rule only when they have no strong opinion on the final form of a bill or when they have been compelled to bring a bill they do not support to the floor. When the Shays-Meehan campaign finance reform bill came to the floor in 2002, House leaders did not support it, so they allowed the Rules Committee to issue a modified open rule, in the hopes that bad amendments would sink the bill. Once the Committee of the Whole has acted on each amendment and voted for passage of the bill, it "rises" and reports its action to the House. The mace then returns to its place, the Speaker takes the chair, and the House formally adopts the Committee of the Whole's recommendation.[61]

Once a bill is adopted by the House, it is sent to the Senate for its consideration. At this point, three things can happen: the bill could pass the Senate in the same form, it could pass in another form, or it could die. Every bill introduced has to be passed within the two-year window of a Congress, or it dies and must be reintroduced into the next Congress if it is to have a further chance of passage. If the Senate adopts the House bill, it is ready to go to the White House for presidential signature into law. If the Senate adopts a different version, the two chambers must appoint a committee of conference to resolve the differences between the two chambers' versions of the bill. Conference committees represent the House and Senate and usually consist of members of the committees that worked on the bill. If the conference can agree to a revised version of the bill, it goes back to the House and Senate for another vote. Conference reports do not face amendments and must be approved or defeated as is.[62] As an indicator of how tough it is to get through the whole process, of the nearly 8,500 bills introduced in the House and Senate during the 108th Congress 2003–2004, only 498 made it to President Bush's desk for signature into law.[63]

The Founders and the House Today

The Framers' design for the House of Representatives works. It is not perfect, but the House does what the Framers intended. The House is close to the people, its members reflect their political views and desires quite well, and the House is a paragon of majoritarianism. If anything, the House does "all representation, all the time" a bit too well. As the Framers intended, the House passes laws that take care of the individual members and their constituents, even if that does not necessarily help any national interest. But one issue does limit the modern House's faithfulness in reflecting the goals of the Founders. Partisanship overwhelms the House's balance between representation and lawmaking; the Framers' design cannot compete against today's organized political parties and their efforts to use the House to advance party, rather than constituent, interests. Two examples demonstrate the challenge of party.

The Framers expected the House to change personnel regularly in the face of changing voter preferences. If the states devised some nonpartisan redistricting mechanism that would make most House races competitive, the return of strong partisanship might even be a boon to democracy. Conflict between the parties can help to make meaningful participation possible: harried voters with little detailed policy information or expertise can still make the key choice between a Democrat or a Republican—and know that the choice of one candidate over the other means something.[64] But citizens do not always get a fair opportunity to choose. In many states, the state assembly has drawn congressional districts with other ideas in mind—usually maintaining partisan control over seats or protecting incumbents from serious challenges. Since the House decided to maintain its size at 435 members in 1911, House seats have to be reapportioned after every decennial census. States that grow in population may deserve additional House seats, while states with falling populations might lose seats. Every state has to study its districts after the census to make sure they all remain about equal in population, as well. Once the census is complete, Congress agrees to the number of seats each state will have in the next congressional election. Then each state government decides how to redraw district boundaries. There are a number of ways to make this decision. Most states rely on their legislatures to pass a law that identifies the new district boundaries. State legislatures are partisan, and they tend to promote boundaries that help the majority party's candidates in House elections. Many states have divided government, so they draw boundaries that protect incumbents of both parties, leaving few seats truly competitive at election time. Many states also face the challenge of building districts that would be likely to elect a minority candidate to office. Several states have been embroiled in fractious court cases challenging the validity of their redrawn districts. After the 1990 census, North Carolina's congressional districts were challenged by a citizen who contended that they were unconstitutional because they used race as a key factor to decide district borders. The Supreme Court agreed with this argument and in 1996 struck down the districts, requiring the state to try again. North Carolina created new boundaries, which were also challenged, and it was not until 1998 that the districts passed court muster—just in time for a new round of redistricting based on the results of the 2000 census![65]

Eleven states have decided to avoid partisan bickering by assigning the task to a nonpartisan commission.[66] The practice of politically motivated boundary drawing is as old as the country, but has gotten more sophisticated with new technology. Computers and comprehensive voter information databases allow campaign and party political consultants to draw boundaries that can pinpoint precincts. Incumbents already have significant resources to aid reelection. Challengers rarely unseat them especially if the district has been drawn to protect the incumbent. With their much higher name recognition, their experience and understanding of the district, and their ability to raise big donations from organized interests that already know them in Washington, incumbents start an election campaign way ahead of their challengers. This helps explain why over 90 percent of incumbents win every election, as Figure 3.4 indicates.[67] States that have chosen a nonpartisan route to select their new congressional district boundaries tend to see more meaningful elections: incumbents still win frequently, but at least they must run good races for reelection against solid challengers with a chance to win.

The House offers a second example of the challenge of partisanship. In 2004, the *Boston Globe* published a series of scathing reports attacking GOP abuses in managing Congress. Congressional leaders ignored House rules in many cases: in one egregious example, House leaders kept the vote open for President Bush's Medicare drug benefit bill for nearly three hours instead of the fifteen minutes allowed by the House rules as they worked to convince unhappy GOP representatives to support the bill; it eventually passed by three votes. According to the reports, many bills were drafted without minority party involvement at all, and some bills came to the floor for final action only hours after having been introduced, leaving no time for anybody to review them. Perhaps the most telling challenge has been the failure in recent years of the House's ethics process. House GOP leaders used the ethical lapses of Speaker Jim Wright D-TX to drive him from office in 1989, but they worked hard to ward off a similar fate for GOP leaders since they took over the chamber. After a series of embarrassing admonitions from the Ethics Committee in 2004 targeted House majority leader DeLay they engi-

Figure 3.4   **House Reelection Rates, 1964–2004**

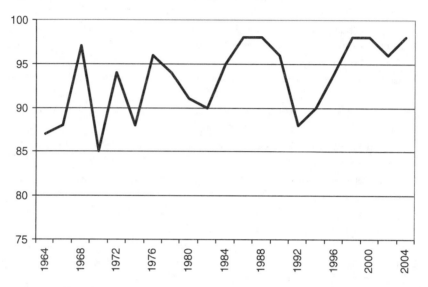

Source: OpenSecrets.org.

neered the replacement of Ethics Committee chair Joel Hefley and two other GOP committee members, as well as a series of committee rules changes that essentially defanged the ethics process before further allegations of misdeeds could harm DeLay.[68]

The House does what the Framers hoped it would: it represents the interests of the constituents that vote for majority party members. But it does not do its job as well as the Founders might have hoped; party influence trumps the delicate balance between lawmaking and representation in the House, leading to an institution that is too effective at advancing the desires of the majority party—instead of the majority of the citizens.

Summary

The House of Representatives is a collection of 440 individual offices, each organized by the members to meet their own needs, and dedicated to advancing the interests of the members and their constituents. But the House could not operate if it were merely an agglomeration of so many individual offices. What makes the House function is its parties. The parties make it possible for like-minded members to join together in an organized way. The parties give shape to the House, manage its committees, and make it work for the members, as much as the parties help to make the members work for the House.

The House of Representatives is a majoritarian legislature. In the House, 218 is the way and the truth. Its rules help the majority party's leaders to manage the large, unruly chamber successfully. Committee chairs have significant autonomy from the leadership, and individual members have their own power bases back home, but the leaders have tools to entice their committee chairs and their members to support them. But it is not a bureaucracy: as we saw with Shays-Meehan, members and committees have a few tools themselves to get a bill to the floor over their leaders' objections.

The Framers did not leave the task of representation to just the House, though. Knowing that they had created a House operating with short time frames, small, particular constituency interests, and rabid partisanship, they sought to balance it with a different chamber, where the balance between representation and legislation was not so one-sided—and where a slower, more deliberative political style could flourish. That is why they built the Senate.

Web Resources

U.S. House of Representatives: www.house.gov.

THOMAS: The Library of Congress maintains this comprehensive Web site, which provides detailed information on bills considered by Congress, laws passed, treaties, and historical documents. A special page also tracks appropriations bills in each Congress (http://thomas.loc.gov/).

The Dirksen Congressional Center: Allied with Bradley University in Illinois, the Dirksen Center works to improve understanding of Congress. Named for former Senate Minority Leader Everett McKinley Dirksen, the center hosts several national educational programs to improve teaching of civics and government (www.dirksencenter.org/).

Carl Albert Congressional Research and Studies Center: Named for former Speaker Carl Albert, the center at Oklahoma University studies Congress and offers scholars a variety of programs to enhance their research (www.ou.edu/special/albertctr/cachome.html).

U.S. Congressional Serial Set: This compendium of official publications tracks all the important documents produced by Congress. Many libraries around the United States contain all or some of the set's volumes, as well (www.gpoaccess.gov/serialset/index.html).

GPO Access: The Government Printing Office GPO manages this Web site, which collects interesting committee documents (www.gpoaccess.gov/congress/index.html).

4 • Representing the States

The Individualistic Senate

*The equal vote allowed to each State is at once a constitutional
recognition of the portion of sovereignty remaining in the
individual States, and an instrument for preserving that
residuary sovereignty. So far the equality ought to be no less
acceptable to the large than to the small States; since they are
not less solicitous to guard, by every possible expedient,
against an improper consolidation of the States into one simple
republic. Another advantage accruing from this ingredient in
the constitution of the Senate is, the additional impediment it
must prove against improper acts of legislation. No law or
resolution can now be passed without the concurrence, first, of
a majority of the people, and then, of a majority of the States.*
—Federalist No. 62[1]

The 107th Congress opened its first session in January 2001 to confront an
odd situation: the Senate was evenly divided, with fifty Democrats and fifty
Republicans. Vice President Richard Cheney broke the tie in favor of the
GOP, and Senator Trent Lott (R-MS) was elected majority leader. Then the
fun began. With an evenly divided Senate, minority leader Tom Daschle (D-
SD) argued that each committee should have cochairs, that resources should
be split evenly between Republican and Democratic staff on each committee, and that power-sharing should be the rule in the Senate until the next
election. Lott tried to hold the line, but after three weeks of negotiating,
Daschle got him to agree to divide staff resources evenly under GOP chairs.[2]

The idea of sharing power with the minority party could not come up in
the House. But it is not outlandish in the Senate. Collegiality and consensus
are the mode of Senate politics.[3] The Senate, after all, is an individualistic
chamber. Its tradition of full and free debate gives every member a chance to
shape bills. The Senate manages disputes on the floor rather than in the committees, as the House does. The Senate successfully achieves the Framers'

intent of serving both the general interest and the senators' constituents, the citizens of their states. Despite some fraying of Senate traditions and a bit of "Housification," the Senate can deal with the large challenges facing the country in a less partisan, less particularistic manner than the House because the Framers' design works to insulate the Senate and individual senators from the pressure of day-to-day politics. The Framers wanted the Senate to be a voice for the states to counter the voice of the people, as expressed by politics in the House. And they also wanted their second chamber's calm demeanor and careful deliberation to counter the frenetic whirl of partisan activity in the House—they hoped that through a melding of the two styles, good policy could emerge. The Senate's evolution preserved the basic goal of the Framers, even with the switch to direct election of senators in 1913, the institution of majority and minority party leadership during the 1920s, and the broad expansion of leadership roles in the chamber throughout the twentieth century, culminating in the empowerment of subcommittee chairs and ranking members in the 1970s. The long terms, staggered elections, and strong protections of minority rights in the Senate continue to preserve its character as a consensus-driven institution.

Unlike the House, where the majoritarian impulse gives the majority party leaders and committee chairs the power to manage the actions of the chamber, the egalitarian impulse in the Senate makes it a body of (near) equals. Nearly every senator is a leader, in the sense that they all are or recently have been chair or ranking member of a committee or subcommittee, and the Senate's rules give only weak powers to the majority leader to manage the floor.

In this chapter, we will review the Founders' intent for the Senate; then we will look at what service in the Senate is like, how its committees work, what its leaders do, and how the Senate passes bills. We will also look at the two special powers granted to the Senate in the Constitution as checks on presidential authority: ratification of treaties and confirmation of senior executive branch officials. The chapter will close with an evaluation of how well the Senate works.

Legislation and Representation

Today's Senate is a clear descendant of the Framers' intended upper chamber. The Framers' fear of tyranny drove them to build the Senate to react to political situations differently from the House. The Senate embodies the principle of equality. Every state has an equal voice in it, as a sign of the states' equal stake in the success of the United States. With only two senators from each state, the Senate is likely to remain small in size, and each senator has a whole state to represent in Washington. Larger and more diverse constituencies make senators think differently about politics than their House counterparts. And with longer terms and staggered elections, the Senate is insulated from the day-to-day politics that drives the House. The principle of equality changes the style of politics and the interaction of senators: Senate rules give each senator more of a role in the chamber than individual House members have. And the small size of the Senate ensures two things: the senators know each other better than House members do, and they all have a chance to take part in most Senate activities, so they have developed a collegial approach to lawmaking absent in the partisan House. The Framers also wanted the Senate to be capable of deliberation, so they insulated each senator from the press of politics with long, six-year terms and no direct election, since the state legislatures originally appointed senators. By staggering elections, so only a third of the senators face reelection each election cycle, the Framers also gave the Senate some breathing room, since a majority of senators in every election year are immune from the political whims that may shape the results of that particular cycle. Whereas the Framers tilted the House toward representation, they hoped the Senate could balance both roles, looking out for their home states, but also detached enough from daily pressures to act in the national interest. Politics in the Senate is therefore quieter, slower, and more consensus-based than in the House.

Serving in the Senate

The Senate is another loose conglomeration of multiple offices, including its hundred members and their staff offices, its twenty committees, and its support offices, which run the three office buildings and maintain the Senate side of the Capitol. Even more so than in the House, the Senate's members are the foundation of the chamber. The Senate is an exclusive club with only a hundred members. While the Senate mirrors the House with its parties and committees, the way the Senate fits the pieces together is completely different. The senators have a greater role in their body than do House members. Senate committees are powerful, but not as dominant as in the House. And party matters less in the Senate. Strong members can vie with committees, and both parties have a role in running the chamber: all this means that leadership in the Senate is much tougher than in the House.

With only a hundred members, the Senate's individual players are more visible, more involved, and more powerful in the politics of their chamber than their House counterparts. Senators tend to be older, and most of them come to the Senate with significant political experience: eighty-eight senators serving in the 109th Congress brought prior elective experience into

Figure 4.1 **Senate Reelection Rates, 1964–2004**

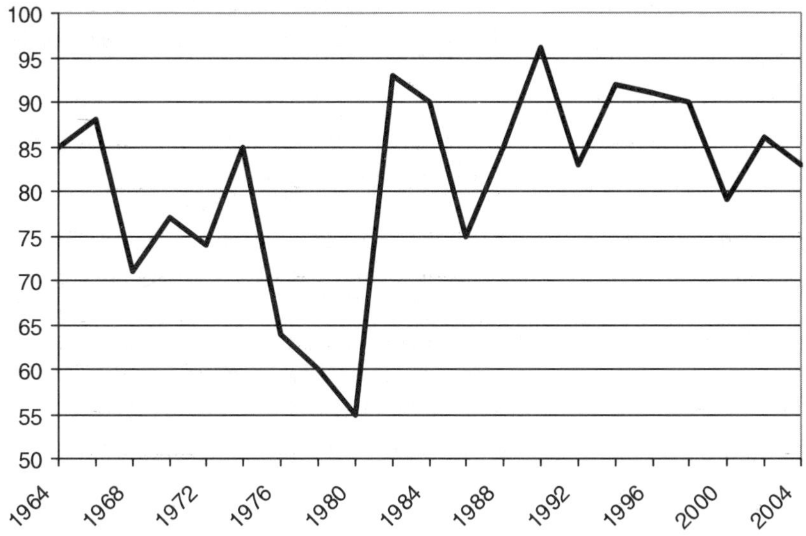

Source: OpenSecrets.org.

office.[4] Fifty-eight senators came to the Senate with experience as lawyers, thirty were formerly in business, and twelve came to their Senate careers via education. Thirty-one of the senators were military veterans, down dramatically from past Congresses; for instance, sixty-nine veterans were senators in the 91st Congress (1969–1970), during the Vietnam War, and sixty-eight veterans served in the 102nd Senate (1991–1992), during the first Gulf War. The 109th Senate also had the highest average age, 60.4, ever recorded in the Senate. Senators have been predominantly white males, with a slow expansion in the number of women and minorities over the past few decades. The 109th Congress followed these trends: fourteen women served in the Senate, alongside one African-American, two Hispanics, and two Asian/Pacific Islanders (ninety-five senators are still white, in other words). And incumbency helped this group as well: only one sitting senator from the 108th Congress lost a reelection bid (this was Tom Daschle, D-SD, the Senate minority leader). Reelection rates have been fairly steady at an average of 81 percent since 1964.[5] Figure 4.1 depicts the reelection rates over time. The average Senate tenure at the start of the 109th Congress was about eight years, which meant that most of the GOP senators had not been in the Senate before the Republican takeover of the chamber in the 1994 elections. So the 109th Senate looks older, and more politically experienced, and with voices from a variety of prior careers, compared to prior Congresses.

Sitting senators rarely face serious primary threats: the expense of mount-

ing a challenge to an incumbent is too much for most of the likely candidates, such as current House members. Knowing the difficulty of knocking
off a sitting senator in a primary, they usually wait to run for the seat after the
incumbent decides to retire.[6] The decision to run for the Senate is a tough
one. Would-be senators have to contend with statewide electorates, and they
must understand statewide issues and become known across the whole state.
They cannot usually focus their campaigns on a few issues as House challengers can. Most states have diversified economies and face numerous economic, environmental, and social challenges, so senatorial candidates must
demonstrate a broad, general expertise from the start of their campaigns in
order to be seen as legitimate candidates. Usually that means that they have
to raise a tremendous amount of money to finance a campaign, since most
states cover multiple media markets. They cannot rely on one good television ad or one radio station to advertise their campaign. With the average
Senate campaign in 2002 costing nearly $5 million, challengers for Senate
seats need to be talented fund-raisers. Many recent victors of Senate races
have entered politics with great personal wealth to draw on, one example
being Senator Jon Corzine (D-NJ), who spent $63 million of his own money
in 2000 to win a seat in the Senate. Given the huge costs involved in running
statewide campaigns for Senate seats, both parties have been aggressively
seeking such "self-funding" candidates to take some pressure of the party
organizations, which cannot raise and distribute enough money on their own
to field good challengers in every Senate race.

  While these candidates do take a burden off of the party organizations,
they add one to the parties' leaders in the Senate. Successful self-financed
candidates enter the Senate with very little obligation to their parties. They
raised their own money, hired their own campaign staff, and got to Washington with little assistance, in most cases, from their party headquarters. They
have their own power base, which makes them less inclined to follow the
directions of the party leaders than their House peers, who tend to receive
financing, advice, and support from the party organizations and leaders in
the House. Added to the Senate's tendency to work for compromise, self-
sufficient senators mean difficulty for the party leaders. Compared to members of the House, senators tend to be older, more experienced politicians,
many of whom have extensive executive experience as former governors.
Many senators have House terms on their résumés, as well, so they are familiar with Washington. They are used to a high profile and they generally know
how to deal with the challenges and opportunities of partisan politics. Even
with this background, however, few senators are prepared for the workload
and varied demands their new office requires.

  Senators have the same constituent and legislative responsibilities as their

House counterparts, only on a larger scale. Senators have to build a staff that can manage the larger challenge of providing constituent services to a whole state's population. The staff will also have a broader range of issues to master in Washington: since senators sit on more committees than do House members, their staffs need broader expertise, too. Senate offices are usually much larger than House offices, with thirty-five to forty people supporting the senator's work. A chief of staff manages the office, supported by administrative personnel to answer the phones, schedule the senator's time, and keep all office technology running. The legislative staff in a senator's office is much larger, too—a legislative director manages a squad of several legislative assistants (LAs) and correspondents (LCs). Senate LAs tend to focus on fewer issues (frequently only one), and they have more advanced education and experience than House LAs. LCs draft all the letters that senators send back to their constituents,[7] leaving the LAs free to concentrate on bills making their way through the chamber. Senators also operate several constituent service offices across their home states, to provide casework and other assistance to citizens.

Legislative work can easily overwhelm a senator. Senators serve (on average) on three committees, compared to the House average of two. Every subcommittee a senator sits on means an additional set of hearings to attend, and an additional set of markups (committee sessions where legislation is drafted and amended). As a result, few senators participate actively in all the committees they serve on; most pick one or two areas to focus on and develop their policy expertise there, becoming a key leader on that issue in the Senate. Senators also devote a great deal of time to floor debate. Given the Senate's tradition of full, free, and open debate, floor action on a bill usually takes much longer than it does in the House. And though few senators attend all of any given debate, committee and subcommittee chairs and ranking members, plus the party leaders in both the majority and minority, must be present on the floor to manage the bill. And the rest of the senators have to be ready at a moment's notice to go to the Senate chamber to vote as debate proceeds. Add the large constituent base, the extensive committee work, and the long, involved floor action together, and senators quickly find themselves swamped by the time, complexity, and diversity of the demands placed upon them.

What motivates people to join the Senate and deal with the long hours and difficult work? Like their House counterparts, senators want to make good policy, and they want to gain influence in the political system. They want to win reelection and remain in the Senate too. And many senators have larger ambitions also, using the Senate to advance future campaigns for executive office. Just since the end of World War II, John F. Kennedy, Robert Kennedy,

Box 4.1

Congress and College II

The Senate Does NOT Rock

Downloaded any good music lately? Whether you did it legally, or not so legally, Congress is interested in what you are listening to on your iPod. The Senate particularly wants to help you listen to the right music, obtained the right way.

What does that mean? Senators do not like rock. Or hip-hop. Or anything else that is popular. Look at your CDs or the next disc you buy (if you still do that)—do you see a "Parent's Advisory" sticker? Thank the Senate for those labels. In 1985, a group of outraged senators (and their spouses), inspired by the raunchy music of 2 Live Crew, a rap act from Miami, formed the Parents Music Resource Center (PMRC) to take a stand against vulgar lyrics. The Senate held a hearing in September 1985, taking testimony from opponents and supporters of free expression in music, including Frank Zappa, Dee Snider of the heavy metal band Twisted Sister, and John Denver! The music industry voluntarily adopted advisory stickers on explicit CDs in order to prevent further congressional action after these hearings.

More recently the Senate waded into the battle over Napster and other file-sharing programs. Senator Orrin Hatch (R-UT) held hearings in 2001 and unsuccessfully tried to get a bill limiting file sharing passed by the Senate in 2004. Every time you download a song or burn a CD for a friend, remember: the Senate is listening in, ready to yell at you to turn that music down!

Sources: Richard Harrington, "The Capitol Hill Rock War; Emotions Run High as Musicians Confront Parents' Group at Hearing," *Washington Post,* September 20, 1985, B1; Christopher Stern, "Hill Takes Notice of Napster Legal Fray; Key Lawmakers Warn Music Industry Could Lose Some Copyright Privileges," *Washington Post,* February 16, 2001, E03.

Edmund Muskie, Edward Kennedy, Robert Dole, Albert Gore, Joseph Lieberman, John Edwards, John McCain, and John Kerry (among many others) sought the White House from perches in the Senate, and Kay Bailey Hutchison sought the governorship of Texas. The Senate gives each member a high profile in political reporting, and many senators use that visibility to push their personal goals, including both career advancement and policy goals. For instance, John McCain (R-AZ) used his 2000 White House run to build a successful national political base, which allowed him to champion several policy positions opposed by his own party leaders. He was instrumental in pushing campaign finance reform in the Senate (with his cosponsor, Russell Feingold, a Wisconsin Democrat) in 2001 and 2002, and he became the chief antipork crusader in the Senate in the wake of the large federal deficits that started adding up from 2001.[8]

Senators contend with long hours, multiple tasks, and the full range of issues that confront the Senate. While their large staffs help tremendously, senators are still very busy public servants. The Senate is a much looser institution than the House, and it is much more a collection of known personalities. Despite their own independent political base back home (or nationally in the case of a few high-profile members), senators do look to committee work to advance their policy and career goals, and to their parties for guidance and advice on key policy issues. In this flexible chamber, the committee system helps senators get things done.

Senate Committees

The Senate took nearly a century to build a permanent committee system, but since those committees began to take shape after the Civil War, they have become a vital part of Senate legislative work. The sixteen standing and four special or select committees of the Senate look much like their House counterparts, and they perform the same functions, but they are not as dominant in the legislative process as the House committees are. The Senate has legislative and nonlegislative committees, as in the House. Fifteen of the standing committees and two of the special committees (Intelligence and Indian Affairs) are legislative, with the authority to produce bills on their own. There are three nonlegislative committees in the Senate: Rules and Administration, the special committees on Aging and Ethics, and the joint committees on printing and the library, and the economic committee. Unlike the powerful House committee, the Senate Rules Committee has no part in the legislative process; it is responsible for overseeing the administration of the Senate—its office buildings, staff spaces, and such, and the rules of the Senate. Figure 4.2 lists the Senate's committees in the 109th Congress (2005–2006).

Senate committees prepare the bulk of legislation for floor action. They hold the hearings, investigate issues, and draft or revise bills.[9] When a bill comes to the floor for debate, the committee chair and the ranking minority member manage the debate. The chair and the ranking minority member are usually the two most important players on most committees, although they

Figure 4.2   **Senate Committees of the 109th Congress**

Legislative/Oversight	**Legislative/Money**	**Nonlegislative**
Agriculture, Nutrition, and Forestry	Budget	Rules and Administration
	Appropriations	Indian Affairs
(Special)		
Armed Services	Finance	Ethics (Select)
Banking, Housing, and Urban Affairs	Taxation (Joint)	Aging (Special)
		Printing (Joint)
Commerce, Science, and Transportation		Library (Joint)
		Economic (Joint)
Energy and Natural Resources		
Environment and Public Works		
Foreign Relations		
Health, Education, Labor, and Pensions		
Homeland Security and Governmental Affairs		
Judiciary		
Small Business and Entrepreneurship		
Veterans' Affairs		
Intelligence (Select)		

Source: U.S. Senate.

are not always the most senior members of the committee. Seniority is a guideline rather than a law when the parties choose their committee leaders, and some members choose to give up seniority on one committee in order to focus on other committee work. In 1995 Senator Jesse Helms (R-NC) was the ranking Republican on the Agriculture Committee but gave up the chance to chair that panel so he could chair the Foreign Relations Committee. Chairs have control over the committee agenda, and that allows them to focus the committee's work, particularly in Senate committees where the subcommittees do not mark up or amend bills, but only hold hearings. Subcommittees that do work on legislation independently of the committee can constrain the chair's power by the choices (and deals) they make before a bill gets to the full committee. Ranking minority members play a more active role in Senate committee work than do House minority members since the minority can influence outcomes more effectively in the Senate.[10] Senators are spread much thinner than their House counterparts, so many of them cannot devote much time to every committee and subcommittee they serve on; as a result, only a few senators usually put in much work on any given sub- or full committee, making them powerful during both committee deliberations and floor action on their bills. The committee's expertise and control of the initial steps in producing bills allows the committees to define the outlines of future floor debates on key issues; after all, the committees select among competing alternatives and send their favored one to the floor for debate. Even with the open floor procedures of the Senate, this control gives committees great ability to shape legislation.

Senate committees cannot keep their jurisdictions to themselves, however. Senate rules allow every senator the opportunity to speak on any bill before the body, which means that every senator can participate in any floor debate. And any senator can offer amendments for bills on the floor, making it difficult for committees to protect their bills once they get to the floor. If the few senators who actively participate in committee work happen to disagree with the committee's version of a bill, they can take their fight to the floor and debate the issues again, with the whole Senate taking part in the decision. Most committees are largely successful in preserving the main components of their bills on the floor, but they do not get the deference (or the procedural assistance) that House committees expect when they bring bills to the House floor for action.

Parties and the Senate

Senate party leaders confront challenges in every direction they look. Senators all have a good deal of individual power, and committees control the basic shape of bills coming to the floor for action. Senate leaders do not benefit from any of the centralized authority or discipline that helps their House peers manage their chamber.[11] Party means a lot to senators, but partisanship does not dominate the Senate as it does the House.[12] Senate rules protect the minority party, giving it a role in managing the chamber. While the majority party controls the agenda, manages the committees, and oversees the administration of the Senate, the minority has staff on each committee, too, and has the power to prevent controversial bills from coming to the floor for debate. The key feature of party politics in the Senate is compromise: since neither party can achieve what it wants in the Senate alone, the two parties have to work together to pass bills that most senators can live with.

The majority does have control over the floor agenda, committees, and administration of the Senate. Since the Senate rules go to great lengths to ensure that all senators have a say in how the Senate deals with important business, the majority party may be able to run the administrative side of the Senate, manage the committees, and set the floor agenda, but it has incomplete control of the outcomes once debates begin on the floor. The key formal power held by the majority party is its control of Senate administration. The majority party has the responsibility to set up and run the Senate. It hires the staff that supports the Senate, including the sergeant at arms, whose duty it is to maintain order in the Senate chamber, and the parliamentarian, who monitors procedure during debates and advises the majority leader whenever a dispute arises over a particular procedural matter.

The Senate majority also manages the Senate's committees. The senators assigned to each committee are appointed by each of the parties, in a proportion that reflects the partisan split in the Senate. Majority party senators serve as chairs of all the committees and subcommittees. They hire the bulk of the committee staffs and set the legislative agendas for their committees and subcommittees, as well. Control of the committees allows the majority to shape the legislation that comes to the floor, and to block minority proposals unless they earn significant majority support. Each committee does have a small minority staff, but most of the resources go to the majority, and as we saw previously, the chairs control their committees' scheduling, meetings, and agenda. But the key power of the Senate majority is that the majority leader controls the floor agenda. Senate rules allow for a much less structured process on the floor than in the House, but if a senator cannot get a bill to the floor, it cannot pass the Senate. The Senate has no formal set of calendars as the House does, so it is easier for the majority leader to move bills around in order to adjust the schedule as needed. Once the bills are on the floor, though, majority party control starts to slip. Most complicated or controversial bills come before the Senate under carefully negotiated arrangements called "unanimous consent agreements," which can be derailed by a single senator.

The Constitution is almost silent on the matter of Senate organization and leadership, whether by majority party or some other mechanism. Only one officer is mentioned at all: the vice president of the United States is president of the Senate, but what that means is left unsaid. The Framers left it to the members of both chambers to decide their internal organization, procedures, and leadership for themselves. In practice, the Senate has been happy to organize itself, with its majority and minority leadership—and no role for the vice president, except for the constitutionally mandated casting of deciding votes in cases of tied votes. Since the vice president is not a member of the legislative branch, the early senators had no desire for him to participate in any other substantive way in the business of the Senate. In practice, no vice president since John Adams (1789–1797) has bothered to visit the Senate except to break tie votes. After their experience with Adams (one of the most capable and experienced legislators in the United States at that time, who participated forcefully in Senate debates), senators adopted rules that relegated the presiding officer to a calm, inactive silence.[13] Since the job no longer has power, the vice president is rarely in the Senate chamber. The majority party appoints a president pro tempore to serve as the presiding officer of the Senate. Usually the longest serving majority senator, the president pro tem also rarely presides over debate, as this position is more honorary than substantive. Instead, another senator is selected on a rotating basis to preside over the chamber. The president's job is to maintain order during floor debates, to recognize the senators who want to speak on the bill under debate, and to record all votes as they occur. If there is a dispute over the procedure being used, a senator may call a point of order, which the president decides upon with the advice of the parliamentarian, who studies the question raised using the precedents of the Senate. Although this can be an occasional duty, if a presiding officer makes a decision on a point of order and is sustained in a vote by the chamber, that decision becomes part of Senate tradition, shaping all decisions about similar disputes in the future.[14]

The real leader of the Senate is the Senate majority leader, who has the duty of scheduling floor action for bills and setting the broad outlines of the party's plans for each session of Congress. The majority leader is aided by three other key leaders: the majority whip, who monitors support for bills and works to win floor votes, and the chair and vice chair of the party conference caucus, who work together to craft policy positions for the majority party. The majority leadership team also coordinates closely with the minority leaders to schedule bills for debate on the Senate floor.

The filibuster is among the best tools that the minority has for shaping outcomes in the Senate, but long before a minority party senator threatens a filibuster, the Senate minority has enjoyed more capacity to shape legislative outcomes in the Senate than its counterpart in the House. Senate tradition, history, and rules give the minority a voice in the proceedings of the Senate, unlike the House, where the minority is just along for the ride. The Senate minority leader and the minority whip meet together with the majority leader to define the rules for every bill that comes to the floor of the Senate, and without majority ability to force the issue by defeating a filibuster (which requires sixty votes), minority concerns get addressed in preparing for bill debates. Why does a filibuster threat work so well to prevent strong majority party rule in the Senate? The Senate's floor schedule is overcommitted: there are more bills on the agenda than the Senate can ever hope to debate. If the majority leader faces a filibuster threat and cannot get the needed votes to defeat it, then it is smarter to pull the bill and move on to another bill, rather than waste valuable time in a losing fight. On occasion, a majority leader may allow a filibuster on a politically sensitive bill in order to paint the bill's opponents as obstructionists; such as the failure to end the filibuster against a constitutional amendment banning gay marriage in July 2004.[15]

The minority has some power in the Senate because the chamber's tradition preserves the right of every senator to take part in debate, and senators of old devised the filibuster to take advantage of the Senate's tradition of full participation. While the majority has the power to set the agenda, as well as to block minority party initiatives, the minority has only the negative power of preventing the most partisan proposals from clearing the Senate. The minority has little ability to select among the alternatives presented to the Senate early in the process of crafting bills, but their power does allow minority members to limit the alternatives that can successfully pass the Senate. And because the minority party has some power in defining outcomes in the Senate, it shares some responsibility for governing with the majority party. If its efforts are seen as obstructive, its members may pay a political price for their limited power in the Senate. This key difference between the Senate and the House makes for very different politics, and for very different challenges facing the senators chosen by their two parties to lead the efforts of the Senate.

A Senate Full of Leaders?

We have seen that the Senate gives individual senators and committees power to get things done and that leaders have few powers themselves to counter the members and committees. The Senate is much better at meeting the needs of individual members than the House, and that complicates the job of the Senate's leaders. Floor action in the Senate therefore looks very different from floor action in the House, where the leaders have the tools to shape the debate and consequently the bills passed by the House. Many observers of Senate politics have noted that the party structures, committee and subcommittee chairmanships, and ranking minority slots make the Senate a top-heavy institution. In the 108th Congress, for instance, eighty-three of the hundred senators held some leadership position in the chamber. If everybody in the Senate is a leader, is anybody really a leader?[16] Does leadership matter? The answer is that leadership in the Senate is more important and much more difficult than in the House, requiring more skill and more diplomacy than needed to make the House respond to its leaders' desires.

When a committee completes its action on a bill and reports it to the Senate majority leader for floor action, the committee chair and ranking member already know two things about the upcoming debate: they will manage the bill on the floor, and they will not be the only participants in the discussion. A few committee members interested in the policy area will also take part in the floor debate, as will any nonmembers who want to add something to the bill. As we saw earlier, only a few senators usually devote themselves to mastering the details of any specific policy, and those few who commit to a particular issue tend to be the ones who take part in shaping Senate bills on that particular issue.

When scheduling the bill for floor action, the majority leader faces three limitations that make it difficult to help the committee chair and ranking member to pass their bill. First, the majority leader does not have extensive formal power to enforce discipline on the floor when bringing a bill to the Senate for debate. Senate majority leaders have only two powers: they decide what bills will go to the floor, and in what order; and they are entitled to be recognized first during debate. In the past twenty-five years, majority leaders of both parties have been forced to work with very narrow majorities, giving the minority ample opportunities to derail Senate action on unpopular bills. Narrow majorities also mean that the moderates in both parties—those most comfortable working with other middle-of-the-road senators—wield significant power. In addition, the majority leaders have to work with a group of legislators who usually do not owe the party much for winning their seats, and these independent-minded senators are not always inclined to go along with their party's program. Add the fact that the senators do not have enough hours in each legislative session to take up all of the bills they would like to discuss, and you have created the recipe for a very difficult, if not impossible, leadership task. The time crunch has forced recent majority leaders to leave many important bills undone at the end of a session, no matter how hard they tried to get the bills passed. For example, GOP leaders in the House passed their version of a bankruptcy bill in 1997, 2001, and 2003, and each time the Senate could not complete its version of the bill in time for it to go to the president for signature. Not until 2005 did the Senate finally finish its version of the bill.[17]

Second, the Senate majority leader also has to contend with the minority party. Senate minority leaders have enough votes to stop any bill they oppose strongly, so the majority leader usually works very closely with the minority party counterpart to head off any serious issues before a controversial bill makes it to the floor. Committee chairs and ranking members tend to know which parts of a bill might excite opposition, so they frequently adjust their bills in committee, anticipating possible floor fights.[18] For the past four decades, the minority has had enough votes to threaten a filibuster—that is, to prevent a final vote on a bill by endlessly debating it until the leadership gives up and pulls the bill—in all but six years (1963–1967 and 1977–1979), forcing majority leaders to accommodate minority concerns.

Finally, the majority leader cannot limit debate on a bill to the issue at hand. The House has a germaneness rule that requires all amendments to a bill to concern the same subject; the Senate does not. So senators can try to attach anything they want to an important bill, as when GOP senators supported an amendment to the Fiscal 2006 budget resolution that would allow drilling for oil in the Arctic National Wildlife Refuge.[19] Such amendments can kill a bill: if enough irrelevant material is attached to it, it may not get enough votes to pass the Senate, or it might be impossible to get the House to agree to the Senate's extras.[20]

The floor is where the Senate makes its decisions, and unlike in the House, the committees have to share control over the final shape of bills with individual senators, and they cannot rely on rules or strong leaders to protect their bills. It is time to see how the Senate conducts floor debates.

The Floor of the Senate: Where the Action Is

With no standing committees before the Civil War, no party leaders until 1925, and with powerful individual members, the Senate has used the floor for making important decisions since its inception. As one scholar puts it, "the Senate has a far more informal, floor-oriented, and collegial decisionmaking process" than the House.[21] Floor procedure still looks much as it did in the 1950s.[22] Although seniority still matters in the Senate, younger members do not automatically defer to the older members, and every senator can take individual concerns (and amendments) to the floor. And the Senate gives members the right to place a "hold" on a bill, which prevents floor action, if they want to slow a bill down. Many senators use holds to give themselves time to work out a deal to amend the bill with the sponsoring committee, or to make a point. Senator Howard Metzenbaum (D-OH) placed so many holds on bills during his Senate service that Democratic leaders added a check box for him on all of their routing forms, to make sure they knew if he was planning on yet another hold.[23]

The Senate does not have rigid floor procedural rules, nor does it use a complicated system of calendars to track legislation. The Senate majority leader uses a legislative calendar for all bills ready to go to the floor and an executive calendar for all treaties and nominations pending before the Senate. (We will look at the executive calendar in the next section.) Under the regular rules of the Senate, bills come to the floor with no time limit for debate, no limit on amendments, and no germaneness protections. As a result, the majority leader can only estimate how long it might take to complete work on any given bill. But since most bills are relatively uncontroversial, this loose approach suits the Senate fairly well.[24] The majority and minority leaders can use their right to be recognized during a debate to remind their peers of other, more pressing business, if they need to keep the chamber on schedule. The best possible outcome is to bring a bill to the floor with no issues left to discuss; if the committee has been successful in anticipating and dealing with all potential objections, the majority leader can simply ask for unanimous consent to pass the bill without debate.[25] The flexibility also allows the majority leader to drop a bill, or pull it from the floor, if a sudden problem arises or if a senator who wishes to speak on a bill is not available for the debate.

Some bills are controversial, though, and can fall victim to the filibuster. The Senate has always had its tradition of full and open debate, and some senators use this tradition to talk an unpopular bill to death. With the many tasks facing the Senate, the majority leader cannot afford to lose too much time on any one bill, so the threat of a filibuster usually keeps a bill off the Senate floor. If the majority leader can forge an agreement on the bill that meets the opponents' concerns, then the bill can go back on the schedule, and a new version of the bill will be debated. If the sponsors of the bill do not want to compromise, they have the option of cloture. If the majority can gain a three-fifths majority (sixty votes), it can force an end to the debate and have a final vote on a bill. Under the current rules, the Senate has an additional thirty hours of postcloture debate, to be used to record votes and complete any other required actions before final passage of the bill. The Senate did not have a cloture procedure until 1917, when it adopted a rule requiring a two-thirds majority to invoke cloture. In 1975, after several unsuccessful attempts, the Senate dropped the needed majority from sixty-seven to sixty, except for filibusters on rules changes, which still require sixty-seven votes to end.[26] The filibuster protects the minority party and forces the majority to collaborate with the minority on major legislation. Senate bills thus tend to reflect a middle-of-the-road approach that both parties can support, rather than the strongly partisan bills that the House majority can force through.

Since the 1960s and the tenure of Mike Mansfield (D-MT) as majority leader, the Senate has used a procedural mechanism to manage controversial legislation and avoid filibusters. Working with Robert Byrd (D-WV), Mansfield devised agreements with the minority party leaders that hammered out all of the issues on tough bills. These unanimous consent agreements (UCAs) can contain time limits on debate, they can limit amendments, and they waive other Senate rules that could prevent the bill's passage. Not every UCA does all three; each UCA concentrates on whatever tough problems could prevent a particular bill's consideration and passage. During Byrd's stint as majority leader (1977–1981, 1987–1989), the Senate's UCAs became hugely complicated, but they worked to set the ground rules for debating difficult bills, and Byrd was quite successful in pushing legislation through the Senate. Majority leaders of both parties after Byrd's tenure have not crafted UCAs as massive as his were, but the UCA has become a regular feature of Senate floor practice now, since it allows majority bills to get to the floor without the constant fear of filibusters—an even more potent threat in recent years than previously. Tight party margins mean that the majority leader cannot afford to lose the support of too many fellow party members without losing votes on bills. And as UCAs have become commonplace, several senators have used strategic threats to filibuster as a bargaining tactic, to force the leadership to accept some proposed change at the last minute or face collapse of a bill. When brinkmanship works, other senators take note and use the technique themselves. The annual debate over spending bills is one of the easiest targets for such efforts (since they all must be passed to fund the government), as is the authorization bill for the State Department, which always excites strong opinions in the Senate.[27] UCAs also privilege senators who understand the rules of the Senate; only careful legislators can keep track of all the rules and procedures of the chamber. The most fearsome rules expert in the past century has been Senator Byrd, who joined the Democratic leadership team in 1967 and has been at the center of most UCAs in the nearly forty years since. Byrd's mastery of the rules means that West Virginia gets lots of federal largesse—even in the GOP-dominated Senate, Byrd knows how to use the rules to get what he wants.

Once the Senate crafts a UCA and proceeds through debate to pass a bill, it must send its version to the House. Formal House-Senate interactions are infrequent, complicating the work of the conference committees of House and Senate members, which are created to resolve differences on specific bills. Committee staffs discuss issues and hearings with each other, and legislators from the same state occasionally work together to push a project good for folks back home, but in general, the House and the Senate do not deal with each other. Conference committees allow the legislative committees of the House and Senate a final chance to protect their bills. Although only about 10 percent of bills go to conference, they are almost always the most important bills.[28] If one chamber accepts the other's version, or if informal methods (such as amendments or leader-to-leader discussions) can resolve the difference, then a bill can be passed without conference. But the important bills go to conference, and that gives the committees a chance to work on the bill one more time. Conferences usually consist of originating committee members and are apportioned according to the number of Republicans and Democrats in each chamber. Occasionally the House "instructs" its conference attendees to demand that certain House provisions go into the final bill, and some senators will call for recorded votes on the Senate floor to constrain Senate conferees.[29] House and Senate rules prevent the amendment of conference reports. Once a conference agrees to a compromise bill, each chamber can approve it, or oppose it, but they cannot change it.[30] The House does allow members to make a point of order against nongermane matters attached by the Senate or in conference, which can change a bill, requiring either a new conference or Senate agreement to the change.[31]

"Advice and Consent": The Senate's Special Powers

In addition to passing bills, the Senate has two other responsibilities granted to it in the Constitution: it also ratifies treaties made by the president, and it votes to confirm the nominations of senior administration officials, ambassadors, and federal judges. The Framers gave the "advice and consent" powers to the Senate as a check on the power of the presidency in two key areas, foreign policy and personnel decisions. The Framers built the Senate to be more deliberative than the House, and they required senators to be older and more mature than their House counterparts. The Senate therefore holds these special powers without House participation.[32] A simple majority of votes cast is enough to confirm a presidential appointment, while treaties require a two-thirds majority for ratification.

Treaties go to the Senate after the president has signed them. The Senate ratifies treaties by conducting hearings in the Foreign Relations Committee, then voting on the floor if the committee agrees to support the treaty. In two centuries the Senate has defeated only about twenty treaties and has approved almost 950, so in general the Senate supports presidents in their role as chief diplomat for the United States. However, this trend has shifted in recent years. After the disastrous failure of the Senate to ratify Woodrow Wilson's Treaty of Versailles, presidents have been very careful to include the Senate in most treaty efforts before ratification. By working with leading senators beforehand, the White House can learn of any concerns and incorporate them into the negotiations, making ratification easier. In several recent cases, though, George H.W. Bush and Clinton administration officials negotiated two treaties on weapons without much senatorial input. In 1997, a flurry of last-minute deals with the Senate by Clinton's Secretary of State Madeleine Albright was necessary to achieve a close vote to support a treaty to ban chemical weapons.[33] The Comprehensive Test Ban Treaty[34] went down to defeat in 1999 after a small group of hawkish GOP senators expressed their opposition on the grounds that the treaty would jeopardize the safety of the U.S. nuclear deterrent.[35] In both cases, two administrations failed to include senators in the negotiations and did not inform the Senate of progress on the treaties until they were ready for ratification. The Senate did not react well to these perceived slights to its constitutional role in treaty making.

Nominations to high-level executive branch positions, ambassadorial posts and federal judgeships all must go to the Senate for confirmation. While presidents have tended to get the executive officials and ambassadors they nominate, the Senate has been more aggressive in dealing with the lifetime appointments that federal judges receive if confirmed. In addition to the requirement for confirmation of appointments, the Constitution checks presidential power by giving Congress the responsibility to structure the executive branch. Over the years, Congress has specified the executive branch positions requiring confirmation; as of 2004, this amounted to over 7,000 slots.[36] Why would Congress give itself so much work? Congress reserves the right to call any confirmed official to testify at committee hearings. Although no formal judgment prevents it, most officials serving in positions that do not require confirmation do not testify regularly. For instance, in 2004, Congress called on President G.W. Bush's national security adviser, Condoleezza Rice, to testify on the intelligence problems uncovered in the wake of the 9/11 terrorist attacks. The White House refused to allow Rice to testify because her position had not required Senate confirmation. For weeks the White House and Congress jousted over the issue, until public opinion and the powerful testimony of other witnesses convinced the White House that Rice should speak to the investigatory commission.

Nominations fall under the same jurisdictions as legislative matters, so the Senate committees do the initial work of confirmation. After the White House announces a nomination, the candidate usually meets with the leaders of the committee involved to discuss the confirmation schedule and to address any issues that might cause problems with the vote. Under the tradition of senatorial courtesy, presidents usually clear a nominee with the two senators from the state where the person will serve or from the candidate's home state if the position is in Washington. Without the support of the home senators, confirmation becomes very difficult.[37] Senatorial courtesy is especially important for judicial nominations, because the Judiciary Committee has a system of holds for nominations that requires at least one of the home state senators to support the candidate. And many candidates face long waits for a Judiciary Committee hearing, given the difficulty every president since Ronald Reagan has had in confirming judicial nominees. Once the home state senators accept a nomination, the committee conducts hearings on each nominee. For most of the positions, a slate of nominations is considered together and approved as a group, speeding up the process. Candidates for senior positions, however, such as cabinet secretaries and heads of independent agencies, all receive individual attention. Committees review the background checks done by the Federal Bureau of Investigation. During the committee hearings on a nomination, committee members will ask the candidate about any troubling FBI information and also discuss the nominee's policy goals and plans. Once the hearings are complete, the committee votes, and if a majority approves the nomination, it goes to the floor for a final vote. Although most hearings are businesslike, controversial hearings can get exciting. In 1991, when Clarence Thomas was nominated to the Supreme Court, accusations of sexual harassment led to contentious hearings, while the confirmation hearings for Alberto Gonzales, who was nominated to be attorney general in 2005, revolved around a memorandum he had written for President Bush concerning treatment of Al Qaeda fighters and other prisoners in military detention centers after the Afghanistan and Iraq wars. Despite strong reservations, the Senate eventually confirmed both men.[38] The Senate does reject nominations on occasion. President George H.W. Bush's first nominee for defense secretary, John Tower, a former Texas senator, was defeated in 1989 over concerns about his qualifications for the job and his alleged drinking problem. In 2001, President G.W. Bush's first choice for labor secretary, Linda Chavez, was derailed by a whirlwind of protests from labor unions and Democrats in the Senate; the president accepted her request to withdraw the nomination and selected another nominee, Elaine Chao, who was confirmed for the office.[39]

The Senate does not need to vote against a nomination to kill it. Several of President Bill Clinton's judicial nominations, and both Zoe Baird and Kimba Wood, his first two choices for attorney general, withdrew their names from consideration when information surfaced that they had failed to pay the Social Security taxes for housecleaning employees.[40] Over the past two decades, the contentious process of confirming federal judges has devolved into a bitter, partisan fight. Although confirmation has always been difficult, particularly with Supreme Court judges, President Reagan's failed 1987 nomination of Robert Bork ushered in a new period of ideological battle over nominations. Clinton-era judicial nominations regularly ran afoul of the GOP majority, with many of his choices never receiving a Judiciary Committee hearing because of holds put on their files by various conservative GOP senators. The trend continued into the Bush administration, with several of his selections filibustered to prevent a final floor vote. When Orrin Hatch (R-UT) took over as chair of the Judiciary Committee, he changed the committee's rules to make it harder to stop committee action on controversial nominees; Senate Democrats responded by filibustering several conservative nominees on the floor.[41] No senator on either side of the battle has advanced a workable solution to the nomination issue that allows noncontroversial judges to advance while the tougher ones receive higher levels of scrutiny, and none of the presidents involved in these battles with the Senate has agreed to any real "advice and consent" from the Senate. No solution is possible until the White House and the Senate agree to some system that keeps controversial nominations from going to the Senate in the first place.[42]

The Senate and the Framers

The Framers wanted a Senate that could balance representation of specific constituencies with lawmaking for the good of the country. Their Senate does a fairly effective job of balancing the roles.

Like the design for the House, the Framers' plan for the Senate has held up well. The Senate's original principles still apply: it is an egalitarian chamber, and the long terms and staggered elections of its members do work to insulate the Senate from the constant political pressures that bedevil the House. If anything, the Senate has fully embraced the ideal of the Framers in the way its internal rules have evolved over time. Two criticisms of the current Senate do raise questions, though, about its ability to do its job. The first is an imbalance of representation in the Senate: the citizens of the small states, in effect, have more power in the Senate than their fellows in large states do. This condition was built into the Senate to entice the smaller states, such as South Carolina, Rhode Island, and Connecticut, to adopt the Constitution. But the unequal results of state equality become more obvious with time. The most populous state in the Union is now California, with 36 million citizens, and the least populous is Wyoming, with 493,000. Yet both have two senators. Federal funding goes to many of the sparsely populated Midwestern and mountain states, while large states like New York end up paying more in taxes than they receive back in federal programs. Small state senators (judging against one-fiftieth of the total population of the United States, thirty-one of the fifty states are "small," five are about equal, and fourteen are "large")[43] have no incentive to accept any sort of reforms or limitations on their enhanced influence in the Senate—and with sixty-two votes in their hands, nobody else can force the issue.[44]

A far more pressing issue is the rise in partisanship in Washington. Although not as prominent in the Senate as it is in the House, the increased partisan and ideological fighting in Washington influences the Senate, as well. Fifty-two senators serving in the 109th Congress, for instance, had prior House experience, and many of them were quite ideological. Used to the party discipline that shapes the House, they sought to "shape up" the Senate in a similar way. Where collegiality once governed everything that the Senate does, party divisions have made the Senate less friendly. Most of the recent partisan senators have been Republicans—which makes sense, given that the GOP has been increasing in strength in both chambers. Conservative politicians like Tom Coburn (R-OK), John Kyl (R-AZ), and Rick Santorum (R-PA) all brought a House-honed, hard-nosed, partisan approach to politics with them into the Senate. Several well-respected senior senators have retired over the past several years, in part to escape the increased partisanship emerging in the Senate; one such example is Warren Rudman (R-NH), who continued to serve the public as a leader of the Concord Coalition to press for budget discipline in Congress and as one of the chairs of a commission to assess U.S. national security after the Cold War. Ideological combat is also at the root of the nomination fights of the past two decades, especially the judicial battles. Hardliners at both ends of the political spectrum think nothing of tying up the Senate in nasty confirmation hearings and votes to advance their particular view of American politics. The tension that this conflict brings to the Senate is exemplified by the amazing story of James Jeffords (I-VT), a lifelong Republican who left the party to serve as an Independent in 2001 following the passage of President Bush's first round of tax cuts. Angered by what he saw as arrogant White House treatment and undue pressure from the Senate leadership, Jeffords switched parties and announced that he would vote with the Democrats on institutional issues. The evenly divided Senate, which had been run by the GOP because the vice president gave them the tiebreaker, thus suddenly shifted to Democratic control in midterm. This unprecedented shift happened because Jeffords, a moderately conservative but independent-minded New Englander, did not like the direction in which the Senate GOP was going under the leadership of its Southern conservatives and the White House.[45]

As in the House, the Framers' intent for the Senate is not quite strong enough to withstand the pressures of modern partisanship. Unlike the House, however, the Senate's long traditions of individualism and equality, though, do inoculate the chamber from the worst excesses of partisanship, unlike the House.

Summary

The Senate is a tradition-bound, conservative institution designed to allow the several states to have an equal voice in debating important national matters. This spirit of egalitarianism is alive and well in today's Senate, where the power structure, resources, and actions all operate to assist the senators in pursuing their own individual goals and interests. The Senate is a collection of equals working together in loose affiliations; senators do not look to their leaders for strong, central direction, and the Senate is more attuned to compromise and bipartisanship than is the House. Senators work in an institution designed to insulate them from the day-to-day political pressures that fuel much of the political agenda in the House.

Acting in consonance with the plan of the Framers, the members of the Senate have the opportunity to balance state and national concerns. The Senate has breathing room to think about the national interest in its lawmaking, even as it allows plenty of freedom for individual senators to work for their voters back home. The Senate is a good counterweight to the more partisan House. It also serves as counterweight to the White House through its advice and consent powers. The Senate is a personal place, where each senator matters and helps shape legislation. Parties and committees play supporting roles to the senators themselves. Sixty votes makes things happen in the Senate: over the past two centuries, the principle of equality has sunk into everything the Senate does.

In these two chapters we have seen what motivates the majoritarian House and the individualistic Senate. We have examined their members, structure, and parties, and we know how each chamber fits those similar pieces into different patterns. We know now how the Congress makes law and how it represents the people and the states. Every law represents a series of policy decisions made by Congress. But Congress does not get to put its laws into effect; it needs the executive branch to go and do the things set forth in law, and the judicial branch to administer justice as expressed in law. Congress has a few tools to guarantee that the rest of the government puts its policy decisions into effect. Now we turn our attention to those mechanisms.

Web Resources

U.S. Senate (www.senate.gov/).

Office of the Majority Leader: In the 108th and 109th Congresses, Senator Bill Frist (R-TN) served as majority leader; his site contains information regarding Senate scheduling and also information for his constituents (http://frist.senate.gov/).

Minority leader's Web site: Senator Harry Reid (D-NV) became minority leader at the start of the 109th Congress, following Tom Daschle's defeat in the 2004 elections (http://reid.senate.gov/).

National Republican Senatorial Committee: NRSC recruits, trains, and helps fund Republican contenders for Senate seats (www.nrsc.org/).

Democratic Senatorial Campaign Committee: The Democratic Party's headquarters for recruiting and funding would-be senators (www.dscc.org/home).

Congressional Information Center, C-SPAN: A handy Web guide to members, activities on the Hill, and issues currently before Congress (www3.capwiz.com/c-span/home/).

II • Enforcing Policy Decisions

In part I, we saw that Congress makes laws for the nation and that its members represent the constituents who sent them to Washington. In terms of government activity, though, Congress does not "do" anything—it does not pave roads, deliver mail, or patrol the streets of Baghdad. Executive branch agencies do all of the things that Congress declares to be national policy.

How does Congress get the executive branch to follow its guidance? Here is where things get tricky for Congress and for the rest of the national government. The Framers lived in a small world, where most people lived out their lives in the area where they were born: when you have to walk everywhere you go, even twenty miles is a day's journey. In such a world, people expected very little from government, and they got that from their town or state authorities. The citizens in those early years of the United States expected very little from their new national government—they wanted their borders free from Indian raids, their coasts clear of pirates, their states' Revolutionary War debts dealt with, and their mail delivered. Everything else they could get for themselves or from their states. The Framers were a part of this society when they met in Philadelphia to craft the Constitution. They had no idea that the future would require an enormous expansion of the size, power, and missions of the federal government. So they did not craft a comprehensive toolbox of powers for the Congress to wield in its battles with the executive branch.

This might have been fine in the early years of the Republic, before Washington grew in size and ability to have an impact on citizens' lives. After the Civil War, however, and through the years just after World War II, Congress engaged in a seventy-year program of government-building. Congress created agencies to deal with the myriad new challenges facing the growing, industrializing, and technologically maturing society in the United States. From Reconstruction through the Progressive Era, the Great Depression, two world wars, and the start of the Cold War, Congress created the federal government as we know it today.

Faced with the complex policy apparatus of Washington today, Congress faces many difficulties as it tries to enforce its policy choices on the rest of the federal government. As we learned in the first chapter, policymaking involves many players, requiring Congress to compete with others for influence. The White House, the press, interest groups, think tanks, industry, and public opinion all take part in important decisions.

Against that backdrop, Congress is not as well-armed as it might like to be. Its own structure—two very different chambers, which have delegated their powers to parties and committees—diffuses congressional power and invites confusion and competition. And Congress has only three constitutional tools to use to manage the executive branch's agencies.

In part II, we will examine the three enforcement powers of Congress. We will look at them in order of usage, from the most commonly deployed power to the least-used of the three. Chapter 5 explains oversight, Congress's power to investigate and evaluate the actions of federal agencies in order to ensure that the agencies comply with congressional intent. Committees and individual legislators devote much of their energies to some sort of oversight, so it deserves first attention. Chapter 6 discusses the power of the purse; the Constitution gives full power over the raising and spending of federal money to Congress, and control over the budget can be crucial in disciplining federal agencies. The budget process shapes Congress's annual schedule. The congressional calendar revolves around Congress's responsibility to make budgetary decisions, such as setting budget totals, aligning revenues with funding needs, and making spending decisions. Chapter 7 details the third power, *organizing*. The Framers wanted Congress to check the president's power, so Congress gets to set the missions, structure, and rules for every federal agency. In current terms, we can think of this power as "reorganization" as much as "organization"—Congress established the bulk of the federal government's agency structure years ago. That means that now Congress uses this power to rearrange agencies when the need arises—a challenge Congress does not enjoy, as it is difficult to do well, it is time-consuming, and it also demands that Congress look at its own structure. If reorganizing agencies is difficult, then reorganizing committees is nearly impossible; hence, this power, while mighty, is rarely used.

5 • The Oversight Power

It will not be controverted that the legislative is
the highest delegated power in government, and that all
others are subordinate to it.
—Centinel No. 1[1]

In a hushed hearing room on Capitol Hill, former National Security Council staffer and one-time national counterterrorism czar Richard Clarke testified at the National Commission on Terrorist Attacks Upon the United States (9/11 commission) hearings on his actions in the wake of the attack and on his thoughts about the policy priorities of the Clinton and Bush administrations. Clarke's testimony was tough, insightful, and controversial. A knowledgeable insider, he sought to help the commission make sense of how the federal government had failed to get a good grip on the threat of terrorism. In a powerful moment captured by the many news cameras filming the hearings, Clarke electrified the audience, the commission, and an already-polarized Washington by doing what nobody else had been willing to do: he apologized to the families of people killed in the attack: "I want the families of the victims to know that we tried to stop those attacks, that some people tried very hard. I want them to know why we failed and what I think we need to do to insure that nothing like that ever happens again."[2] Clarke's testimony put the White House on the defensive and emboldened critics of the Bush administration. White House personnel, including National Security Adviser Condoleezza Rice, suddenly confronted a much tougher commission, shocked by Clarke's bleak assessment.

The commission, in other words, was working: it was uncovering what happened before 9/11, in the hopes of learning how to prevent another such disaster in the future. Congress and President Bush had created the commission to seek answers to the tough questions surrounding 9/11. The commission was an extension of congressional oversight of the executive branch; when Congress cannot pursue good oversight because of time, resource, or political constraints, it can use other methods, like independent commissions, to seek the truth and develop good policy alternatives.

As we saw in part I, Congress has the constitutional responsibility to make law for the nation, but it does not implement policies. Congress needs a mechanism to enforce its decisions, and oversight is its best tool for making sure that the executive branch is following laws passed by Congress and that those policies work well. The Constitution does not explicitly grant the oversight power to Congress, but from the beginning it has been considered an essential function of Congress's legislative duties.[3] Britain's Parliament had the power to conduct hearings and investigate matters before deciding on legislation, so the Framers expected their new Congress to be able to do the same thing. Federal courts have recognized Congress's right to oversee the executive branch in a series of decisions that made it clear that oversight is fundamental to good public policy and to Congress's ability to execute its lawmaking responsibility.[4] The Legislative Reorganization Act (LRA) of 1946 gave each of the standing committees the responsibility to perform oversight within its jurisdiction.[5] With the LRA as guidance, the House and Senate Rules Committees mention oversight in the specific rules that grant the committees their jurisdiction. Congress also standardized the rule-making responsibilities of the various agencies in 1946. The Administrative Procedures Act (APA) extends legislative goals to the actions of rule-making agencies, requiring them to seek public comment through hearings, much as Congress's committees study legislative proposals.[6] Growing out of its British heritage, court approval, and legal grounding, oversight is the central mechanism Congress uses to keep track of the actions of the executive branch and to signal to federal agencies what Congress wants them to do.

Members of the House and senators are well aware that they do not work in a vacuum. At the same time that Congress seeks to influence agency actions, the White House, political appointees, interest groups and industry, the media, and the courts also impact on agency actions. For Congress, then—as for all of the players involved—influencing agency actions is a difficult, time-consuming task. And it is difficult to assess congressional success, given the many other influences simultaneously impinging on agencies.

When Congress uses its oversight powers, these other factors have to be considered. For instance, when a committee drafts a bill containing instructions to an agency, the committee's staff and members must account for White House statements on the issue and respond to any recent court actions on the matter, as well. Recent research into the question points out that several factors seem to influence the amount of specific instructions on policy included in legislative attempts to shape bureaucratic actions. When political conflict rises among the committees overseeing an issue, or between the House and

Senate, or when the president or the courts are likely to take issue with congressional intent, legislation tends to contain more specific policy guidance.[7]

In fact, frequently congressional oversight must *anticipate* the influences of the other actors, particularly the courts. If a committee is aware that recent court decisions have changed the way an agency does its work, then it can write future bills to accommodate those court decisions. Congress does not always know about court actions—only the precedent-setting appeals and Supreme Court cases tend to earn much coverage.[8] In his classic study of government agencies, *Bureaucracy,* James Q. Wilson notes that court action has grown in importance over time; whereas the courts deferred to the executive and Congress in the nineteenth century, since at least the 1950s the courts have been much more willing to step into disputes over agency instructions and how the agencies interpret those rules.[9] Knowing that the courts have allowed more people to bring cases on agency actions, and knowing that the courts are also now more willing to interpret congressional intent, committees have responded by crafting legislation that specifies judicial review in many cases. Congress knows that the courts are open to allowing lawsuits over agency actions, so they anticipate that possibility by writing bills with clear intent and with careful limits on judicial review.[10]

Congress exercises oversight in the complicated, multiplayer context of the U.S. public policymaking system. We saw in part I that Congress does not do anything as a body, and that is true of oversight as well. As with legislation, the task of oversight is split up among the committees of the House and the Senate. The legislative committees are Congress's primary agents for managing the executive branch agencies, and although there are a few other avenues for overseeing the agencies, the committees are the main actors in performing congressional oversight. Because the legislative committees also do oversight, they are sometimes referred to as "oversight committees" as well. (The Appropriations Committees of the two chambers conduct very thorough budgetary oversight every year as they produce the appropriations bills that fund the federal government; we will examine their work in chapter 6.) In this chapter, we will examine the oversight power. We will answer three questions. First, what is oversight and what broad patterns emerge in use of the oversight power? Second, who oversees whom—how does Congress use this power? And third, how effective is Congress in using this power to enforce its policy decisions?

What Is Oversight?

Oversight means many things, and it has no formal definition in the Constitution, law, or rules of the two chambers. Many of the daily activities of members, committees, and staff can be called oversight: they seek information on policy execution, help constituents deal with agencies, research issues for committee hearings and markups, and study programs to evaluate performance and compliance with congressional intent.[11] Congress's oversight interests reach into every aspect of the federal bureaucracy's operations, from policy decisions and processes to personnel, budget,[12] and organizational[13] issues.[14] Oversight is what we call the mechanisms Congress has designed to ensure that agencies perform their assigned tasks according to congressional intent, that programs work as expected, and that congressional solutions have solved the problems Congress identified. Oversight is nearly constant, but it is not usually thoroughly planned or regularly scheduled.[15] In many cases, when legislators have seen compliance in the past, they trust agency personnel to follow congressional guidance so there is no need for extensive oversight.[16] Congressional committees are also quite busy with legislative work, so they do not have the time or resources for constant oversight,[17] preferring to respond to specific events or perceived changes in public mood that demand tighter congressional control over executive branch actions.[18]

Oversight is a constant feature of congressional activity because it meets two important needs for legislators: it helps them get reelected, and it improves policymaking. Oversight gives legislators many opportunities to demonstrate to their constituency that they matter in Washington and that they are effective champions for the voters back home. Constituent service is the clearest way for members and senators to do this, but conducting hearings or calling for investigations on behalf of constituents can also help legislators when the next reelection campaign begins.[19] Legislators also care a great deal about good policymaking, and they pursue oversight to advance their preferred programs and policies.[20]

Oversight is also ubiquitous because it is tough to do. *Oversight* is a neutral term, but presidents and agency personnel treat most congressional attempts at oversight as intrusive, confrontational, or inappropriate—and in the normal conditions in Washington over the past fifty years, when one party controls Congress and the other holds the White House, even the simplest exercise of oversight becomes partisan. That is the context facing Congress when it pursues oversight to make sure that executive branch agencies act in accord with congressional intent.[21] But Congress faces many obstacles to performing good oversight. The most important is that the federal government tends to be conservative with respect to major change, preferring the status quo to change, and small, incremental changes to large ones.[22] This incremental tendency means that the long-term, key players in Washington— the executive agency leaders and staff, senators and members of the House, and interested outside groups like lobbyists, industry, and advocacy organizations—prefer to move slowly for change, if at all.[23] This is not to say that major changes never occur. In the face of a major failure, or when the agency and committees that usually manage a policy issue fail to address ongoing concerns, then it can be possible for other committees, or party leaders in the House or Senate (or in the White House), to step in and craft a more comprehensive reform proposal. This is a relatively infrequent occurrence, but at times major change punctuates the usual, incremental style of governing.[24]

How does Congress use the oversight power? Before we can examine that question, we need to recall Congress's role in policymaking and how that can affect oversight. The primary reason oversight is so hard to do well is the complicated policymaking process in Washington. As we saw in chapter 1, policymaking is messy, so oversight has to be ubiquitous and multilayered if it is to be successful. Washington policymaking rarely follows the neat charts in introductory textbooks, with each step clearly defined—starting with problem identification, moving through alternative formulation, testing, selection, and implementation. In reality, all these steps can happen out of order, or nearly simultaneously, making oversight difficult.[25] Along with every step happening almost at once, the players shift from time to time, their goals are not always clear (even to themselves), and sometimes nobody can clearly sense the consequences of their policy decisions.[26] This sort of organized anarchy makes oversight confusing. In this kind of challenging environment, Congress may prefer small, politically safe forms of action: incremental actions, which may never fully address problems. Congress also tends to prefer quiet oversight to any large, public investigation.[27] In the face of tough choices, Congress sometimes chooses ambiguous solutions, which allow many legislators to support them without necessarily agreeing on what they are trying to accomplish.[28]

Who Oversees Whom?

"Congress" does not really do oversight. It is too big, too slow, and too unwieldy to manage the task as a whole. So when we say that Congress oversees the actions of the federal bureaucracy, we are using shorthand—Congress as an institution parcels out the oversight to its members and, most important, to its committees. Members perform some individual oversight through personal investigations and their casework operations. Legislators with policy interests may also take on a watchdog role.[29] But the main agent for oversight is the committee system. As we saw in part I, the committees of the House and Senate divide the legislative work of Congress into segments, with each committee having jurisdiction over a specific range of issues. Oversight follows the same pattern, with each committee having responsibility to oversee executive branch agencies that perform tasks under the committee's jurisdiction. Many agencies fall under the jurisdiction of one committee in each chamber, but agencies with many responsibilities may find that they must report their activities to several committees. For instance, the Department of Defense falls under the Armed Services Committees of the House and Senate, but since the Pentagon also operates several intelligence-gathering agencies, its leaders must also report to the House Permanent Select Committee on Intelligence and the Senate Select Committee on Intelligence. Whenever agencies must report to multiple committees, they must spend more time interacting with Congress than departments with single committee oversight. In addition, since the committees exercise exclusive oversight over those matters under their jurisdiction, the committees only rarely coordinate their hearing schedules or the guidance they issue to the agency heads. This leads to confusion: what congressional guidance should an agency heed when it receives multiple, conflicting instructions? Even agencies that answer to only one committee in each chamber have this problem, since the House and Senate often see the same issue in two completely different ways.

Oversight is complicated by another factor as well: committee jurisdictions are not always as exclusive as they seem to be in the rules of the two chambers. Complicated policy issues frequently require actions from many agencies, so congressional oversight of an issue can fall under the jurisdiction of several committees. In addition, how leaders, committee chairs, and the policy community frame an issue can influence which committees exercise oversight on certain issues—and which committees get left out. In the early 1990s, for example, House Subcommittee on Health and the Environment chair Rep. Henry Waxman (D-CA) sought to confront cigarette manufacturers over the health effects of their products. Congress had for years taken no serious steps to combat smoking-related health problems, partly because the Agriculture Committee had jurisdiction over the issue, since tobacco is a major farm crop in many Southern states. Legislators from both parties who represented tobacco-growing states sat on the Agriculture Committee, defending the growers and cigarette manufacturers from regulation. Waxman successfully reframed the issue by focusing on the potential illnesses caused by smoking; by changing the issue from a farming issue to a health issue, Waxman was able to wrest the issue away from Agriculture and move it to his own committee, which then held a series of powerful, and damaging, hearings, during which the heads of several cigarette companies were forced to render embarrassing testimony about the known ill effects of their products.[30]

Committee Oversight

The committees carry the weight of oversight: only they have the requisite resources of staff, expertise, and jurisdiction. Oversight is part of the legislative jurisdiction of the committees, which have developed a wide range of tools to use to perform oversight in their areas of responsibility. Each committee sets its own schedule for oversight activities, as well as setting goals to achieve through oversight. Oversight helps committees to pursue several possible goals:

> [T]he focus may be on promoting administrative efficiency and economy in government, protecting and supporting favored policies and programs, airing an administration's failures or wrongdoing, or its achievements, publicizing a particular member's or a committee's goals, reasserting Congressional authority vis-à-vis the executive branch, or assuaging the interests of pressure groups.[31]

Oversight is not a coordinated, systematic process managed by the leadership of either chamber; it is part of what committees do in pursuing their legislative responsibilities. Despite increased staff size and expertise since the 1960s, oversight is incomplete and sometimes irrational.[32] Given the policy patterns discussed in chapter 1, some committees have a larger role than others in policymaking; these committees will have more opportunities to use oversight effectively to ensure that the executive branch does what the committees want. In particular, committees in cooperative or committee-driven situations, where the committees have a large role in shaping policy, will be likely to have more success in overseeing agencies compared to committees working on issues that display top-down or nonparticipatory patterns. In those cases, committee oversight tends to be less effective. Top-down issues see leaders dictating goals to committees, while nonparticipatory policy (crisis response) leaves no work for the committee to do until long after the fact. Figure 5.1 reproduces the policy patterns described in chapter 1.

But the committees do have a wide array of techniques to use to oversee their jurisdictions, including informal methods, hearings, authorization, sunset clauses, inspectors general, reports, confirmations, the legislative veto, evaluation standards, and general oversight committees. We will now look at each of these techniques.

Not every interaction between the oversight committees and the federal bureaucracy is a formal meeting. Committees use a range of informal methods to shape agency behavior, and if those methods are successful, then there will be no need for a hearing, investigation, or any other oversight.

Figure 5.1 **Policy Patterns, Committee Oversight**

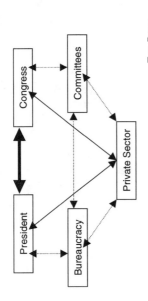

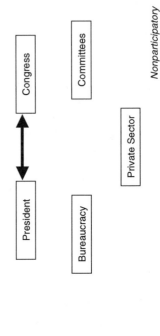

Source: Adapted from Ripley and Franklin, 1991.

Committee staff and members communicate with the agencies regularly by phone, e-mail, and letters, and these informal contacts can be very effective signals of congressional desire. Many agencies respond quickly to congressional inquiries as a way of maintaining good relations with their oversight committees.[33] Another informal method is to include guidance in the report filed with a bill passed by a committee, which suggests congressional intent without formally requiring compliance in the text of the bill.[34] Agencies keep track of these sorts of cues, often working with supportive committee members to shape such report language in specific ways to show willingness to work with Congress, making the agency's job easier.[35] Legislators also form caucuses to press for specific programs; these informal groups work to preserve favored programs or to call for new ones to address some perceived challenge.[36]

The most recognized method of committee oversight is conducting hearings and investigations into the operations of the federal agencies. Hearings allow committees to evaluate the performance of federal programs, to gauge public support for those programs, and to signal committee interest in specific programs.[37] Hearings allow committees to gather information needed to decide whether new legislation is required and what form it should take. Since collecting information is so important for legislative deliberations, oversight committees have subpoena power and can hold agency officials in contempt if they refuse to share needed information.[38] Each committee and subcommittee has a hearing room on Capitol Hill for its meetings and hearings, and on occasion some members will conduct hearings in the field to collect public testimony about specific programs.[39]

Every federal cabinet department and agency exists because Congress has authorized it to exist; congressional legislation sets the mission, size, and organization of each agency. For many specific programs, this authorizing legislation expires after several years. Every time a committee considers reauthorizing an agency or program, the members have an opportunity for comprehensive assessments of every activity within the program or agency.[40] Every dollar appropriated for a federal program must first be authorized by one of the oversight committees, so the authorization process is a powerful tool for oversight.[41] Some programs, such as federal highway and transit assistance to the states for transportation projects, come up for reauthorization every six years; each reauthorization is a huge challenge for the committee to manage.[42] On the other hand, the Defense Department faces reauthorization at the beginning of each two-year Congress, with a smaller round of defense authorizations the following year to revise any programs in need of adjustment.[43] Since each authorization bill has to clear the floor to make it into law, it is not only the committees that can use authorization to influence agency actions. With the largest proportion of the federal discretionary budget (the part of the budget Congress decides how to spend each year), the Pentagon sees a flurry of legislative activity each year when the annual defense authorization bill comes up for floor debate. The bill now takes as long as two weeks, with hundreds of amendments considered before the final approval of the bill.[44] A similar technique is to include a sunset clause in a program's authorization bill, which ends the program unless Congress decides to keep the program in operation.[45]

In 1978, Congress passed a law establishing an inspector general (IG) in each of the major federal agencies. In addition to producing regular reports on their agencies, IGs conduct investigations of reported problems within agencies, and Congress can use the IG system to ensure that performance standards are being met in the agencies. In addition, committees can call on the IG to testify and share any information gathered in investigations.[46]

Whenever a committee wants to emphasize its interest in having a program run in a specific way, it can require the agency involved to report on that program on a regular basis. Many agencies already produce an annual report to the president and Congress outlining their activities for the year, and many of the agencies include these statutory reports in that document. The Defense Department, for instance, has seen as many as 1,100 demands for reports on specific programs in the defense budget.[47]

The Senate has a chance to perform oversight every time the president submits a candidate for confirmation to a federal office. The committee of jurisdiction holds hearings for all major positions, using the hearings to probe the candidates for their views on any important or controversial issues they will deal with while in office.[48] While the media frequently report conflicts over confirmation of federal judge nominees,[49] the confirmation hearings for many other appointees can also make the news, as when the Senate Armed Services Committee refused to confirm John Tower to serve as President George H.W. Bush's secretary of defense in 1989.[50]

Starting in the 1930s, Congress devised another tool for oversight, which is called the legislative veto, a provision in a bill that gives Congress the opportunity to prevent an agency action by passing a resolution disapproving the proposed action. Legislative vetoes usually gave Congress a set period, such as ninety days, to act, or the agency proposal would take effect. About 200 of these veto provisions were enacted through 1983, when the Supreme Court invalidated the use of legislative vetoes. Congress does still use a form of the legislative veto, but in order to comply with the court's instructions, now all legislative vetoes pass by joint resolution, which must be passed by the House and Senate before taking effect.[51]

Congress devised a new oversight tool in 1993 with the passage of the

Government Performance and Results Act (GPRA). The act sets government-wide standards and calls on each agency to audit its activities using measures of results, rather than indirect measures such as inputs (budgets and staff) and outputs (so many citizens helped, so many investigations performed).[52] GPRA has not been fully successful, since many agencies do not produce easily measurable results (how can we tell if the State Department is producing more, or better, diplomacy?), and many agencies have had severe difficulties in shifting from older indirect measures to results-oriented evaluations.[53] But the GPRA evaluation requirements do give the Congress another tool for overseeing executive branch agencies.

Two standing committees have a special responsibility for oversight. Realizing that many oversight issues will necessarily involve examining government actions across several of the standing committees' jurisdictions, the House and the Senate each established a committee devoted to general oversight of the government. The Senate committee was established in 1921, and the House committee in 1927. The House Committee on Government Reform and the Senate's Governmental Affairs Committee both conduct broad hearings dealing with management issues, such as the civil service, personnel pay and retirement systems, paperwork reduction, governmental efficiency, accounting, and executive branch reorganization.[54] Both committees also accept the reports of the comptroller general, the head of the Government Accountability Office (GAO), and make recommendations to their parent chambers based on those reports. They also oversee any reorganization proposals brought before Congress and evaluate any reorganization after enactment. The Senate Governmental Affairs Committee managed the Senate's work on the establishment of the Department of Homeland Security in 2003.[55]

Congressional committees have developed a broad array of techniques for overseeing the agencies they monitor, and the two chambers have set up committees to deal with issues that cross the jurisdictional boundaries of the standing committees. This is how most of the oversight happens, but what happens when an investigation is too complicated or too time-consuming for a committee to manage? Congress has established a number of support agencies to deal with such difficult situations.

Congressional Agency Oversight

Sometimes the committees do not have the time or expertise to conduct an investigation of a complex issue. Rather than give up, Congress has responded to this challenge by creating support agencies that can help the committees with the oversight challenge. Congress recognized the need for extensive support early in its history, creating the Library of Congress to provide a repository of references for congressional use. Several other congressional support agencies have followed, each giving Congress new capabilities in a variety of academic, technical, and professional fields. These agencies are the Congressional Research Service (CRS), the Government Accountability Office (GAO), the Congressional Budget Office (CBO), and the (now-defunct) Office of Technology Assessment (OTA). All told, 10,000 staffers in these agencies support the oversight efforts of Congress's committees.[56]

The oldest, broadest, and most widely used resource is the world-renowned Library of Congress, established in 1800 to provide Congress (and the rest of the federal government) with references and studies that might be of use to the members during debates on legislation before the House or Senate. Since its humble beginnings, the library has become the premier research library in the world, with over 129 million books and, in the past decade, a growing digital collection of films, music, and other media. Over 5,000 employees work at the library, maintaining its collections and assisting legislators, staff, and scholars. The Library provided sufficient assistance to Congress until the growth of the federal government during the Progressive Era (1890–1910) outpaced the library's ability to support the research needs of Congress. In 1914, Congress added to the library's capabilities by creating the Legislative Reference Service. This office helped Congress to deal with the organizational, technical, and regulatory complexity of executive agency operations. The office was renamed the Congressional Research Service in the 1970 Legislative Reorganization Act. The CRS is charged with serving as an in-house think tank for Congress. CRS experts perform research for members and committees, and their work is scrupulously nonpartisan.[57] They submit their research directly to the requestor, and their studies are generally not made public. In addition to research on legislation and policy proposals, CRS experts also meet with legislators and staff to give briefings on their work, and they train Hill staffers in legislative research skills. Nonpartisan, private studies allow CRS researchers full freedom to report accurate findings, regardless of potential difficulties. Members rely heavily on the CRS's work because it is so careful, complete, and dispassionate.

Congress needed more help, however, particularly after the passage of the Budget Act of 1921, which required the president to submit to Congress an annual unified budget proposal for the federal government. In the act, Congress created two agencies to assist in managing the new budget process: the Bureau of the Budget for the executive branch (now called the Office of Management and Budget), and the General Accounting Office, to support congressional budget work. The General Accounting Office initially performed a purely accounting function, checking the executive budgets and assessing the accuracy of federal spending records. In the 1950s and through the 1970s, the GAO's duties expanded into program evaluation. Now the GAO acts as Congress's government-wide inspector general. In recognition of the broad management and program evaluation duties performed by GAO's 3,200 employees, the agency was renamed the Government Accountability Office in 2004.[58] The GAO produces over 1,000 analytical reports every year, examining policies and programs across the full spectrum of federal agency activities, and GAO researchers frequently testify before congressional committees in support of the research they conduct.[59] In 2003, for example, the GAO sent researchers to testify before committees 189 times, making over 2,000 recommendations on how to improve federal programs.[60]

Two other agencies have had some role in assisting Congress with its oversight role. The Congressional Budget Office was established during the 1974 budget reforms, which also created the Budget Committees of the two chambers. CBO provides the budget expertise needed by the Congress to compete with the executive branch's Office of Management and Budget, whose budget work reflects the priorities and programs of the president. CBO's mission is to support congressional budget work with objective, nonpartisan evaluations of program costs and estimates, so congressional budget debates can proceed with solid information. CBO's mission area is very specific. The bulk of CBO's support goes to the two Budget Committees. CBO's staff is a "professional, nonpartisan staff" that "does not make recommendations on policy."[61] Since its establishment, CBO's rigorous analyses and ferociously nonpartisan approach have made it a respected agency throughout the government.

One other agency formerly provided Congress with comprehensive, technical data designed to help congressional committees oversee complicated defense, space, and energy programs. Established in 1972, the Office of Technology Assessment (OTA) conducted in-depth analyses, some of which took several years to complete. The thoroughness, complexity, and detail of OTA reports could not be matched by the other agencies, but some legislators complained that OTA's long-term studies took too long to produce, since they were frequently completed after bills were passed. Arguing that its research activities could be managed within CRS or GAO, the GOP majority closed down OTA in 1995 to demonstrate its commitment to a smaller, more economical government.[62]

Congress looks to its committees and support agencies to manage the bulk of the oversight tasks. Committees conduct most of the oversight, conducting hearings, small investigations, and requiring frequent reports on sensitive issues. In some cases, more complicated questions get handed off to the support agencies for a thorough investigation. The committees with oversight jurisdiction use these support agency reports and investigations as a tool to understand complex programs, so Congress can enforce its policy preferences in the bureaucracy. While this division of labor helps Congress to conduct oversight across the full range of executive branch activities, it means that congressional oversight is fragmented and limited by the jurisdictions of the various committees. On occasion a major event occurs that requires a broader, more comprehensive oversight approach by Congress. Rather than trying to get several committees to work together to deal with such difficult (and frequently politically controversial) issues, Congress uses special oversight mechanisms to assess the situation, evaluate government responses, and recommend any changes needed to address the issue.

Beyond Regular Oversight

If large programs or policies require revision, or if a major government failure occurs, Congress cannot always rely on the usual oversight tools to find out what went wrong and craft a legislative response to address the issue. In these cases, Congress has two options for oversight: it can create a select committee to deal with the investigation internally, or it can establish an independent investigation to review the situation and deliver recommendations to the Congress for future action. In particularly complicated cases where Congress fears that its members will not have sufficient time to investigate the issue completely, the independent investigation route has become the favored option. In some cases, Congress takes both routes simultaneously, creating an internal select committee to investigate certain factors and creating a parallel independent commission to study other aspects of the situation. Usually, the more controversial or partisan the potential results of the investigation, the more likely Congress will create an independent commission, to give more credence to the findings and to get some distance between those findings and Congress.

The House and the Senate both have procedures in their standing rules governing the creation of select committees, which specify how they are to be organized and how they are charged with their duties. Select committees usually exist for a short period of time, generally no longer than a two-year session of Congress, unless approved to continue to the next Congress. Select committees are established to investigate specific issues and to craft a suitable legislative response if necessary.[63] For example, in 1997 reports surfaced suggesting that Hughes, an aerospace firm that builds satellites, might have illegally shared technical information about one of its satellites with officials of the People's Republic of China after the failed launch of the Chinese rocket scheduled to lift the satellite into orbit. The House of Representatives appointed a select committee, under the leadership of Christopher Cox (R-CA), to investigate the charges and to assess whether existing licensing regulations protected American technology sufficiently. After a year of hearings and investigation, the Cox Committee issued a report that questioned the integrity of the export license program. But since the House GOP supported the committee's creation and the report attacked the (Democratic) Clinton administration's handling of the license program, many observers did not embrace the report's findings.[64]

Many of the most important issues Congress needs to investigate are controversial, or partisan, or both. In those situations, no standing or select committee has the objectivity to conduct a legitimate investigation. In such difficult cases, Congress appoints an independent commission to deal with the topic. For instance, congressional Republicans disagreed with the Clinton administration's slow approach to national missile defense (NMD), but despite passing a law making NMD official U.S. national security policy— which President Clinton signed!—House and Senate leaders could not force the Clinton White House to move fast enough on the issue. So in 1997 they created the commission to Assess the Ballistic Missile Threat to the United States (Rumsfeld Commission) in an effort to make their case more effectively. The Commission reported in 1998 that many nations around the world, including several unfriendly to the United States (North Korea and Iran), were closer to fielding dangerous ballistic missiles than U.S. intelligence had estimated. Even with the publication of this report, however, the Clinton administration continued its original, slow NMD research plan.[65]

Another independent commission had been working for several years on the difficult question of adapting U.S. national security policy to new challenges, releasing two thorough reports on how to think about the challenge. Appointed in 1998, the bipartisan U.S. Commission on National Security/ 21st Century (also called the Hart-Rudman Commission) had examined every aspect of national defense. In 2001, the commission issued a third report, which included a proposal to create a new department to manage the defense of the continental United States against potential attacks by terrorist or rogue nations. Nothing happened with the report's recommendations at the time.[66]

Six months after the final Hart-Rudman report was issued, everything changed when nineteen terrorists attacked the World Trade Center in New York and the Pentagon in Washington, DC. The terrorist attack on 9/11 represented a tremendous government failure: the attacks took U.S. intelligence and law enforcement agencies by surprise, despite years of antagonism from Osama bin Laden's organization (and years of other attacks on U.S. and allied targets around the world, making it clear that bin Laden had the organizational resources and planning capacity to strike against the

United States). Congress responded using a combination of internal and external investigations to determine what went so wrong in the years leading up to the 9/11 attacks; its inquiries were targeted not at any specific administration, but on any structural and procedural liabilities extant in the executive branch that allowed an attack as large as 9/11 to occur. Both chambers agreed to order a joint inquiry by the Senate Select Committee on Intelligence and the House Permanent Select Committee on Intelligence, which explored the intelligence problems prior to 9/11 and issued a report in December 2002. Congress also worked with the president to appoint an independent commission to investigate the intelligence failings that allowed the 9/11 attacks in New York and Washington. The commission's report, issued in the summer of 2004, questioned long-term issues in the management and organization of the intelligence community, particularly its lack of focus on the full range of threats after the end of the Cold War and its inadequate intelligence-gathering capabilities in the Middle East and the larger Muslim world. Congress enacted many of the commission's recommendations in late 2004.[67]

Congress performs oversight of numerous federal government activities all the time. Working through standing committees, select committees, and independent commissions, Congress makes broad use of its many oversight powers to investigate issues, resolve policy problems, and devise new legislation where necessary. How effective is Congress's use of the oversight power? What are the strengths and weaknesses of the various methods of oversight?

Assessing Congressional Oversight

Congress does a great deal of oversight; does it work? The answer seems to be "not very well." Congress can be fairly successful at using oversight to ensure compliance with policy decisions and to respond to major problems, but its fragmentation and the various patterns of policymaking complicate oversight. Congressional agencies study executive branch actions frequently and report their findings to Congress, but their reports have no force of law and may not lead to policy changes. The same limitation confronts independent commissions. Finally, Congress faces several institutional challenges to good oversight.

Oversight is hard to do effectively; many observers feel that Congress is not very successful at using oversight to shape the actions of the bureaucracy. It is tough to measure oversight or define its impact. With each committee pursuing its own oversight goals, there is nothing systematic in Congress's approach to oversight. Two researchers aptly describe Congress's preference for "fire alarm" oversight that targets emergencies as they happen, instead of regular "police patrols" to keep agencies in line before they violate congressional intent; the fractured power of the committee system makes it tough to do police patrol oversight.[68] And the many techniques Congress has developed for oversight all have strengths and weaknesses. For instance, reporting requirements become routine, so committees may not study them in detail. Hearings are not always well attended; given the number of committee assignments members of Congress have, they cannot attend every hearing.

Congress's research agencies and independent commissions can get good information through their investigative work, but their reports are nonbinding on Congress, which may or may not act on any recommendations. In addition, commissions lack subpoena power, and with their fixed terms of service, recalcitrant executive branch officials can wait them out. And commissions have less power to effect changes than GAO or CBO; once they report their findings and publicize their recommendations, they go out of business, leaving Congress free to use their ideas or not. Select committees avoid some of the problems facing commissions (they have subpoena power, for instance, and can report a bill for the House or Senate to vote on), but they are temporary, disorganized, and usually under tight time deadlines to get something done.[69]

The final challenge to full use of the oversight power is institutional. Congress is a conservative institution: leaders and legislators prefer the status quo, which preserves current power relationships and interactions between the committees, congressional leaders, the president, bureaucracies, and interested outside groups. If change is called for, Congress prefers incremental change. Oversight is tough and time-consuming and has a low political payoff: as long as that is true, the current level of unsystematic, decentralized oversight is probably about what we can expect from Congress.[70] Partisanship also limits Congress's institutional ability to use oversight effectively; when one party controls both the Congress and the White House, there is a tendency to do less oversight. This has been particularly the case since George W. Bush took office in 2001.[71] An excellent recent study of bureaucratic policies can serve as the last word on Congress and the oversight power:

> With hundreds of different constituencies enfranchised in the Senate and House of Representatives, Congressional control of the bureaucracy is fundamentally uncoordinated. . . . Specific committees and subcommittees . . . may influence what goes on in particular agencies . . . but the bureaucracy as a whole does not operate under the direction of Congress as an institution.[72]

Summary

Congress looks to the committees for oversight. But committees have to compete with the president, congressional leaders, the bureaucracy, and outside groups to shape policy and ensure that the government agencies do what Congress intends. And since not all policies are made in the same way, some committees have more power to wield effective oversight than others do. Committees overseeing crisis policy do not get to do their oversight until after the crisis ends; committees with strategic, regulatory, and redistributive policy oversight also have limited oversight capability because of their limited role in setting policy; but committees involved in distributive and structural policy can make oversight work, since they are immersed in policymaking. All the oversight committees have a set of techniques to use for oversight: informal methods, hearings, authorization, sunset clauses, inspectors general, reports, confirmations, legislative vetoes, and evaluation standards. Congress also has a general oversight committee in each chamber and the power to appoint select committees or independent commissions to deal with tough oversight challenges.

With the oversight power distributed across the committee structure, it is not likely to be comprehensive. But committees do have the capacity to shape short-term agency response very effectively and force the administration and agency officials to move toward Congress's view of the world. Especially when public pressure forces an issue to the forefront, congressional oversight can be a powerful mechanism for discovering what has happened and how the government could do better.

Richard Clarke's appearance at the 9/11 commission is a great example of how good oversight can force bureaucracies—and the White House—to pay attention to Congress: in the wake of his powerful testimony, the president ended up allowing his national security adviser, Condoleezza Rice, to testify before the commission, a move that he had opposed until Clarke's strong performance forced him to allow Rice's testimony.[73]

Web Resources

Committee listing, U.S. House: This page contains links to all the oversight committees in the House (www.house.gov/house/CommitteeWWW.shtml).

Committee listing, U.S. Senate: This page links to all the Senate's committees (www.senate.gov/pagelayout/committees/d_three_sections_with_teasers/committees_home.htm).

Congressional Budget Office: CBO offers its publications on it Web page, including extensive reviews and background on budgetary issues (www.cbo.gov/).

Government Accountability Office: GAO conducts many investigations for Congress and studies program implementation in the executive branch. Its reports are available on its Web site (www.gao.gov/).

Library of Congress: The Library is home to a vast collection of volumes, but also includes a great deal of interesting historical information on its Web site (www.loc.gov/). The Library also lists a wide array of useful links on its legislative information page (http://thomas.loc.gov/home/legbranch/legbranch.html).

Open CRS: This Web site contains a public archive of Congressional Research Service reports produced for members and committees (www.opencrs.com/).

National Bipartisan Commission on the Future of Medicare: Congress established this commission in 1997 to explore Medicare reform (http://medicare.commission.gov/medicare/index.html).

U.S. Commission on National Security/21st Century: This bipartisan study group, chaired by former senators Gary Hart and Warren Rudman and including former Speaker Newt Gingrich, issued three reports between 1999 and 2001 concerning the United States' role in the world and how to provide for a more adaptable national security policy. They anticipated 9/11 by noting the threat of terrorism and called for a new homeland security department (http://permanent.access.gpo.gov/nssg/www.nssg.gov/addedumpage.htm).

6 • The Power of the Purse

It is necessary that the power of the general legislature should extend to all the objects of taxation, that government should be able to command all the resources of the country; because no man can tell what our exigencies may be. Wars have now become rather wars of the purse than of the sword. Government must therefore be able to command the whole power of the purse. . . . A government that can command but half its resources is like a man with but one arm to defend himself.
—Oliver Ellsworth, January 7, 1788[1]

Tensions in Washington ran high in the fall of 1995. The new GOP masters of Congress refused to compromise with President Bill Clinton on the federal budget, and time was running out. Speaker of the House Newt Gingrich (R-GA) insisted that Congress not budge, and Senate majority leader Robert Dole (R-KS) grudgingly went along. House leaders wanted a significantly smaller budget and a smaller federal government, too. But President Clinton, stunned at first by the GOP victories in the 1994 elections, had begun to regain his political footing. Sensing that the GOP leaders supported an unpopular position and that their stubbornness would hurt them, he refused to meet their demands. The budget impasse meant a government shutdown—all of the agencies that had not yet been funded in annual appropriations bills would run out of money in mid-November. Neither side budged, so the shutdown occurred, lasting for six days before a stopgap agreement reopened the government, but then that failed, shutting the doors for twenty-one more days. Speaker Gingrich thought that everyone would blame Clinton, but the president forcefully took control of the story in the media, and by the end of the shutdown, the White House won the day—not only did the budget reflect a win for Clinton, but the press and the country largely blamed Gingrich and Congress for the whole mess.[2]

How could this happen, when the power of the purse is the most fearsome weapon in Congress's arsenal? Observers offered many explanations for the failure of Congress to impose its will on the White House in 1995. Gingrich misread the political winds and overplayed his hand, while Clinton worked political magic to turn the whole story into a disaster for Gingrich. But more than that, Congress's own internal budget process could be blamed in part for the mess.

What is the federal budget? How does Congress manage the budget process? The budget is more than a single document listing revenues and spending for the year. The budget is really a vast array of decisions, programs, and policies that reflects the multiple goals of the many players in Washington who have some role in creating it—the various money committees, the party leaders, and active individual legislators.[3] Since the budget is the final and most concrete statement of a government's priorities, it has a special place in any consideration of congressional power. Of the three powers for enforcing decisions we have been discussing, it is the only one clearly expressed in the Constitution.[4] It is the most feared and most talked about of Congress's three powers, and it excites great attention among agency heads and political appointees since they have to seek funds from Congress every year to pay for their agency activities.

But great as the budget power is, Congress's complex internal structure and its difficult budget procedures combine to make the power of the purse an unwieldy weapon. The complexity of the budget makes it hard for legislators to use the budget power as forcefully as they might like. Three problems challenge Congress's power of the purse as a tool for enforcing its policy decisions. First, much of the federal budget is actually spent before the "budget process" even starts, limiting Congress's reach. Second, since there is little coordination among taxers, budgeteers, and appropriators, Congress sends mixed signals to the agencies it seeks to control. And finally, the appropriators have become so powerful over the past few decades that their dominance over the policy committees seriously jeopardizes the quality of congressional oversight in general.

In this chapter, we will examine Congress's budget power. We will first sketch the history of the federal budget process and how it evolved into the system we have today. Next, we will discuss the current process. Then we will explore how the budget process drives Congress's whole schedule, effectively crowding out other legislative priorities if those are not timed very carefully. Then we will describe the committees that manage budget decisions for Congress, examining their roles and limitations. This chapter will end with assessment of how successfully Congress uses its budget power to enforce its policy decisions on the executive branch agencies.

Congress and the Federal Budget

Budget matters have not always been central to the work of Congress. At first there was no central budget process; the executive branch departments reported their expenditures and made their budget requests directly to Congress. From 1885 to 1921, the House did not even have a centralized appropriations process: many of the larger agencies made their budget requests to their oversight committees, which had both authorizing and appropriating powers.[5] World War I ushered in a new era requiring more attention to fiscal matters. From then until 1974, the White House had better budget development capabilities than Congress. But in 1974, Congress enacted a major reform that allowed it to take a more active and central role in the federal budget process. Congress is now the key player in the budget process, so much so that its own legislative calendar is dominated by the budget cycle. From the submission of the president's budget in February through final passage of the twelve[6] appropriations bills (one passed by each Appropriations Subcommittee) in late September or early October, the calendar in both chambers is built around the budget resolution and the appropriations bills.

In this section, we will take a look at the development of the modern budget process, starting in the late nineteenth century. Following that, we will see how the Congress makes budget decisions today and how the budget process has come to dominate the whole legislative schedule.

The Development of the Budget Process

For more than a century after the founding of the nation, budgeting was not a concern in Washington. The federal government had few responsibilities, and those could be supported with tax revenues derived from imports (tariffs) and on certain goods traded within the United States (excises). From the founding of the country until about 1910, there was no real "budget process" to study. Congressional committees and the few federal agencies worked together to pay for the small number of tasks the federal government performed in those years. But as the federal government began to expand in the years after the Civil War, so did federal expenditures. Budgeting became more important to government leaders after the growth spurt in Washington caused by the reformers of the Progressive Era. The Sixteenth Amendment, allowing an income tax, was approved in 1913. This new revenue was needed to pay for the expanded federal bureaucracy. Besides creating the Internal Revenue Service to manage the income tax, Congress did little to change its own budgeting practices or to monitor revenue and spending in any meaningful way. Congressional management of federal spending was fragmented and partial—in fact, between 1885 and 1921, the House Appropriations Committee did not oversee the whole of the budget; much of the federal budget went through the oversight committees for both authorization and appropriations. For example, the Military Affairs Committee drafted the army budget every year in that period, and the Naval Affairs Committee produced the navy budget. These two committees did not share any information with the Appropriations Committee, and nobody in Congress (or in the executive branch) collected all of the budget bills and checked expenditures against federal revenues![7]

America's involvement in World War I (1917–1918) demanded budget discipline. The government ended the war with deficits and debt, so in 1921, Congress passed the Budget Act in order to streamline federal budgeting. On the executive side, the act required the president to create a unified federal budget covering the activities of the executive branch agencies. The act also established the Bureau of the Budget (now the Office of Management and Budget, OMB) to help the president develop the annual budget submission. On the legislative side, the Budget Act returned all spending authority to the House and Senate Appropriations Committees. To ensure adequate financial oversight capabilities, Congress also created the General Accounting Office (GAO, renamed the Government Accountability Office in 2004) to audit executive branch agencies and ensure good budgeting.

Federal budgeting has been a complicated process since Congress decided to create a formal process with the passage of the Budget Act in 1921. Since the beginning, budgeting has been a tug-of-war between Congress and the White House. If we think of the period before 1921 as a period of *Congress-centered* (or even committee-centered) budgeting, the Budget Act changed the relative strengths of the Congress and the president. The act started a period of *president-centered* budgeting; the White House had more capability than Congress did, since the Bureau of the Budget gave the president a cadre of skilled budgeteers that Congress could not match, even after creating the GAO.

The tide began to turn in the wake of budget problems under Presidents Lyndon Johnson and Richard Nixon. Deficit spending and inflation concerns at the end of the Vietnam War, coupled with major policy differences between Congress and both of those presidents, led to a set of budget reforms in 1974. The reforms effectively ended the president-centered budgeting process operant in Washington since 1921, ushering in a period of relatively balanced budgeting, with president and Congress more or less equals in the process. The Congressional Budget Reform and Impoundment Control Act of 1974 introduced two new players into the budget process: the Budget Committees and a new staff organization, the Congressional Budget Office (CBO). The Budget Committees are supposed to manage the budget process by coordinating the revenue work of the House Ways and Means and Senate Finance Committees with the federal spending work of the Appropriations Committees. By putting an overarching step into the process, the act sought to make Congress more effective at controlling spending. CBO gave Congress its own budget experts to counter the OMB, which works to advance presidential budget priorities. The new Budget Committees and the expertise of the CBO have made Congress more effective in the budget process—so the 1974 reforms did balance the process between Congress and the White House.

This is not to suggest that the *budget* has been balanced: while the process now involves roughly equal players, they have not managed to balance the federal books very well in the past several decades. The original understanding of government budgeting—that revenues and expenditures should be matched—collapsed under the threat of the Great Depression. Economists such as John Maynard Keynes argued that government spending should be focused not on maintaining balanced books, but on maintaining a stable economy. Under Keynesian economics, the government would be acting wisely to engage in deficit spending during economic downturns in order to spur growth and end the recession (or depression). Ever since President Franklin Roosevelt's New Deal, in fact, the federal government has used spending to regulate the American economy, even if it has caused deficit spending.[8] Since 1981, Washington has spent far more than it has taken in. President Ronald Reagan oversaw a series of huge deficits in the 1980s, which saddled his successor, George H.W. Bush, with a severely strained budget.[9] President Bush famously promised in his election campaign in 1988, "Read my lips—no new taxes," but the deficit he inherited forced him to agree to a budget deal in 1990 that included small tax increases as well as spending cuts.[10] In 1993, President Bill Clinton and the Democratically controlled Congress were able to hammer out a budget deal (with no House or Senate Republican votes) designed to balance the federal budget through spending cuts and new taxes. Although the Republicans voted against that budget deal, they worked with Clinton, after taking control of Congress in 1995, to end deficit spending, even running small surpluses in 1998 to 2001. Believing that those surpluses should be returned to the voters rather than being used to pay off the national debt, President George W. Bush asked Congress to pass tax cuts in 2001, 2002, and 2003. Coupled with a recession brought on in part by the collapse of the dot-com market and the terrorist attack of September 11, the government faced deficit spending again, much as it had in the late 1970s and 1980s; the deficit condition was made worse by the need for higher defense spending for military operations in Afghanistan and Iraq.[11] Figure 6.1 shows the long-term trend of rising total federal debt from 1960 to 2005. This graph indicates that federal debt rose most dramatically after 1980. Large annual federal deficits, beginning under President Reagan, drove this debt increase, as Figure 6.2 reports. The federal government has

Figure 6.1 **Total National Debt, 1960–2005** (in trillions of 2005 dollars)

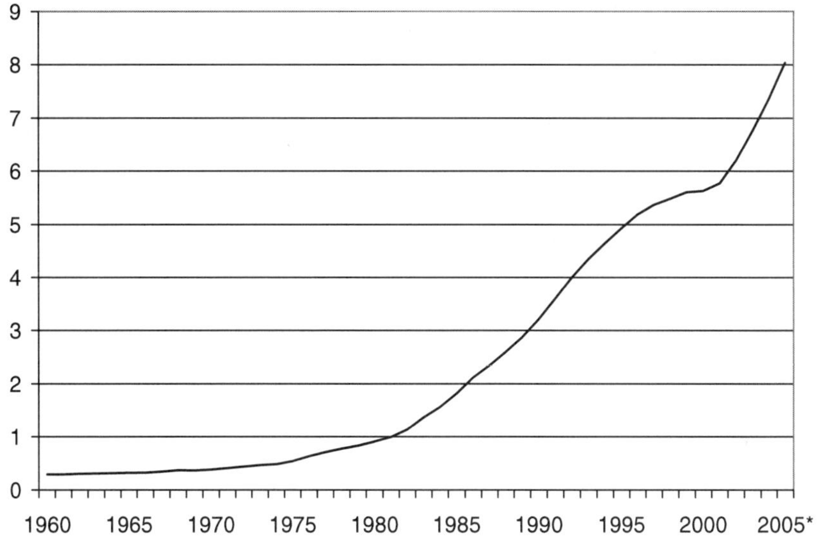

Source: Office of Management and Budget.
*Estimated total for 2005.

Figure 6.2 **Federal Deficit and Surplus Totals, 1960–2005** (in billions of 2005 dollars)

Source: Office of Management and Budget.
*Estimated total for 2005.

run annual deficits for much of the period from 1960 to 2005, with the 1980s and the years after the turn of the century showing especially large annual budget deficits.[12]

In the wake of a decade of annual deficits and increasing national debt, Congress built its new budget system in the 1974 reforms. How has Congress used its power of the purse under the 1974 Budget Reform Act and the spending challenges it has faced in the past two decades?

The Budget and Appropriations Process Today

When politicians and students of Congress talk about the budget they are not talking about all the spending that the federal government does every year. In fact, the budget process accounts for just over a third of total federal spending. Federal revenues come from four main sources: corporate income taxes (10 percent in fiscal 2005), individual income taxes (43 percent), excise taxes and all other taxes, like customs duties (8 percent), and social insurance taxes (39 percent).[13] Figure 6.3 displays graphs of revenue and spending for fiscal year 2005. Revenues for fiscal 2005 were estimated by OMB to total $2.05 trillion.[14] Federal spending falls into three broad categories: mandatory payments based on formulas (entitlements), debt service, and the discretionary budget. Entitlements are programs such as Medicare, Medicaid, and Social Security, and their spending levels are set by formula; Congress at some point in the past agreed that such programs served a need so important that they should no longer be subject to the annual cycle of budget negotiations. Entitlement programs deliver payments to all citizens or groups that meet eligibility requirements, as decided upon by Congress and defined in a law, which also sets forth the formula for calculating payments. Since these entitlements are not negotiated every year, the entitlements budget is thought of as "automatic" spending. In fiscal 2005, spending on Social Security was $515 billion (21.4 percent), Medicare and Medicaid was $384 billion (13 percent), and other mandatory programs cost $337.4 billion (14 percent). The second category, debt service, requires the federal government to pay interest on the national debt, which was $7.99 trillion at the start of fiscal 2005, requiring interest payments of $177.9 billion for the year, or 8 percent of the total budget. Finally, the remaining 42 percent was discretionary—that is, Congress could decide how to spend the money during the budget process. This money is traditionally divided into two main categories: defense discretionary ($400 billion or 21 percent), and nondefense discretionary ($391 billion or 21 percent).[15]

Why would Congress decide to make certain programs entitlements, exempting them from the annual budget process? Some programs, such as Social Security, may have seemed so important to the government's conception

Figure 6.3 **Federal Revenue and Spending, FY 2005**

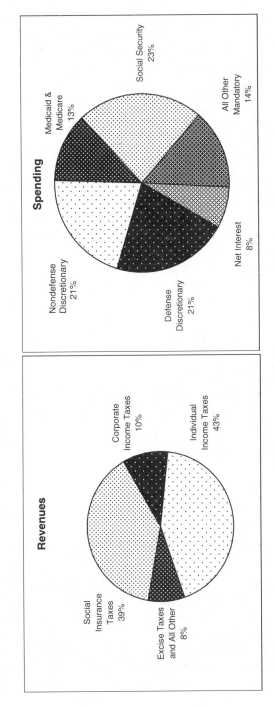

Source: Office of Management and Budget.

of social justice that they should not need annual consideration. Or perhaps a program's payment formula, such as that for farm price supports, is so complicated that it became too difficult to recalculate every year, so it was placed off budget as an entitlement. Entitlements, in general, reflect programs that Congress sees no need to reexamine regularly, so they are set outside the regular budget cycle. This practice has three consequences. First, broadly speaking, the tendency is for entitlements programs to grow regularly over time in size and cost.[16] Since these programs do not face regular scrutiny in the budget process, they can grow without anybody really noticing. Second, entitlements programs make budgeting harder. More than half of all federal expenditures fall into the category, meaning that mandatory spending places over half of annual spending off-limits when budgetary decisions get made. In other words, congressional committees seeking to balance the budget can use only the 40 percent of the total budget that is discretionary.[17] Finally, given the popularity of entitlements programs and the automatic nature of the spending that supports them, it is extremely difficult politically to change the programs—particularly if program cuts are on the table. The enormous popularity of Social Security has made it nearly untouchable since President Franklin Roosevelt and the 74th Congress created the program in 1935.[18]

So in reality, congressional budgeting takes over after the federal government has already committed itself to spending half of its budget on entitlements and another 8 percent on debt service. Congress's power of the purse thus involves only about 40 percent of the total budget. Budgeting, in other words, rests atop a floor of automatic spending that would require major effort and significant political risk to change. With this sobering point in mind, we can now look at how Congress decides to spend the discretionary portion of the annual federal budget.

Running, or Ruining, the Calendar?

How does Congress execute the budget process every year? Budget decisions are so difficult and time-consuming that Congress's budget work drives the annual congressional calendar. The annual budget cycle begins within the executive branch agencies, which start formulating budget requests every spring, sending them forward to OMB, which produces the draft budget in the fall of each year. The draft goes to the White House for final decisions in November; then OMB produces the final budget proposal for submission by the president to Congress in the first week of February. Congressional budget work begins immediately after Congress receives the president's budget. The budget committees are expected to hammer out their budget allocations by April 15. The authorizing committees (discussed in the last chapter) begin drafting any necessary authorizing bills, which the House can consider after May 15. The Appropriations Committees begin their work in subcommittees[19] on the funding bills that make up the discretionary budget. Once the budget committees finalize their resolution, which apportions the spending into the appropriations categories, usually around May 15, the Appropriations Subcommittees can finalize their spending bills and send them to the floor for action, first in the House and then in the Senate. Floor action on needed changes to authorization in order to align any bills with budget targets (called reconciliation) occurs in May and June; then the House and Senate can move to finalize their appropriations bills. If all goes well, those bills are approved in the House by June 30, and shortly thereafter in the Senate, and conference committees meet to resolve all differences on the bills, so they can be dealt with in September, just in time for the start of the fiscal year on October 1.[20]

The first session of each Congress tends to run longer than the second session—usually until about Thanksgiving—which allows Congress to deal with other major legislation, in addition to the budget and appropriations bills. One of the most difficult authorization bills, the defense legislation, is produced every year, but the first session bill usually covers all major programs for the entire two-year session of Congress, allowing the second session bill to be smaller and easier to complete. And at the end of the second session, Congress usually rushes to accomplish everything so the members of the House and Senate can return home to run for reelection. With all the members trying to finish their legislative work by mid-October in order to maximize their time at home campaigning, there is plenty of opportunity for budget mischief at the end of the session. Despite this risk, many recent Congresses have ended in just such a fashion, by passing a few large appropriations bills combining many of the bills into giant "omnibus" packages—as has happened all but one year since 1999. And in many years, Congress does not complete all its appropriations in time for the new fiscal year, requiring the passage of continuing resolutions (CR) to keep the whole government operating. A CR is a temporary measure that maintains the spending levels of the previous fiscal year, allowing Congress a few more days or weeks to complete its appropriations work. CRs have become a regular feature of budgeting since the mid-1980s.[21]

It is clear that working on the budget can crowd out other important policy debates. Congress can find the time for major policy debates only in the spaces that fall between consideration of the budget resolution and the authorization and appropriations bills. As a result, if an oversight committee is working on an important bill, but cannot finish it in time to get it to the floor during one of these windows, then the bill might not be considered at all in the course of a Congress. In both the 107th (2001–2002) and 108th (2003–2004) Congresses, for instance, legislation to reform bankruptcy had made it out of committee and was ready to be debated on the floor (in October of 2002 and again in 2004), but both bills ran into conflict with omnibus spending bills that tied up the floor in the crucial final weeks prior to the start of reelection campaigning, and the bankruptcy bills never got passed by either Congress.[22]

The budget reforms of 1974 produced a complicated budget process, but they have had some success in moving Congress back to center stage in the process. But the reforms have come at a steep cost, too. The legislative time needed to set up the budget resolution, appropriate to the targets in the allocation, and move to conference and final passage of all the bills is tough to fit into a calendar year! Even with broad agreement on spending goals, members and staffs of the committees have so much work to do to complete the bills in time that they face terrific pressure to get their bills done fast. This pressure leads to lack of coordination among the oversight and Appropriations Committees, since there is not enough time for a thorough examination of every issue before the spending bills have to be done. This in turn leads to a preference for incrementalism—that is, this year's spending bills will look an awful lot like last year's, with only marginal changes. This makes it hard for Congress to envision and to enact major reforms or wide-ranging reviews of federal agency activities.[23]

With this overview of the budget process in hand and some idea of how it stresses the calendar for each new Congress as it starts its work, we can now turn our attention to the three pairs of committees that Congress relies upon to wield the power of the purse: the Senate Finance and the House Ways and Means Committees, the Budget Committees, and the Appropriations Committees.

Congress's Money Committees

If the budget process is successful, it links raising federal revenues and spending in some logical way, so income and expenditures are more or less equal. In order to accomplish this goal, Congress looks at three separate tasks: revenue, budgeting, and spending. As with its other legislative responsibilities, Congress manages the budget process using committees. Each chamber has assigned responsibility for raising money, for budget decisions, and for spending to a specific, and different, committee. The House Ways and Means Committee and the Senate Finance Committee handle revenue issues, the Budget Committees set the overall targets for further legislative action, and the Appropriations Committees make the spending decisions. And although the revenue committees do have jurisdiction over many entitlements programs, re-member that we are not talking about how Congress decides to spend every dollar in the federal budget; we are talking only about the discretionary part of the budget—that is, about forty cents of every federal dollar spent.

The next section will introduce these six committees, and we will exam-ine three characteristics of each committee: its jurisdiction, its policy func-tion, and its organization. We will look at them in order: the money raisers, the budgeteers, and the spending committees.

The Tax Committees

Congress's two revenue committees, the House Ways and Means Committee and the Senate Finance Committee, are responsible for federal tax policy, raising the revenue needed to run the programs of the federal government. In the House, Ways and Means is a powerful committee that works closely with the leadership to ensure that any bills it produces will reflect leadership goals. And closeness to House leaders helps Ways and Means preserve a long tradi-tion of deference on the floor, where most of its bills do not face major amend-ments. The House Ways and Means Committee has six subcommittees that monitor sources of federal revenue and entitlements programs (Trade, which considers tariffs, excises, and the like; Oversight, which monitors overall revenues issues for the full committee; Health, which oversees Medicare and Medicaid; Social Security; Human Resources, which monitors unemploy-ment issues; and Select Revenue Measures, which handles special cases as-signed by the committee's chair).

The Senate Finance Committee is a fairly independent-minded commit-tee compared to Ways and Means, and it has tended to be more fiscally sen-sible in the past few decades, compared to its House counterpart. Unlike the House, where both Ways and Means and the Appropriations Committee have been open to increased spending, the Senate Finance Committee tries to en-sure that revenues are sufficient to spending plans. Like its House partner, the Finance Committee has five subcommittees (Taxation and IRS Oversight, Social Security and Family Policy, Long-Term Growth and Debt Reduction, International Trade, and Health Care) to oversee federal income and entitle-ments programs.

Congress also looks to the Joint Committee on Taxation (JCT), estab-lished in 1926 to provide nonpartisan, expert analysis of the effects of tax legislation proposed to Congress. The JCT consists of five members each from the House Ways and Means Committee and the Senate Finance Com-mittee. The staff includes tax lawyers, accountants, and economists, who provide the JCT (and any member of Congress who makes a request) with advice on likely outcomes of tax legislation—how revenues and administrative issues might change, and potential legal or economic consequences.[24] Every tax proposal that comes before either chamber goes through thorough analysis by JCT staff, so legislators have a detailed report to work with before they decide on a bill. The JCT provides its estimates on a confidential basis to any member who requests it, making the information publicly available only if it has been released in an official document, such as a revenues chart in a committee report.

A constitutional requirement dictates that all tax bills originate in the people's House, rather than in the Senate, so whenever tax legislation comes up, it must originate in the House Ways and Means Committee. The Senate Finance Committee does not take up any such bill until Ways and Means has acted, and in conference between the two committees, the House is customarily in charge of the negotiations. Thus, the Senate must always wait on House action, a requirement that can put the Senate behind through the whole budget process if any significant tax changes are required.

The House Ways and Means Committee and the Senate Finance Committee are among the most powerful and important committees on the Hill. They are responsible for crafting the bills that generate all the revenue of the federal government, from personal and corporate taxes, to excise and customs duties, to Social Security and Medicare payroll taxes. Once they raise it, it is time to decide how to spend it. For that purpose, Congress looks to two other pairs of committees: the budgeteers and the appropriators.

The Committees on the Budget

The two Budget Committees set the spending targets for the appropriations work in each chamber. They were created in the 1974 budget reform act, which also established the Congressional Budget Office (CBO), which provides expert analysis for Congress on all budgetary matters. Each year, the Budget Committees receive the president's budget proposal in early February. They also receive projections from the appropriations and oversight committees of their chambers in the month following the president's budget submission, and they work with CBO to produce a thorough assessment of the budget proposal, including deficit projections, revenue estimates, and total spending. With all that data in hand, the committees set to work crafting the budget resolution for the upcoming fiscal year. The budget resolution is a concurrent resolution (adopted by both chambers) that sets the spending targets for the appropriators across the various categories of spending; the resolution is necessary not only to set spending limits, but to translate OMB's budget categories into useful numbers for the subcommittees of the Appropriations Committees, which are different from the OMB budget groupings.[25] The two chambers produce their resolutions by March, and then the House and Senate Budget Committees meet in conference to resolve any differences so both chambers will work to the same budget goals.[26] Under current law, the concurrent budget resolution is supposed to be adopted by both chambers by April 15.

The House Budget Committee (HBC) consists of thirty-five members, selected in a unique way. Members of the Budget Committee cannot serve more than eight years in a ten-year period. The Appropriations Committee assigns five members, the Ways and Means Committee assigns five, twenty-three come from other committees, and the House majority and minority leadership each appoints a rotating member of the leadership to the committee, as well. The HBC was originally intended to serve as the forum in which all the money committees could work out a plan for the annual spending bills together, but over time the HBC has developed its own personality, and with so many members serving on the committee, the Appropriations and Ways and Means members of those two committees have a smaller voice now in the affairs of the Budget Committee. The Budget Committee tends to hew closely to the House leadership as well, given the importance of the budget resolution in setting the terms of the annual appropriations process. The House leadership supports the HBC. When the budget resolution comes to the floor, the leaders usually protect it with a closed rule, preventing most floor amendments. This makes a lot of sense politically and practically: since the HBC reflects the leaders' desires, it is a smart move to protect its bill on the floor, and given the complexity and technical detail that go into HBC calculations, it would be hard to craft a floor amendment that was as well-informed as the HBC's original resolution.[27]

The Senate Budget Committee (SBC) has no restrictions on length of service and no membership connections to the other money committees. As is usual in the Senate, the committee is more independent than its House counterpart, and non-SBC members take an active interest in the work of the committee. In order to protect the SBC's resolution when it comes to the floor, though, the Senate has instituted a special expedited procedure that allows the resolution to be debated without the usual raft of amendments. In the years before the 1974 reform created the Budget Committees, the Appropriations Committees saw themselves as the guardians of the federal treasury, but over the three decades since the passage of the 1974 law, the Budget Committees have stepped into that role, and they use the concurrent budget resolution to impose some spending discipline on the rest of Congress.[28]

Once the House and Senate adopt the joint budget resolution, the Appropriations Committees know what their total budget allowances will be for the upcoming fiscal year, and they can begin making spending decisions. In addition, the oversight committees sometimes have to produce a revised authorization bill through the Budget Committee, as part of the reconciliation process, which aligns previous spending decisions with the updated budget picture expressed in the budget resolution. But once the reconciliation package, if needed, has been approved by the House and Senate, the HBC and SBC have largely completed their work, and the attention and energy shift in both chambers to the work of the appropriators, who have to decide how to spend the budget approved in the resolution.

Now we have seen how Congress raises the money and how it sets spending totals among the various spending categories. Now let us look at how final spending decisions occur in the two Appropriations Committees.

The Committees on Appropriations

The Appropriations Committees are perhaps the most powerful bodies in each chamber. They make all the discretionary spending decisions for the Senate and the House. Their bills fund all the federal executive branch agencies, as well as the operations of the judiciary and the legislative branches. The two committees were organized in the same manner until the House reorganized its committee at the start of the 109th Congress in an effort to make the appropriations process more manageable. This is a laudable goal, since in recent years Congress has not managed to pass all its appropriations in time for the start of the new fiscal year.[29] Both committees begin their work on spending bills in much the same manner: each of the subcommittees holds a series of hearings, usually running from mid-February through April, during which they hear funding requests from the agencies whose spending they control. In addition, each subcommittee accepts letters from members of their chamber, making specific spending requests or recommendations about specific programs. The subcommittees then prepare their spending bills, using the information from the president's budget, the hearings, and other members of Congress, as well as the work of the subcommittee staff. Once a subcommittee considers and passes its bill, the bill then goes before the full committee, where each bill is reviewed, amended if there is support for changing specifics, and then passed. Following committee consideration, the bills all go before the full chamber for passage, under a different process in each chamber.

The Senate Appropriations Committee (SAC) is among the most desirable assignments for a senator. In the Senate, members can serve on more than one major committee, so most senators who serve on SAC also serve on one or more of the main oversight committees. This means that SAC members bring a good bit of substantive understanding of policy issues into their discussions about spending levels. The SAC has twelve subcommittees, each of which is responsible for producing one bill; these subcommittees are Agriculture, Commerce, Justice, and Science, Defense, District of Columbia, Energy and Water, Homeland Security, Interior, Labor, Health and Human Services, Education, Legislative Branch, Military Construction and Veterans Affairs, State and Foreign Operations, Transportation, and Treasury, the Judiciary, Housing and Urban Development.[30] The SAC, like most other Senate committees, does not see itself as the final arbiter of bills, since every senator has the right to debate any bill once it comes to the floor. So the SAC's job is to draft the bulk of each appropriations bill, determine the major areas of disagreement, and sketch out the points that will need final adjudication during floor debate. With many of its members serving on the other committees of the Senate and with its commitment to full debate on the floor of the Senate, the SAC is tied into the life of its parent chamber. The one requirement of Senate debate on spending bills is its "germaneness" rule, which demands that only spending matters directly related to the bill be included in any specific appropriation bill. Since spending bills are "must pass" legislation, the germaneness rule in the Senate prevents crafty legislators from attaching pet provisions to key spending bills in an effort to get them passed along with the spending bill.[31]

The House Appropriations Committee (HAC) is a different animal altogether. In the House, members are limited in their service on major committees, with the result being a far sharper distinction between "substantive and financial" decisions.[32] The chair of the full HAC and the subcommittee chairs are very powerful members who are nicknamed the "cardinals" as a reflection of their power. As with its other committees, the GOP-controlled House has sought to maintain majority leadership control over the HAC by requiring term limits of eight years for all chairs, thus preventing them from accumulating too much power and independence.

At the start of the 109th Congress in 2005, the HAC's new chair, Rep. Jerry Lewis (R-CA), announced a reorganization of his subcommittees, from the thirteen that had been used since 1973, to a more streamlined ten-subcommittee structure. Three old subcommittees (District of Columbia, Legislative Branch, and Veterans, Housing, Independent Agencies) were disbanded and their duties assigned to other, reorganized subcommittees. The new subcommittees are Agriculture; Defense; Energy and Water; Foreign Operations; Interior and Environment (which assumed control over spending for the Environmental Protection Agency and other environmental regulatory bodies); Homeland Security; Labor, Health and Human Services; Education; Military Quality of Life, Veterans Affairs (including several Department of De-

---

Box 6.1

Congress and College III

Just Say No to School Loans

Remember Nancy Reagan's admonition to "Just say no to drugs"? Congress does. In 1998, Congress amended the federal school loan program, making anybody with a drug conviction ineligible for federal support to pay for college. It is the only conviction that will prevent students from receiving loans.

Said Rep. Mike Doyle (D-PA) in 2005, "It seems a little unfair to me that somebody could commit a murder or another violent felony, serve their time and still be eligible for a student loan. Yet if a high school student, because they're young and not thinking straight, gets caught on a marijuana charge, they're banned for life from getting a student loan." Department of Education figures indicate that 101,434 students were denied federal loans from 2000 to 2005 because of the law.

Congress is interested in your personal choices. Read the small print on your aid forms carefully the next time you apply for federal financial aid, and try to figure out what Congress wants you to do— or stop doing. . . .

Source: Bill Zlatos, "Federal Student Drug Law Under New Scrutiny," *Pittsburgh Tribune Review,* April 4, 2005.

---

fense programs, such as Basic Allowance for Housing, facilities funding, and health care programs); Science, State, Justice, Commerce; and Transportation, Treasury, Housing (which will also handle District of Columbia funding).[33] When the HAC's bills go to the floor for debate, they are generally protected by the House leaders with relatively restrictive rules, which limit the number of amendments that can be offered during debate. Senate appropriations bills go to the floor without the strong protections of their House counterparts. And with twelve subcommittees instead of the House's ten, finalizing appropriations bills could be difficult in the future.

One important feature of House appropriating needs special mention: the HAC's special position in the lineup of House committees. Since the creation of HBC in 1974, the HAC has seen itself as the forum for funding programs. Where it was once a fiercely budget-minded committee, now it looks to the HBC to serve that role, and it seeks means of increasing spending for popular programs. This willingness to spend and its privileged position as the House's owner of the federal checkbook have made the HAC's bills targets for members' pet projects. Although appropriations bills are not allowed to contain policy statements under the House rules, HAC bills containing policy pronouncements regularly pass through House floor action without successful challenges from other committees. Despite the efforts of the authorizing committees to retain their control over policy decisions, the HAC finds it easy to poach on their territory; after all, the appropriating power is explicitly listed in the Constitution, whereas authorization is only a congressional tradition. And since the House acts on authorization bills first and finishes with appropriations bills, the HAC serves as the court of last resort for any member seeking to support a favored project. While the practice of earmarks (setting money aside for specific projects in a spending bill) has a long history in Congress, the GOP-controlled Congresses since 1995 have mastered the art of filling appropriations bills with pork.[34]

Now we have reviewed the process Congress uses to set budget policy and the six committees responsible for raising the money, setting spending limits, and making final spending decisions. In the next section, we will consider how well these committees make use of Congress's power of the purse—and we will see that the challenges of federal budgeting rob the budget power of much of its usefulness.

Assessing Congress's Power of the Purse

Control over the national government's finances was the Framers' key gift to Congress. They well knew that power over money is true power in political battles between the branches of the government, and they intended Congress to retain its dominant position in the federal system by controlling the government's money. Even when used poorly, this tremendous power still allows Congress to keep control of the federal agencies reasonably well. And it is used poorly by Congress, despite long hours and tremendous effort put into the crafting and debating of the budget resolution and the appropriations bills every year, as well as any tax reform bill that comes to the floor of either chamber. The old norms that once allowed Congress to see its way through budget debates frayed in the twentieth century, and no new consensus has emerged to replace the constitutional ideals of balance, annularity, and comprehensiveness. Under the old understanding, "balance" meant that government revenues and expenditures should be balanced. "Annularity" meant that Congress would consider the whole budget every year, and "comprehensiveness" meant that the budget should include all federal spending and revenues.[35] Since the Great Depression, though, these three norms have slowly collapsed. Keynesian budget politics, under which government spending is aimed at balancing the economy (high employment and low inflation), pressures the norm of budget balance; entitlements, large defense procurement programs (such as multiyear spending needed to buy a new aircraft carrier), and debt payments throw off the traditional one-year budget process; and entitlements also reduce comprehensiveness, since these programs do not fall under the regular budget process. The 1974 Budget Reform Act, the 1986 tax reform, and the 1993 budget deal all attempted to revive the old norms, but they were not successful. And without a consensus as to the goals of government budgeting, it is nearly impossible to achieve "success" in managing the budget process. Without that consensus to guide debate, Congress confronts several challenges in effectively using its power of the purse, particularly the burden of automatic spending, which overwhelms the discretionary budget process; the complexity of the congressional budget process, which limits coordination among the key committees; and the growing imbalance between authorizing and appropriating committees, which undercuts the legitimacy of congressional oversight.

First, much of the federal budget is actually spent before the budget process even starts, limiting Congress's reach. As we have seen, entitlements and debt service create an annual spending baseline that consumes about 60 percent of the annual federal budget. The budget process treats that spending as automatic and then largely ignores it to focus on the discretionary budget that makes up the other 40 percent. No matter how hard they try, Congress cannot hope to use the power of the purse effectively if over half of the purse is emptied every year before it *starts* budgeting! Congressional Democrats and Republicans in the 1990s both deserve credit for making difficult spending decisions to balance the budget. They raised taxes to increase revenue and lowered discretionary spending, leading to federal budget surpluses for the first time in memory, and they agreed to an aggressive plan to reduce the national debt, which would lower future interest payments for the federal government. But Congress lost interest in fiscal discipline after the 2000 elections. Congress thus can only blame itself for the financial pressures it faces today. Its decision to raise entitlements spending, cut revenues, and approve supplemental budget requests all added to the deficit and the national debt, thus effectively raising the level of mandatory spending and further limiting Congress's ability to manage the federal budget using the regular budget process. House and Senate GOP leaders agreed with President George W. Bush to cut taxes, drawing down the surplus almost immediately. In the wake of an economic slowdown and the 9/11 terrorist attacks, those tax cuts drove the federal budget back into deficit in 2001, and deficits have grown every year since then. In addition to the loss of revenue due to the tax cuts, military expenditures rose dramatically as U.S. forces took on the Taliban and Al Qaeda in Afghanistan and later toppled the regime of Saddam Hussein in Iraq. The dismal fiscal picture was completed by Congress's approval of in the Medicare drug benefit requested by President Bush in 2002. The result is less revenue, more mandatory spending, and a corresponding drop in the discretionary budget that Congress can manage through the budget process.

That brings us to the second limitation on Congress's power of the purse: its complexity. Different committees manage the three steps in the budget process—raising money, setting budget targets, and making spending decisions. The revenue committees make tax policy decisions with little real analysis of how those decisions link to spending priorities, as the Bush tax cuts of 2001–2004 make clear. The House Ways and Means Committee, particularly, supported the White House's tax cut proposals despite CBO analysis that warned they might be too large to sustain over time without returning to deficit spending.[36] The budget committees did not react well to the changing revenue situation, setting budget targets higher than revenues. In every year since 2001, HAC and SAC leaders produced spending bills that relied upon deficit spending to achieve their desired spending priorities, following the lead of the Budget Committees.[37] And the HAC and SAC continued a long-term trend of largely ignoring the authorizations produced by the various House and Senate oversight committees, approving funds for programs never authorized, and approving sums in excess of authorized levels.[38] This trend reflects a lack of coordination between the authorizing and appropriating committees, which is particularly bad in the House, where HAC members are limited in their other committee assignments. In addition, the authorization-appropriation disconnect sends mixed signals to executive branch agencies. Which committee should an agency obey? If the oversight committee fails to approve a requested program or approves less funding than desired, is it acceptable to ask the Appropriations Committee to help out?[39] With no coordination among revenue committees, budgeteers, and spenders, and with multiple messages coming from the oversight and Appropriations Committees, Congress loses its ability to wield the budget power effectively.

This point raises the final issue that limits the effective use of the power of the purse. The 1974 budget reforms did bring Congress more forcefully back into the budget process, as intended, but the reforms had a serious side effect. As the HAC and SAC lost their self-conceived role as guardians of the treasury to the new Budget Committees, their self-image seems to have begun evolving to a view of themselves as the courts of last resort for harried programs. The appropriators have become so powerful over the past few decades that their dominance over the policy committees seriously jeopardizes the quality of congressional oversight in general. The Appropriations Committees of both chambers regularly approve spending without authorization, and the rules preventing that are either waived or ignored.[40]

The power of the purse is not all that it could be. Automatic spending limits the reach of the budget process and makes fiscal discipline tough. Multiple committees with separate budget tasks and little coordination fragment the process and reduce its effectiveness. And the disconnect between the increasingly powerful appropriators and the policy experts on the authorizing committees means that budget decisions frequently trump policy decisions.

Summary

The power of the purse is still tremendous, and Congress does use it to ensure that federal agencies follow congressional priorities. By funding certain programs and starving others for cash, Congress makes its policy preferences clear to the agencies administering those policies. But Congress would be more powerful if it coordinated the parts of its budget process and if it linked the two powers we have discussed so far. Authorizing committees performing oversight and the money committees managing the budget power sometimes seem to exist in totally different worlds, and this results in Congress sending very mixed messages to the executive branch.

Even when congressional leaders overcome the independent-mindedness of their members and committees, the power of the purse can backfire if not used judiciously. Despite building strong support for their budget and appropriations decisions in 1995, the new GOP leaders could not enforce those decisions on the executive branch. Speaker Newt Gingrich overplayed his hand badly in the fall of 1995 during the showdown over the federal government shutdown, and his poor political performance undercut even the power of the purse. President Bill Clinton's adroit political performance in the face-off with Congress demonstrated the limitations of the budget power. Even armed with the federal checkbook, Speaker Gingrich could not best President Clinton: Gingrich's stubbornness trapped both House and Senate GOP leaders in a corner, Clinton capitalized on the growing unpopularity of the GOP position, and he prevailed in the budget negotiations that ended the government shutdown.[41] Gingrich's grandstanding on the shutdown sowed the seed of distrust in GOP ranks; that loss of confidence in his leadership would later force him out of the Speaker's chair and the Congress after the 1998 elections.

Web Resources

American Enterprise Institute (AEI): A leading conservative think tank that works on limited government and fiscal issues (www.aei.org).

The Brookings Institution: The oldest Washington think tank, Brookings, considered center-left in its perspective, publishes reports on nearly every aspect of governing, including budgets (www.brook.edu/).

Bureau of the Public Debt, U.S. Department of the Treasury: This office tracks federal debt and offers a wide range of facts and figures relating to the national debt (www.publicdebt.treas.gov/).

The Cato Institute: Cato is the leading libertarian voice in Washington, producing studies from its small-government perspective (www.cato.org).

Center for American Progress: One of Washington's newest think tanks, CAP was founded in 2004 as a progressive alternative to the Heritage Foundation and American Enterprise Institute (www.americanprogress.org/).

Center on Budget and Policy Priorities: One of the premier public advocacy organizations that focuses on budgetary matters. The CBPP is progressive/left-of-center, which of course influences its analyses (www.cbpp.org/).

Committee on Appropriations, U.S. House (http://appropriations.house.gov/).

Committee on Appropriations, U.S. Senate (http://appropriations.senate.gov/).

Committee on Budget, U.S. House (www.house.gov/budget/).

Committee on Budget, U.S. Senate (http://budget.senate.gov/).

Committee on Finance, U.S. Senate (http://finance.senate.gov/).

Committee on Ways and Means, U.S. House (http://waysandmeans.house.gov/).

Congressional Budget Office (www.cbo.gov).

Council of Economic Advisers: The council advises the president on economic matters (www.whitehouse.gov/cea/).

Heritage Foundation: One of the leading conservative think tanks in Washington, it produces many budget briefs as well as policy proposals (www.heritage.org/).

Joint Committee on Taxation (www.house.gov/jct/).

Office of Management and Budget (www.whitehouse.gov/omb/).

7 • The Organizing Power

*[T]he federal government must have a complete set of
judicial officers of different ranks throughout the continent;
then, a numerous train of executive officers, in all the
branches of the revenue, both internal and external; and
all the civil and military departments. . . . If these numerous
offices are not at once established, they are in the power of
Congress, and will all in time be created.*
—Melancton Smith, June 25, 1788[1]

On a remote airstrip deep in the desert of Iran, American helicopters and
cargo aircraft met in early 1980 to attempt a daring and unconventional mission. The aim was to transfer Special Forces troops from the airplanes into
the assault helicopters, which were to fly into downtown Tehran. There the
troops would find and rescue the Americans held hostage after the U.S. Em-
bassy was overrun during the Iranian Revolution in 1979. Landing in a blind-
ing sandstorm, the pilots of the various aircraft could barely see each other.
Coming from the U.S. Air Force and the U.S. Marine Corps, they had never
trained together, either. In the confusion, a helicopter and a C-130 transport
ran into each other, killing eight personnel and forcing the mission commander, U.S. Army Colonel Charlie Beckwith, to abort the mission and pull
out the remaining troops.

The failure of the Desert One mission demonstrated that the Defense
Department had a problem with unconventional warfare. Congressional
defense reformers, conducting a series of harsh hearings to uncover the
reasons for the failure of Desert One, discovered that the problems ran
deep in the structure of the Pentagon. Each service had developed its own
Special Forces in the 1960s and 1970s, but those units never trained with
each other and did not know how each operated. Congress responded by
reforming defense budgeting for the Special Forces and by establishing the
United States Special Operations Command (SOCOM) in 1987. SOCOM

commands the Special Forces of the army, navy, air force, and marines and oversees their training in peacetime to ensure that all these units can cooperate with each other easily.[2]

Congress has the power to organize the agencies of the executive branch. When a new demand arises, Congress can create an agency to deal with it, and when existing agencies fail to meet expectations, Congress can reorganize them, as well. Congress looks to its committees to manage this power, much as it does with oversight. In addition, each chamber has established a committee with broad responsibility for government reorganization, to handle larger questions about restructuring. But since reorganization is a tough, demanding challenge that usually requires a great deal of time to investigate, Congress frequently outsources the task to select committees or to independent commissions, which can focus on the need for restructuring and leave the regular committees free to continue their normal oversight duties.

Congress does not rely often on large-scale uses of the organizing power; in that sense, it is a "Use only in emergencies" power. But there is always some reorganizing going on in smaller ways, given the nature of the bureaucratic politics model that the United States adopted in the early twentieth century. In this chapter, we will first examine the nature of American bureaucracy and federal agencies. Then we will review the slow creation of the federal bureaucracies and trace their development through the twentieth century. We will then consider how Congress uses the organizing power to keep the bureaucracy focused on congressional desires, and we will close with an assessment of Congress's use of the power of organization.

Organization as Policy

How the executive branch of the federal government is organized says a lot about the priorities of Congress; if there is a department or agency to do something, it is because Congress felt it was sufficiently important to commit resources permanently to dealing with that issue. And while many champions of good public policy over the years have striven to make the case that administration should be as separate as possible from politics, in the end Congress defines its policy goals by creating agencies and programs to pursue certain issues. So managing the organization of the government is an expression of Congress's policy preferences, and organizational decisions are inherently political.[3] This is not to say that Congress is the only influence that matters when it comes to agency behavior! As we saw in chapter 1, government policymaking involves five actors: the president, the congressional leaders, the committees and subcommittees, the agencies, and the outside parties interested in specific policies. Agencies must account for presidential directives, influences from congressional leaders, and interactions with interest groups, industries, the media, and the public, as well. In this chapter, we will focus on how Congress uses its power to organize the bureaucracy to enforce its own policy goals.

The structure of the executive branch reflects generations of congressional decisions about what policies matter enough to pursue. The federal government agencies were not created at once, based on a comprehensive plan. The agencies were created one at a time, in response to specific challenges facing the government at that moment. As noted in chapter 1, administration was only mentioned in passing in the Constitution, because the Framers did not imagine a world that would demand a larger, more capable federal government. The government started out small, and it took over 150 years to expand the executive branch into the large operation it is today.

The slow, almost organic process of government growth has the advantage of directly linking agencies and the tasks they were expressly created to accomplish, giving the U.S. government far more flexibility and adaptability than the older, centralized bureaucracies in most European countries.[4] But this flexibility comes at a price. It leads to a sprawling executive branch that Congress struggles to oversee effectively, and it requires constant adjustment.[5] As tasks change, organizations that no longer operate effectively may need to be reorganized to succeed. And reorganization is tough. Congress cannot simply shut down an agency and rebuild it; reorganization has to happen on the fly, as the agency continues to perform its assigned tasks. Any change in an agency's structure generates opposition: every office that could lose some power after the change is likely to fight the reforms, making the process slow and difficult.[6] In the end, reorganization frequently occurs in two stages: in the first stage, a number of small changes are implemented within the existing organizational structure; in the second stage, the accumulated weight of small changes can force a more substantial change.[7]

Executive agencies and congressional committees operate within a fragile, complicated web of relationships. The complexity of the interactions means that few players are willing to consider major change. The preference in Washington is for slow, incremental change. Major reform can happen, but usually only in the face of a major challenge that demands swift action. So Congress has muddled through over time, creating agencies to deal with issues as they arise.[8] But three great bursts of agency creation have occurred. Congress responded with a swath of new agencies designed to meet the challenges of the Progressive Era at the turn of the twentieth century, the Great Depression, and the start of the Cold War.

Development of the Executive Branch

The Framers had no idea that the federal government would become the large bureaucratic institution it is today. In their day, government did very little for the citizenry, and what little the citizens needed from their government came from local authorities or from the states. European visitors to the new United States of America noted that the Framers had achieved a strange feat, the creation of a stateless state.[9]

The Framers did not anticipate the changes that would drive the expansion of the national government from its small beginnings. And the national government stayed quite small through the first decades of the new country's history. Not until after the Civil War did Washington start to grow at all, with the establishment of the Justice Department in 1870 to enforce the Thirteenth and Fourteenth Amendments. Other agencies followed during the 1880s, each designed to address a specific challenge as it arose. The first regulatory agency, for example, was the Interstate Commerce Commission, established in 1887 to manage business disputes involving commercial activities crossing state borders.[10]

Congress realized that the executive branch was growing rapidly in this period and that the system as it had evolved was driven predominantly by patronage rather than skill. Although the idea of political appointees appealed in the early 1800s as a means of allowing many citizens to cycle through government service, thus retaining a democratic cast to the executive, by the late 1800s the system was demonstrably corrupt.[11] Congress took the first step toward building a cadre of trained, nonpartisan civil servants with the passage of the Pendleton Act in 1883, which identified a small number of executive branch jobs as civil service positions and set basic standards for the skills and other qualifications office seekers would need to be hired. Although the Pendleton Act targeted only about 10 percent of the jobs in the executive branch, it marked the beginning of a slow process of professionalizing federal workers, and it provided the Progressives with a strong foundation for their reform program.[12]

As the scale and complexity of everyday life increased in the late nineteenth century, the federal government faced increasing demands to participate in more activities. This process led to three waves of agency creation. The first was driven by the reforming zeal of the Progressive Era (1890–1910), the second was Washington's frantic response to the Great Depression (1929–1939), and the third created the national security establishment needed for the Cold War (1949–1989). Most of the federal bureaucracy is a product of those periods, but Congress has created smaller agencies frequently and still engages in larger reorganizations of the federal government.

Congress created the groundwork for the federal bureaucracy as we understand it during the Progressive Era, both by devising the model for government agencies that we still use today and by establishing a broad network of new agencies designed to keep workplaces and commercial products safe. The agencies added a new layer of expertise to the federal bureaucracy and connected it to Congress through more sophisticated rules for managing the agencies and better oversight.[13] Progressive notions about accountability, specialization, hierarchy, and rules still shape the way civil servants, legislators, and the media think about government.[14]

Even with the expansion of governmental capability in the early 1900s, the Great Depression overwhelmed Washington and the state governments. The federal bureaucracy was not prepared to meet the collapse of the stock market and the subsequent flood of joblessness. After the election of Franklin Roosevelt in 1932, though, Washington began a rapid expansion of agencies dedicated to economic regulation, job production, and public works projects designed to get the nation back to work. Although not all these new agencies proved successful, the enlargement did give the federal government the capacity to shape economic decisions and safeguard citizens in ways it had never been able to before the Depression, using new agencies such as the Securities and Exchange Commission, the Federal Reserve System, and Social Security.[15]

A final bout of agency creation gave the United States its centralized national security establishment. After World War II, leaders in Washington, sensing the rising challenges of the Cold War as it slowly emerged, unified the nation's military services into a single Department of Defense and also created the Central Intelligence Agency and the National Security Council to help the president craft and manage a global security strategy.[16]

Congress has continued to use its organizing power to refine the structure and mission of the executive branch's many agencies, adding new ones when situations warrant. For instance, Congress established the Environmental Protection Agency in 1970 to track compliance with the antipollution statutes passed in the late 1960s and early 1970s.[17] Congress also created the Departments of Energy (1977)[18] and Education (1980)[19] to manage federal programs in those issue areas. And most recently, Congress established the Transportation Security Administration (TSA) in 2001 after the September 11 terrorist attacks, following that up in 2002 with legislation reorganizing twenty-two separate agencies (including the new TSA) into the Department of Homeland Security (DHS). (We will discuss the creation of DHS in the next chapter.)

Organization and Reorganization Since the Progressives

Why did the Progressives push Congress to reform government by creating a set of bureaucracies? The Progressive movement sprang out of a deep

Box 7.1

Congress and College IV

Welcome to the Army, Mr. Smith

Here is another thing to think about if you are looking at federal loans to pay for school. Have you registered with the Selective Service for the draft?

In 1982, Congress enacted the Solomon Amendment, which mandates that all student loan recipients who are eligible for the draft must be registered with the Selective Service, or they cannot receive any federal student aid for their education. The Thurmond Amendment in 1985 requires that anybody who wants to work in the federal executive branch must also have a registration number.

If you are a male under twenty-five years of age and do not have a Selective Service number, no loans for you!

Source: Selective Service System Web site, "Registration Information" (www.sss.gov/reg5.htm).

distrust for the political system of the late nineteenth century, which had evolved into a harsh conflict between the parties. Partisanship shaped everything that the federal government did: every position in government was assigned through patronage; each new president replaced the whole executive branch with his cronies. Government services, like government jobs, went to the politically connected, not to citizens who needed the most help.[20] And repeatedly majorities in Congress sought to maintain their friends in federal positions by passing laws that protected them, making it impossible for a new president to sweep all these partisans of the wrong party from their federal offices.[21]

Confronted with rampant partisanship and poor performance by the government, the Progressives called for the sweeping reform of the whole system. The Progressives were a coalition dedicated to government reform for many different reasons. Populists in the West and South called for government regulation of large industries that dominated rural life, particularly the railroads.[22] Civil service reformers wanted to see better-educated people placed into government jobs, rather than party loyalists.[23] Middle-class taxpayers wanted to see low-quality government services brought up to standard.[24] Urban commercial interests saw the need to improve local government services and reduce corruption.[25] Social reformers wanted to improve the quality of life of the urban poor and the working class.[26] While each of these disparate groups pursued reform for different reasons, once they came together under the Progressive umbrella, they could all agree on the need for government reform.

Progressives called for depoliticizing public administration—they wanted to separate politics and administration.[27] Instead of political loyalty, they stressed expertise and responsibility. Instead of favors for the well connected, they stressed rules that ensured that services went to those who needed them. And instead of responsiveness to the White House, they stressed accountability to the people, through their elected representatives in Congress.

The Progressives were so successful in setting the terms for how to build, manage, and evaluate government bureaucracies that we still look to their standards today. The goal of the Progressives was to create a politically neutral bureaucracy that would provide government services effectively, in line with decisions made by the elected government. Two other principles shape Progressive bureaucracies: accountability and efficiency. Accountability requires that agencies faithfully execute the directives of whomever the voters install as the political leaders of the nation. Accountability connects the administrative agencies to the elected political leaders and ensures that the agencies do what the elected officials desire. Efficiency demands that agencies do their work in a well-managed, cost-effective manner.[28]

To achieve their twin goals of accountability and efficiency, the Progressives developed a set of characteristics that a successful bureaucracy should have, including trained staff, hierarchy, rules, specialization, simplicity, and responsibility. The Progressives called for the creation of a merit system to hire civil servants, so that trained professionals instead of party loyalists would serve in government agencies. Hierarchy both organizes and focuses agencies, allowing clear accountability through the chain of command.[29] Managing the agencies and administering programs by rules that specify the actions of civil servants ensures that all citizens are treated according to needs, rather than political connections.[30] Specialization by agencies created skilled offices that could perform specific tasks; agencies were to divide themselves into subunits with specific responsibilities, so that the agencies of the government would be professional and trained, just like the civil servants working there.[31] Simplicity and responsibility come together: efficiency demands the simplest possible agencies, and simplicity encourages clear responsibility, with agencies and managers within the agencies clearly assigned to tasks for which they would be accountable to Congress.[32]

As they were implemented between 1900 and the New Deal in the 1930s, these ideas became the orthodox approach to creating government agencies in the United States, and they still set the terms of debate about government organization today.[33] Two other schools of thought arose after World War II to contend with the Progressive orthodox bureaucratic model. In the wake of the New Deal and Cold War expansions of the federal bureaucracy, many researchers questioned the Progressive idea that one set of principles could explain all agencies and guide their creation and management. Rather than demanding that every new agency follow the same pattern, these researchers argued that each agency could be organized uniquely to deal with whatever issues it was designed to face.[34] And in the 1980s and later, a wave of market-based reformers argued for business solutions to be implemented in government agencies—that "reinventing government" would lead to better, more efficient operations.[35]

One of the other enduring legacies of the Progressive movement has been a condition of permanent reform of government agencies. The Progressive goal of a neutral administration with accountability and efficiency is impossible in practice: the more accountable an agency is, the less efficient it becomes, and efficiency can limit neutrality and accountability. In every generation, then, elected officials have to struggle with how to balance the three ideals so that federal agencies are neutral enough, accountable enough, and efficient enough to gain congressional support. And that balance shifts from time to time, requiring constant adjustment by Congress and the agencies. For instance, after World War II, Congress, examining the work of the many agencies created during the New Deal and the war, realized that it had delegated important rule-making responsibilities to many of these agencies. Congress passed the Administrative Procedures Act in 1946 to ensure that the rule-making agencies would follow a congressional approach when designing regulations—that is, the act required agencies to open their processes to public scrutiny through hearings and comment periods. This mechanism made the agencies more responsive to public concerns, mirroring Congress's own concerns about responsiveness to public opinion.[36] So agencies constantly review their internal operations, refining their procedures and realigning offices; and congressional committees constantly review these agency actions to ensure that congressional intentions are being met.[37] With this background in mind, we can now examine how Congress uses the organizing power to enforce its own policy preferences within the federal bureaucracy.

Congress and the Challenge of Reorganization

Reorganization is expensive, complicated, and time-consuming. For those reasons, Congress tends to prefer small changes to large ones, favoring an incremental approach over revolutionary change. That is the case with restructuring as well: reform is happening all the time, but most of the time, when it is small and noncontroversial, the agencies themselves get to do it, with Congress happy to use its oversight power to ensure that its goals are being met. It is only when there is a strong disagreement between an agency (or agencies) and the relevant oversight committee that reorganization becomes a congressional matter.

Most of the smaller issues about agency structure fall under the jurisdictions of the oversight committees. When more complicated issues arise or when restructuring requires coordination between several agencies, the House and Senate each rely on a committee devoted to overseeing reorganization, the House Government Reform Committee and the Senate Governmental Affairs Committee. The committees can manage most of the restructuring questions that come before Congress, but sometimes larger questions arise, and Congress looks beyond its regular system to deal with major reorganization proposals. Just as it does with policy oversight, Congress can create select committees or independent commissions to explore the need to reorganize.

Reorganization Within Jurisdictions

The organizing power is closely tied to Congress's oversight power: oversight without the power to change failed organizations would not be much of a tool to keep the agencies in line. And Congress manages the organizing power in the same distributed manner as it manages oversight. The standing committees perform oversight and control the organizing power. Most organizational questions are routine, and Congress has delegated a great deal of responsibility for fine-tuning to the agencies themselves, reserving the right to approve any proposed reorganizations and to initiate restructuring when it seems necessary. Congress does have two standing committees with broad responsibilities for reorganization, as well, to help evaluate and manage any reorganizations that do occur. How do the standing committees use the organizing power to improve agency performance?

Federal agencies constantly review their performance, and so does Congress. Most agencies have been given fairly broad leeway to design their own organizational structure. Until the law lapsed in 1984, presidents could submit plans for reorganization under a special procedure that allowed the plans to take effect as long as Congress took no action to object to the plan.[38] For example, the Office of the U.S. Trade Representative, founded in 1962, was reorganized in this manner in 1979, with a second restructuring passed as a law in 1988.[39]

Agency leaders use their discretionary power to reorganize when they recognize a weakness in their performance, knowing that Congress can step in if they do not reform themselves—and congressional mandates for change conform to congressional desires, not necessarily to those of the agency itself. For instance, in 2003 the Government Printing Office (GPO) initiated a comprehensive organizational review and implemented a far-reaching internal reorganization designed to bring the GPO in line with current business practices. GPO leaders took the step before they were compelled to do so by their oversight committees, the House Committee on Administration and the Senate Committee on Rules and Administration.[40] In some cases, the oversight committees will step in to force agencies to reorganize in the face of questions about agency performance. Following years of complaints from some members of Congress that the State Department and the other agencies involved in foreign relations, such as the U.S. Agency for International Development (USAID) and the Arms Control and Disarmament Agency (USACDA), failed to coordinate programs, the Senate Foreign Relations Committee drafted a reorganization plan that made USACDA and the U.S. Information Agency divisions of the State Department, and ordered USAID to report to the secretary of state. Working with the Clinton administration to resolve some strong differences of opinion, Congress passed the Foreign Affairs Reform and Restructuring Act in 1998.[41]

Sometimes, though, the oversight committees cannot manage the demands of reorganization. Some issues cross jurisdictional boundaries, for example, requiring the attention of more than one committee. When this happens, both chambers have a committee empowered to review the need for reform and devise a suitable plan. The Senate Governmental Affairs Committee and the House Government Reform Committee both have broad oversight jurisdictions, covering civil service rules and personnel issues, and both committees are also responsible for overseeing reorganizations. The committees review any plans submitted to Congress by agencies, and they also examine reorganizations proposed by the standing committees. As an example of what these committees do, in 2004, the Subcommittee on the Civil Service and Agency Reorganization, part of the House Government Reform Committee, undertook a series of hearings on the findings of the National Commission on the Public Services, a bipartisan panel that issued its final report on improving the federal bureaucracies in early 2003.[42] And the Senate Committee on Governmental Affairs held hearings in 2004 to consider reorganization of the fifteen agencies in the intelligence community.[43]

Congressional committees can impose reorganizations on agencies when they identify a need for reform that an agency has not undertaken. In some complicated cases, the two chambers have each set up a committee to manage broader reorganizations. Even so, occasional challenges overwhelm the standing committees and the Government Reform and Governmental Affairs Committees. When Congress confronts a difficult, multiagency reorganization, it can use the same methods to manage the reorganization as it does with tough oversight questions. As we saw in chapter 5, Congress can appoint a special select committee or create an independent commission to study the issue in depth and recommend any needed changes.

Major Reorganizations

Some issues are too complicated for a single committee to investigate thoroughly or in a timely manner. Some reorganization proposals involve changes at several agencies. Sometimes an issue is politically sensitive, and congressional leaders would prefer to distance themselves from the investigation. Rather than relying on the standing committees to handle difficult cases, Congress looks to independent commissions and select committees to deal with the whole question. In the case of reorganization, the commission has been a more popular option. Crises that lead to calls for major governmental reorganization usually excite strong feelings and require a difficult investigation into the actions of many agencies. With this kind of potentially time-consuming and explosive effort, Congress prefers to shift the attention to an independent commission—a select committee may not insulate the legislature enough from the difficult work (and its consequences).

Either chamber of Congress can appoint a select committee with the mission of examining an issue and crafting the reorganization legislation needed to solve the problems that the select committee discovers. Two major select committees have been created in the past few decades to investigate governmental problems and design new organizational structures—the Church Committee in the 1970s and the House Select Committee on Homeland Security in 2002. (We will examine the work of the Homeland Security Committee in chapter 8.)

The Senate Select Committee to Study Governmental Operations with Respect to Intelligence Activities, called the Church Committee in honor of Senator Frank Church (D-ID), its chair, was established in 1975 to review intelligences activities and report on any needed changes to the structure of the intelligence community and congressional oversight of intelligence. President Gerald Ford had also organized a presidential commission, chaired by his vice president, Nelson Rockefeller, to examine problems in the intelligence community. In addition to discovering many instances of improper covert operations undertaken by the Central Intelligence Agency (CIA) in the 1960s and early 1970s, the Church Committee uncovered many significant organizational problems within the intelligence community, as did the

Rockefeller Commission. The Church Committee recommended that both chambers, having failed to oversee intelligence operations properly, should create a permanent intelligence oversight committee, which the Senate did in 1976 (Select Committee on Intelligence) and the House did in 1977 (Permanent Select Committee on Intelligence). These two committees would oversee the intelligence community, authorize its activities, and approve an annual intelligence budget. Further, the Church Committee urged Congress to pass a set of statutory limits to guide future intelligence activities. Finally, the Church Committee recommended internal reorganization of the CIA to bolster intelligence analysis, proposing that two different officers run the CIA and the entire intelligence community.[44]

The Church Committee worked for over a year, and although its work led to significant reforms in the way the U.S. government structures and oversees its intelligence capabilities, it is uncommon for Congress to look to a select committee for such a difficult task. The legislators appointed to select committees all have their other constituent service and legislative work to do as well. The preferred method for dealing with tough organizational questions through most of the twentieth century has been the independent commission. These commissions can focus entirely on the issue they have been created to study. Two examples will show how Congress uses independent commissions to lay the groundwork for executive branch reorganizations.

Perhaps the most comprehensive examination of the executive branch's structure occurred under two commissions, chaired by former president Herbert Hoover, that Congress created after World War II to study the large number of agencies established to deal with both the Great Depression and the war. Many GOP lawmakers who won a majority in both chambers in the 1946 elections felt that the government had grown too large, too fast. In 1947, Congress and President Harry Truman agreed to create an independent commission to examine the structure of the executive branch and recommend changes. The commission was bipartisan and president and congressional leaders appointed the commissioners, who selected Hoover to be their chair. The first Hoover commission met for eighteen months and studied the executive branch in detail, particularly the staff and agencies directly supporting the president. Following submission of the first Hoover Commission's report in 1949, President Truman appointed a presidential commission to review its findings and begin implementing those that Truman supported. In 1949 and 1950, the White House submitted thirty-three reorganization plans to Congress, covering nearly every agency then in existence. Congress eventually approved twenty-eight of the plans. One of the chief features of many of these plans was to vest responsibility for delegating specific responsibilities within a cabinet department to the secretary; previously,

Congress had determined which subunit should do every set task, which meant that even small reorganizations had to be enacted in law. By delegating this responsibility to the relevant cabinet secretary, Congress shifted its own responsibility away from detailed decision making and toward broader, more programmatic review of agency activities and structure.[45] Congress created the second Hoover Commission in 1953, shortly after Dwight Eisenhower became president, with a broader mandate than the first commission. The second commission would consider organizational questions again, but was also charged with making policy recommendations as to whether the federal government should perform certain tasks. Congressional leaders added this policy review because of concerns about the first commission, which had successes in making the executive branch more efficient and better managed by the White House—but had not called for the closing of any agencies or any significant reduction in the scope of government activities. The second Hoover Commission worked from late 1953 until June 1955, submitting twenty reports covering a broad range of issues. Congressional leaders did not receive many recommendations for shrinking the bureaucracies, but did get some excellent ideas. Two of the important reforms recommended by the commission were the creation of a senior civil service (now called the Senior Executive Service) and the reorganization of the Department of Defense to allow for better command and control of forces deployed around the world.[46]

Congress still uses commissions to explore reorganizations. In the fiscal 2000 defense authorization act, Congress called for the establishment of an independent commission to study the management and organization of Defense Department space programs. The Commission to Assess United States National Security Space Management and Organization (or the Space Commission), chaired by Donald Rumsfeld, issued its report in January 2001, recommending a series of structural and administrative changes in the Pentagon. Rumsfeld instituted many of the administrative recommendations after he was appointed secretary of defense.[47] In the end, Congress did not draft any legislation to reorganize the space capabilities within the Defense Department, in large part because the main sponsor of the commission, Senator Robert Smith (R-NH), had lost his influence in the Senate after leaving the Republican Party in the summer of 1999 while on a brief, ill-fated quest for the White House as an independent.[48]

Congress has delegated much of the responsibility for internal structure to cabinet secretaries, and there is a nearly constant background hum of small changes going on across the bureaucracies in Washington. But sometimes crises demonstrate that the federal government needs more significant reorganization. Because restructuring is so difficult and takes so much time to examine properly, restructuring proposals can easily overwhelm the standing committees of Congress. Select committees and independent commissions then help Congress study the complicated business of reorganizing the executive branch. Now that we have seen how Congress uses the organizing power to shape agencies and to get them to respond to congressional desires, we can assess how useful this tool is—especially when combined with Congress's other two tools, oversight and budgeting.

Assessing Congress and the Organizing Power

Each Congress sits for two years. Current members do not expect to be around to see the long-term results of any large-scale reorganization. They will not get any credit for the time-consuming work of reorganization, and they will not know if it worked, because the impacts of major reorganizations take years to play out. And in the short run—in time to cast a shadow over elections—reorganizations can actually cause problems, since the new structure may lead to a loss of effectiveness while agencies relearn their jobs and how they should interact with each other and their (possibly new) oversight committees.

Reorganizing federal agencies is tough work. Not only because of the complicated nature of examining agency missions, staff, and structure. Not only because we rarely know the full consequences of change.[49] Not only because the federal government is fragmented on both sides—the executive branch is a varied collection of agencies and cabinet departments, and the bicameral Congress, already complicated, does all its legislative, oversight, and reorganizational work through committees. The main reason that restructuring is so hard is that reform must first overcome the natural preference for the status quo within the agencies involved (and their friends on the Hill). Reformers must combat the current holders of power in the agency, who will naturally fight to retain their present level of authority.[50] Slow, small, incremental change is preferable because it does not excite strong opposition.

So does congressional use of the organizing power help it to enforce its policy decisions? Yes, it does. Small changes in agency structure are almost always happening, many of which are delegated to the agencies themselves by Congress, so it does not have to step in. Committees are willing to step in and make the changes if they deem it necessary, which helps to keep everybody in line. What committees do not like to do, and what is unreasonable to expect from a fragmented system of oversight in a fractured federal government of shared powers, is big, comprehensive reorganization. Given the realities of the federal structure, it should not be surprising that incremental change is the favored approach. It is only when events force the issue that Congress takes up major reorganizational questions, using select committees or independent commissions, which tend to be free of the commitment to the status quo that the standing committees have.

The most far-reaching and changing power of the Congress is the one it least likes to use. It is difficult to effect major organizational changes because of the fragmentation of the government: both the agencies doing the work and the committees overseeing that work have exclusive jurisdictions, making coordination difficult, never more so than when reorganizing is under discussion, with its clear implication of permanent changes in the power relations among the actors involved.

Federal agencies are created when Congress feels the need to create them. They exist because they were authorized by Congress to deal with specific tasks, and they continue to exist because Congress funds them. In broad terms, Congress controls the federal agencies.[51] But Congress's control over the agencies is far from comprehensive, as we saw in chapter 5. Most agencies, most of the time, seem to meet Congress's expectations, so they receive regular funding and do not face significant demands for restructuring. By delegating most of the responsibility for internal organization to the cabinet department secretaries, Congress has given away a good bit of its power—but in a way that allows the federal executive branch to manage itself without straining Congress's already overworked committees.

When Congress reorganizes the government, it puts new pressures on its own oversight structure. If Congress endorses a major restructuring of the executive branch, it also needs to look at its own structure and consider whether new subcommittees, or new committees entirely, will need to be created. And this means wrestling with the jurisdictions of the standing committees—and the power of their chairs, which is never an easy discussion![52] After World War II, Congress reorganized itself completely in 1946. After constant fighting with the Nixon administration, Congress reformed the budget process, adding the budget committees in 1974. After the Church Committee uncovered decades of abuses in the intelligence community, Congress established its permanent select intelligence committees a few years later—in other words, Congress only looks at its own internal structure occasionally.

The federal bureaucracy was not built in a single step. It is the product of over a century of dedicated attempts to meet national needs by creating agencies specifically designed to meet those needs. When the situation changes, the organization may no longer be effective, requiring change. When major reorganizations occur, Congress finds itself trying to combine agencies designed at different times to meet different missions. The result is rarely a smooth fit—the pieces do not snap into place. As a result, one reform package is rarely enough: Congress will have to return to the issue some number of times before the organization acts the way Congress really wants it to.[53]

And since nobody knows how reorganization will affect government performance, there will be unintended consequences. As we will see in the next chapter, Congress created the Defense Department in 1947, but reorganized it significantly in 1949, 1953, 1958, and 1986.

A final point will round out this assessment of Congress and the organizing power. First, while the Progressive orthodox ideas of accountability, neutrality, and efficiency still guide most of our thinking about federal agencies, those three goals do not work in harmony. Congress must seek a way to balance the three goals, because it cannot achieve a structure that will be fully accountable, efficient, and neutral. Whenever restructuring occurs, Congress must weigh the three goals and choose which one gets priority. For example, when Congress created the Nuclear Regulatory Commission (NRC) in 1974 to oversee the nation's nuclear power plants, it wanted the NRC to move forward very cautiously on approving new power plants. Preferring accountability to efficiency, Congress built a slow-moving five-member panel to run the NRC, rather than a single director.[54] And Progressive ideas about bureaucracy are no longer sacred, either. Multiple concepts about how to organize federal agencies make reorganization efforts even tougher, since it is now harder to decide upon standards to guide congressional efforts.

Summary

Congress uses the organizing power when needed to shape the federal bureaucracy to meet new challenges. While it has delegated much of the power to agency heads to deal with internal organization, Congress can and does step in if agencies refuse to reform in the face of problems. After all, agencies cannot exist if Congress chooses not to support them.

The committees manage Congress's organizing power, just as they manage the oversight power and the budgeting power. So congressional reorganizing efforts are not comprehensive, reflecting the fragmented nature of power on Capitol Hill. The House Government Reform Committee and the Senate Governmental Affairs Committee do provide some broad control over reorganization, but Congress prefers to name a select committee or an independent commission to work on reorganization.

Moving agencies around, creating new ones, means years of effort to get the new structures to meld together into a functioning unit; it also means years of struggling to comply with Congress's intentions surrounding the restructuring. And it opens the door to two unpleasant possibilities, as well: the need to adjust congressional committee structures and jurisdictions, and the looming possibility of unintended consequences. (In the next chapter we will see a good example of both of these effects; homeland security, it turned out, involved nearly every committee in Congress, which nobody realized until after everybody had endorsed the idea of creating a new department.) After all, there is rarely any clear evidence that a new structure will do what it is supposed to do, so even when there is clear evidence that a change is needed, Congress is uncomfortable with major change because that change will reverberate through its own structures and procedures for years to come.

Congress confronted these difficult concerns after the failure of the Desert One mission in 1980. After investigating that disastrous operation, Congress forced the Defense Department to provide better funding to Special Forces, and it established the United States Special Operations Command in 1984 to provide better training and to ensure proper employment of Special Forces in combat situations. Congressional reformers can be proud of the success of their reorganization of the Defense Department: SOCOM troops successfully carried the brunt of the difficult fighting in Afghanistan in 2001–2002 and provided key capabilities to General Tommy Franks when he commanded the invasion of Iraq in 2003.[55]

In the next chapter, we will examine a case that allows us to see Congress using all its three powers to accomplish one goal: improving the security of the United States by establishing a new cabinet-level agency, the Department of Homeland Security.

Web Resources

Committee on Government Reform, U.S. House (http://reform.house.gov/).
Committee on Homeland Security and Government Affairs, U.S. Senate (http://hsgac.senate.gov/).
Federal Government Manual: This manual lays out the structure of the federal government and contains helpful information on organizational issues (www.gpoaccess.gov/gmanual/index.html).
Organizational Change: An Annotated Bibliography: The National Archives produced this listing of information concerning federal reorganizations (www.archives.gov/research_room/alic/staff_resources/organizational_change_bibliography/govt_reorganization.html).

III • Congress and Emerging Challenges

The United States lives in a less predictable world than most legislators like. Used to the stability of the Cold War, the federal government has to confront new challenges today, demanding thorough cooperation among executive branch agencies and congressional committees—a level of coordination that has historically not existed. Neither Congress nor the executive branch is ready to deal effectively with the full range of demands it faces.

The unpredictability of this new world was made clear to all Americans on September 11, 2001, when terrorists flew two airliners into the World Trade Center and one into the Pentagon. Another plane crashed in Pennsylvania before it could strike its intended target. In the months after 9/11, Congress struggled to learn what had gone wrong and how the U.S. might prevent a future attack. Given the seriousness of the attacks and the complexity of reforms needed to prevent future assaults, numerous congressional leaders, committees, and key members started working on several efforts to protect the United States from future attacks, a policy area now referred to as "homeland security." In striving for an answer to 9/11, Congress used all three of its powers.

As we learned in part II, Congress has three Constitution-based powers that it can use to shape the activities of the executive branch agencies. Most of Congress's committees use the oversight power to ensure compliance with legislative intent. Congress's six money committees manage the budget power. And Congress built the executive branch's many agencies over the past century and a half using the organizing power. Nowadays, we might think of this third power more as the reorganizing power, since it appears that the great age of agency creation is behind us.

But the homeland security challenges demanded sustained attention from Congress on all three counts. How did agencies responsible for intelligence and security do their jobs? Did the United States devote sufficient resources to the issue? Were the responsible agencies organized correctly, and were they coordinated sufficiently well to protect the nation from future attacks? Congress had to use all three powers to address the homeland security question, and it did so. How did Congress do?

Chapter 8 is a case study of the effort to build the Department of Homeland Security to protect the United States from terrorist threats. The chapter looks at each of the three powers and assesses Congress's difficulties in using the three powers together to solve problems. As noted in chapter 3, we can use several methods to examine congressional action, such as historical analysis, quantitative tests, and case studies of specific actions. While each of these methods has strengths, we must use the case study approach to examine how Congress uses the three powers together to solve policy challenges. After all, Congress has used all three powers together in a concerted effort to solve a policy problem in only a few instances. Since World War II, this has only happened twice: in 1947, when Congress combined the War and Navy Departments into the Department of Defense (DOD) and also created the National Security Council and the Central Intelligence Agency, and in 2002, when Congress established the Department of Homeland Security (DHS). Although two cases do not provide us with a large dataset to study, the stories of the creation of DOD and DHS certainly illustrate the difficulties Congress faces when it needs to bring all three powers to bear in a coordinated way. Two chambers, each with its own committee structure and its own majority and minority parties jousting over the legislative agenda: all the interrelated moving parts within Congress make coordination difficult, as chapter 8 will show.

Can the Framers' system meet the tests of the next few decades? It can, but the job will likely be tough. The leaders of the House and Senate have to remember that they have both party *and* institutional responsibilities: they have to work to advance the interests of their parties, but they cannot forget that they also have to safeguard the ability of Congress to participate in policymaking as an equal of the other branches. If congressional leaders do not find a way to balance their twin responsibilities, they will not be effective. Chapter 9 outlines the conclusions of our examination of Congress. We will consider how well House and Senate perform their representative and legislative duties, and we will explore some of the conditions that make it hard for the two bodies to accomplish both responsibilities as well as the Framers might have hoped.

8 • Using the Three Powers

Creating DHS

The clause which vests the power to pass all laws which
are proper and necessary, to carry the powers given into
execution, it has been shown, leaves the legislature at liberty, to
do every thing, which in their judgment is best.
—"Brutus" 11, January 31, 1788[1]

In the decade following the collapse of the Soviet Union, the end of the Cold War unraveled the four-decade-long consensus on U.S. national security policy. With the demise of the USSR, containment was irrelevant. By the end of President George H.W. Bush's term in office, congressional leaders began clamoring for a thorough revision of U.S. defense policy. Several prominent legislators offered their own approaches for a new security strategy, and the new Clinton administration began developing its new plan, which the White House called engagement and enlargement—a continuing and active U.S. role in world affairs, with the aim of increasing the number of democratic states around the globe.[2]

Congress did not endorse the Clinton approach and in 1998 created a task force to look into a new U.S. national security policy. Chaired by retired senators Warren Rudman (R-NH) and Gary Hart (D-CO), the United States Commission on National Security/21st Century brought together fourteen distinguished policy analysts and well-known political figures to work on the challenge. The Hart-Rudman Commission produced three interesting and thoughtful reports. In 1999, the commission looked at the state of the world and the nature of the new threats confronting the United States.[3] In 2000, the commission's second report offered a new national security strategy designed to be the centerpiece of a new multinational approach to dealing with challenges such as international crime, drug trading, and Islamist terrorism.[4] The final commission report, issued in February 2001, made recommendations on how to address the challenges outlined in the first two reports. Prominent among these ideas was the creation of a new Department of Homeland Security to protect U.S. territory from threats like terrorism.[5] Commission members fanned out across the media to publicize their recommendations, particularly with a new administration in town.

Nothing happened.

And then on a bright, crisp, beautiful morning in September 2001, Washington's peaceful calm was shattered by a series of horrifying events. Breaking news reports from New York City showed flames and smoke pouring from the north tower of the World Trade Center. As federal employees gathered around televisions in their offices around Washington, they watched a second plane fly into the south tower. By mid-morning, both towers collapsed, killing nearly 3,000 people and swamping most of lower Manhattan in a huge cloud of smoke, dust, and debris.

Washington also reeled from a second attack, this time against the Pentagon. At 9:37 AM, stunned residents of Alexandria and Arlington, across the Potomac River from Washington, looked up to see another low-flying airliner slam into the southwest side of the huge building and explode. Rescue workers struggled all day to pull the wounded from the burning section of the building, and another tall column of smoke curled into the cool September skies.

The United States was under attack by as yet unknown foes. They destroyed the World Trade Center and damaged the Pentagon with three strikes, and they would have hit another key site in Washington if the passengers of the fourth hijacked airliner had not forced it down in rural Pennsylvania.

In the months that followed the September 11 attacks, Congress rediscovered the work of the Hart-Rudman Commission and used its recommendations as the starting point for its design of a new federal cabinet department to combat the challenge of homeland security. Moving swiftly in response to a White House call to complete a bill before the November 2002 elections, Congress created one new agency and moved it and twenty-one others into a new Department of Homeland Security, which opened its doors on March 1, 2003, just eighteen months after the terrorist attacks.

When confronted by a complicated public policy choice, such as responding to the 9/11 attacks, Congress uses all three of its powers to craft a solution and ensure that federal agencies execute it as Congress desires. But using the three powers is a tough challenge. Two chambers and many committees, not to mention 535 members, use the powers. So many decision makers and so many committees enforcing Congress's policy decisions through oversight, budget, and organizing mean confusion: Does every committee share the same interpretation of congressional policy goals? Does each committee have adept leadership that can use the three powers effectively? Do House and Senate agree, and can they overcome their different styles to enforce congressional decisions in a uniform way?

Although far from systematic, Congress can use oversight, budgeting, and organization to get the federal bureaucracies to meet congressional expectations. The story of the Department of Homeland Security (DHS) is an excellent case study of the strengths and limitations of Congress's three powers. In this chapter, we will trace the legislative action that led to the creation of DHS, and we will use that story to evaluate the effectiveness of the oversight, budgeting, and organizing powers of Congress. We will see that each power is quite difficult to use on its own and that combining them to enforce decisions is vastly tougher. In the case of creating DHS, it proved to be too difficult, leaving much work to be done even years after the Department began its work. Finally, we will consider how Congress can use the three powers together and examine a previous policy challenge, the creation of the Department of Defense (DOD) in 1947, to see how it looks when Congress responds well to a policy challenge demanding full use of all three powers together.

The Challenge: Coordination, Intelligence, and Response

The 9/11 attacks made clear to most policymakers in Washington that there were significant weaknesses in federal organization, planning, and preparedness to meet new threats. Congress and the president could use existing agencies to monitor and counter some new security threats around the world, but not all of them. Just as Hart-Rudman had warned, direct threats against the territory of the United States now loomed for the first time since the War of 1812. "Homeland security" refers to the actions required to protect the United States from these threats. And like other spurs to federal action, the definition used by the government for homeland security points directly to the threat inspiring the reorganization:

> Homeland security is a concerted national effort to prevent terrorist attacks within the United States, reduce America's vulnerability to terrorism, and minimize the damage and recover from attacks that do occur.[6]

U.S. defense policy relied on a top-down, centrally coordinated organization that had been created in the 1940s to deal with the emerging Cold War threat of the Soviet Union and its allies. It was a slow, ponderous system designed to deal with one large threat by means of overwhelming force. In the years after the end of the Cold War in 1991, however, it became increasingly clear that the Cold War defense structure was not well suited to the emerging world of multiple threats of varying scale, purpose, and capabilities. Terrorists are a threat as unlike the Soviet Union as one could imagine, and the U.S. national security system was nearly incapable of devising a worthwhile response to such a threat, as 9/11 clearly demonstrated. The events of 9/11 revealed three major problems areas for the federal government. First, the new threats to the United States required multiple agencies to respond in a coordinated fashion, and Washington's interagency process is poor. Second, the fifteen agencies of the U.S. intelligence community (IC) were unprepared for the new security situation of the country. The IC was still too focused on old threats, it did not have the capabilities needed to understand new threats, and its culture of secrecy and compartmentalization made it nearly impossible to share information rapidly among the IC members, or between the IC and other agencies, such as the Federal Bureau of Investigation (FBI). Finally, nontraditional threats required response not just from the federal government, but also from state and local authorities—and there was not much capacity to foster good federal-state-local cooperation.

Interagency Coordination

Most of the agencies designed to handle security issues were put together at the start of the Cold War, and they each played a specific role within the system that provided the United States with a comprehensive national security apparatus. When Congress created the Defense Department in 1947–1949, it also established the Central Intelligence Agency (CIA), to provide strategic intelligence to the White House, and the National Security Council (NSC), so the president could work out security strategy with the participation of all the key departments. For most of the Cold War, those departments were DOD and the State Department; occasionally the Treasury Department also participated. Once the Cold War ended, though, this system started to break down. Facing a broader array of threats, requiring the expertise of many more federal agencies, the NSC was not equipped to provide the same central policymaking it had provided earlier. Threats like terrorism, international drugs, and failed states in the developing world demand skills provided by the attorney general and the Justice Department, the FBI, the Department of Commerce, the Federal Emergency Management Administration (FEMA), and sometimes even the Department of Agriculture, in addition to the Treasury. The attacks of 9/11 demonstrated just how limited the NSC structure was in dealing with this new type of threat. The NSC, the Pentagon, the CIA, and the State Department made quick progress in planning the military response to the attacks, deploying forces into Afghanistan within two months of 9/11. But the remainder of the U.S. response lagged behind, largely because President George W. Bush was forced to rely on an NSC system too narrowly focused to provide him the full range of needed capabilities.[7]

The challenge of adapting the NSC to the new world is only part of the problem, though. Interagency cooperation on any issue has never been easy in Washington—each department has its own operating procedures and plan-ning cell, and they are all used to dealing with their own issue areas without much interaction with other organizations. So when a new problem arises where solution demands the attention of more than one agency, the federal government has to build a new process to allow the requisite agencies to figure out a solution together. Interagency working groups are set up when-ever several agencies need to work together in a coordinated fashion to solve a policy problem.[8]

Intelligence Demands in a New World

The CIA and the rest of the intelligence community developed over the past fifty years to deal with a single challenge: the global threat of the Soviet Union. The USSR's leaders were careful to protect their military and eco-nomic secrets, but their top-down system proved susceptible to technologi-cally driven intelligence gathering. The CIA and the other IC agencies responded to this small vulnerability with an energetic, decades-long flurry of invention. In order to penetrate the web of secrecy surrounding the Sovi-ets and their allies, the IC developed an amazing array of technological de-vices, from satellites to submarine-based probes, in order to monitor Soviet communications, weapons tests, and the like.[9] Although the CIA did recruit a few Soviets to spy for the United States, technology was the key to unlock-ing Soviet secrets, and technological surveillance became the favored espio-nage technique in the IC. This led over time to a withering of U.S. human intelligence assets, not only in dealing with Soviet intelligence, but also in other regions of interest around the world.

September 11 was the last and most fearsome example of how dangerous it was for the United States not to have a strong network of human agents in the Middle East and Central Asia. The 1993 World Trade Center attack, the 1998 attacks on U.S. embassies in East Africa, and the 2000 attack on the USS *Cole* in Yemen all pointed to a serious weakness in U.S. intelligence capability. Understanding a new web of threats not based in, or operated by, specific states and certainly not as centrally organized as in the USSR has proved a daunting challenge for the IC. For instance, Al Qaeda's top leaders are technically savvy but no longer use satellite or cell phones, preferring to send messengers to relay instructions. The new threats confronting the United States are nearly impenetrable using technological means, but the CIA has few agents on the ground in the Middle East or Central Asia, leaving the U.S. government scrambling to build information-sharing agreements with regional states, such as Saudi Arabia and Pakistan.[10]

The IC faces another major challenge at home. Information-sharing among the agencies of the IC has never been a complete success—and sharing between the IC and other parts of the government, such as the FBI and state law enforcement authorities, is next to nonexistent. The 9/11 Commission discovered numerous instances of different IC agencies having bits of information that, if combined, could have uncovered the 9/11 plotters before the attack, but the IC did not have an effective mechanism to induce broader information-sharing among the fifteen IC agencies.[11] Terrorism is also a law enforcement challenge—and CIA-FBI cooperation is infrequent and irregular. Federal law strictly prohibits the CIA and other IC agencies from conducting domestic spying or other intelligence activities, preferring the FBI to take the lead on these activities. Without thorough and regular interaction, though, the CIA could track potential terrorists until they enter the country, then merely hope that the FBI takes action on the tip. Reports in late 2004 indicate that the FBI has no functioning system or internal procedures for sharing information among its Washington headquarters and its field offices. Thus, there is little effective information sharing within the IC, within the law enforcement community, or between the two sets of agencies.[12]

Responding to New Challenges

The NSC system devised after World War II is not well suited to the two main responses the United States needs to meet the challenges it confronts around the world today. Because of its narrow focus on a national security strategy based on military and political power, the NSC system has trouble bringing all of the country's other power to bear, such as its economic, law enforcement, antidrug, and currency expertise. And the NSC system is not designed to cooperate with the state and local governments in the United States that provide police, fire, and other emergency services to the citizenry. One recommendation for responding to the challenge of homeland security has been to copy the efforts at the start of the Cold War by replicating the same system, with a Homeland Security Council set up alongside the NSC.[13] The White House explored several other options to improve coordination between the various agencies that play a part in the emerging area of homeland security, including establishing a new White House office to manage the process and inviting the secretaries of the treasury and commerce into NSC meetings when appropriate.[14]

In addition to these efforts to improve central management, the White House also had to wrestle with the federal issues raised by homeland security. Although FEMA provides federal assistance to state and local governments in emergencies, FEMA's expertise is nowhere as broad as the range of federal support activities that can come into play in a homeland security situation.[15]

But these structural challenges pale before the real challenge, which is re-orienting a large, centrally managed federal security apparatus into a more flexible, adaptable system. To do this requires new personnel rules, new organizational models, and a fundamental change in attitudes. How can the federal government reimagine the world and the likely range of threats that confront the United States—and how does Washington build a flexible planning and coordination process to make it easier to deal with whatever comes next?

Of course, the White House was not alone in thinking about how to prepare for and, if possible, prevent future threats like 9/11. Congress also began to think about the challenge, and in early 2002, several bills were designed to address various aspects of the issue. Although different in details, these bills all shared one key component—a reorganization of the government's agencies with homeland security responsibilities into a new cabinet department. Over the course of 2002, Congress worked on these bills, at times with the White House's assistance, until November, when it passed a bill that established the Department of Homeland Security, and designated March 1, 2003, as its first day on the job. Let us review the path that the DHS legislation followed through Congress and see how Congress used its three powers to address the homeland security challenge.

A New Department for Homeland Security?

Congress reacted strongly to the 9/11 attacks. Within weeks of the attacks, several legislators in both chambers had drafted bills to address the issue of homeland security. Those many reports and recommendations that had been circulating around the Washington policy community came back to the fore, becoming the basis of many of the congressional bills introduced in late 2001 and early 2002. It seemed clear that some sort of federal reorganization would happen in order to bring the disparate agencies with homeland security tasks into closer coordination, if not into a single agency. Support for some sort of new federal department quickly emerged on the Hill, but the White House opposed any new government agencies for months after 9/11. With the 2002 congressional elections looming on the horizon, the White House shifted gears in July 2002, endorsing the new department and pushing Congress to enact authorizing legislation before the legislators left town to campaign for reelection.

Confronting the needs for improved interagency coordination, better intelligence and broader intelligence sharing, and flexibility to respond to a new array of threats, Congress used its three powers to address the challenge of homeland security. Here is how they did it, culminating in the establishment of the Department of Homeland Security on March 1, 2003.

Time Line: October 2001 to November 2002

Between October 2001 and November 2002, consensus in Washington slowly shifted toward the creation of a new cabinet department to meet the challenge, except at the White House. President Bush preferred to manage the effort through a new office within his staff, which he announced on October 8, 2001, when he appointed Tom Ridge of Pennsylvania to direct the Office of Homeland Security at the White House. When pressed to comment on the several bills making their way through Congress, Bush repeatedly stated his opposition to the establishment of a new department, noting that he had not come to Washington to build more bureaucracy.[16] Ridge went to work immediately, identifying all the federal agencies that did homeland security as part of their mission and trying to coordinate their efforts and monitor spending on the issue. Under the executive order creating his post, however, he had little real power to force organizational or budget changes; his only power was the support of the president.[17] More would have to be done to protect the United States from future repeats of 9/11.

By the summer of 2002, though, Congress was making slow progress on the issue. Six bills in the House and five in the Senate offered various views of how to create a new department. Both chambers discovered that using their three powers to address the homeland security issue would prove difficult. Oversight would prove nearly impossible under regular practice—eighty-eight committees or subcommittees had jurisdiction over some aspect of homeland security. Both chambers realized that crafting a successful bill would demand more than regular legislative processes. To coordinate House oversight and to wield the organizing power, the House set up a select committee in June, tasking it with crafting the authorizing legislation for the new department. The Senate chose to proceed on the subject with its Governmental Affairs Committee in the lead. Both House and Senate leaders chose to leave the challenge of appropriating for homeland security until they had dealt with oversight and organization.

Summer 2002 saw political pressure to pass a bill rise. The House Select Committee conducted a series of hearings on the proposed department in July, and the Senate followed suit later in the summer. But the most important political decision was made in early June 2002 in the White House, when the president suddenly reversed his long-standing opposition to a new department and recommended a bill to create the Department of Homeland Security, which he urged Congress to pass before the November elections.[18] The White House realized that Congress was determined to pass some sort of bill and that the president could not allow it to do so without taking part in the debate. White House advisers did not support any of the bills then before

Congress, so they drafted their own proposal quickly by combining parts of several bills into a new package that they could support. In addition to making sure that Congress accounted for White House concerns, swift action on the president's bill could end up helping the GOP in the upcoming congressional elections. And as results would show, it made sense for the White House to endorse its own version of the new department and try to force speedy congressional action on the White House proposal.[19]

The Senate took up legislation creating the new department in its last few weeks in session before the elections, but could not complete work on a bill. Senate Democrats and Republicans could not agree on worker protection in the new department, and the dispute slowed action on the bill. Unions have been strong allies of the Democratic Party since the New Deal era, and the government-employee unions are among the strongest members of the union community, so Democrats in the Senate wanted to preserve the workplace rules that had been negotiated by their union allies for the federal government. But the GOP favored more management flexibility, on the grounds that the new department would need to adapt quickly to changing circumstances and could not do so with the traditional employee unions and other worker protections that were in place in the rest of the federal government. With the Democrats in charge of the Senate, their unwillingness to cut the workplace regulations meant stalemate with the White House. Movement on the bill stalled and the Senate adjourned to campaign.

The elections brought the GOP back into power in the Senate, which returned in mid-November to finalize action on the bill. Bush signed the bill into law on November 23, 2002, and nominated Tom Ridge as the first secretary of homeland security.

The Department Takes Shape

Under provisions of the law, the DHS consists of twenty-two agencies and about 180,000 employees, transferred from across the federal executive branch. Only one of the agencies is new. Congress established the Transportation Security Administration (TSA) in November 2001 to take over security work at the nation's airports. Prior to the TSA, airports and the airlines were responsible for security operations, which was one of the main concerns after 9/11. Congress made airport security a government responsibility (as it is in most other countries) and tasked TSA to execute the mission.[20] Congress also provided more funds to the Federal Aviation Administration for air marshals, who fly under cover on numerous flights to provide further security. The air marshals are now part of DHS. DHS management operates from the Office of the Secretary, as well as the Office of Management, which assists the secretary and handles budgeting and coordination with Congress. Five main directorates house the field agencies of DHS: (1) Border and Transportation Security, including the TSA, Customs and Border Protection, and Immigration and Customs Enforcement; (2) Emergency Preparedness and Response, which manages response to crises through FEMA; (3) Information Analysis and Infrastructure Protection, which handles information security and critical infrastructure protection; (4) Science and Technology, which oversees advanced research into topics of interest for DHS; and (5) U.S. Citizenship and Immigration Services, which brings all citizenship offices into a single operation. The U.S. Coast Guard and the U.S. Secret Service retain some autonomy within DHS.

Congress could not be content with creating DHS, though; under its existing structure, using the three powers would be difficult. So Congress began the slow and tricky work of reorganizing itself as well. The House retained the Select Committee on Homeland Security in the 108th Congress (2003–2005) and directed its chair, Chris Cox (R-CA), to draft House rules changes that would enable the committee to become a permanent standing committee. The intent of the House leaders was to help Cox figure out how to change committee and subcommittee jurisdictions so that the new committee could take over the prime responsibility for DHS oversight. To make the task easier, GOP leaders appointed the chairs of all the key oversight committees to serve with Cox, in the hopes that these key players could work out an acceptable plan together and make the oversight toll more effective by streamlining House jurisdiction over DHS components. Unfortunately, few of the key committee chairs proved amenable, and House leaders did not help Cox resolve the jurisdictional problems. He continued the effort in the 109th Congress.[21]

The new Congress worked quickly to address the second power of Congress. In February 2003, the House Appropriations Committee reorganized, creating a new Subcommittee on Homeland Security; the Senate followed suit in March. With the initial organizing work done, neither chamber did anything with that power, and the House continued to work throughout 2003 and 2004 on the jurisdiction of the select committee, as described above. The Senate, recognizing the challenge of shifting jurisdictions, preferred to wait until the House could devise a workable plan.

With its internal reorganization under way to improve oversight of DHS and to manage appropriations through new subcommittees, and with initial organization of the department done, Congress turned to using the powers to influence DHS in early 2003, just as the new department opened its doors. Oversight hearings by many committees in both the House and Senate focused on how DHS performed many of its tasks; for instance, in May 2004 the Select Committee considered *The Transportation Security Administration's*

Progress in Enhancing Homeland Security, while in June the committee considered strategic ideas in its hearing *Information Sharing After September 11: Perspectives on the Future,* and looked into *Protecting the Homeland: Building a Layered and Coordinated Approach to Border Security* as well.[22] The House Select Committee and the Senate Governmental Affairs Committee also looked into DHS management as it worked on integrating the many old agencies into a single team.[23] The Homeland Security Appropriations Subcommittees produced their funding bills in both 2003 and 2004 and got them passed and signed into law without falling into the year-end omnibus bills, although some politicians complained about low funding levels.[24] Others warned that DHS did not support state and local governments in proportion to their risks: Wyoming, for instance received per capita funding of $38.31, compared to New York's $5.47 per capita, despite the latter being a far more likely target.[25] Reports also questioned the utility of bringing so many agencies under one roof and pointed to management problems in DHS, particularly after Secretary Ridge announced his departure shortly after the 2004 elections.[26]

Assessment: The Three Powers Are Tricky!

DHS is a new department. With so many agencies to integrate into a single team and with so much confusion in Congress about how to use its three powers to enforce its policy goals in DHS, we can be sure that we are a long way from seeing the end of major DHS legislation. How did Congress do in the DHS story? Did it use its three powers effectively to create a solid department? And if not, why not?

Congress did not use its three powers as well as it could have. In part, this is due to the complexity of the powers themselves—it is very tough to use them well. But Congress also got itself into this particular mess, with a strong assist from President Bush. Congressional GOP leaders allowed themselves to be bullied into moving too fast in order to respond to the president's demand for action before the fall 2002 elections. Politics trumped policy deliberation, and that made the difficult task of using the three powers even more tricky. Recall the challenge of balancing Congress's twin roles of lawmaker and representative that we examined in chapters 3 and 4. The electoral pressure on the House in particular gave Bush strong leverage to force a quick resolution to the homeland security issue. House leaders focused on passing a bill to meet the president's political demand, and they did it in a way that obviated most of Congress's strengths.

Before we can assess Congress's use of oversight and budgeting, we have to consider how it decided on DHS's organization. Both chambers realized that they had to assign lead jurisdiction to a single committee in order to make progress on the issue. Even so, given the complexity of the task, both the House and Senate moved quickly to produce bills! Some legislators feared moving too quickly with such a complex task. As Senator Robert Byrd (D-WV) said as the Senate took up its version of the DHS bill, "amid all of this upheaval we run the risk of creating gaps in our homeland defenses."[27] In general, Congress has not been comfortable with major reorganizations such as the creation of DHS. Even small changes in agency structure can lead to many unanticipated side effects, especially involving interagency relations. Congress usually meets new challenges with small adjustments. Big changes are rare, and they follow a pattern too. Major change is usually limited to reorganization, to shifting agencies around and changing the way that existing organizations work together—in other words, Congress prefers to use what already exists in new ways before it considers adding new offices to the mix.[28] DHS is an amalgam of many existing agencies, moved from their old departments into the new department.

Congress followed its usual pattern of rearranging old offices rather than creating new ones. But Congress did not allow itself the time to think the process through carefully. By responding to Bush's challenge to pass the bill before the fall elections, the House limited its time to consider all its options. It held only three hearings on the bill before the floor debate. It was power politics, not the need to address the problem of homeland security, that determined which agencies would be moving to DHS.[29] For example, the House Judiciary Committee tried to derail transfer of the Secret Service, the Immigration and Naturalization Service, and FEMA to DHS, but the final bill ignored Judiciary's attempts to control the creation of DHS.[30] The Senate did not deliberate for very long on the bill either. After no hearings in committee, the Senate debated the bill on the floor for just over a week before the election and returned to Washington to finish the bill after the elections.[31]

The president's bold call in June 2002 to complete a bill before the election short-circuited the usually slow process of crafting complicated reorganization bills. House and Senate leaders can only blame themselves for the reports of poor management, lack of coordination, and confusion in DHS; after all, they designed the department in only a few months—and with many warnings and concerns on record in both chambers.[32] The resultant DHS is a large and very complicated department, with a wide array of missions to be accomplished by agencies drawn from across the federal government. The transition to the new DHS organization could only be complicated, slow, and difficult, and recent reports reflect the difficulty of bringing so many disparate offices together into a single operation.[33]

Having created the new department, Congress now had to fund DHS. Although most of the agencies that moved to DHS already existed, their funding was spread out across most of the thirteen appropriations bills, so Congress could not clearly determine the adequacy—or even the real level—of federal homeland security funding. Several reports made clear the need for increased appropriations for homeland security, including higher levels of federal support for state and local programs.[34] Recognizing the importance of both the level and priorities for homeland security spending, the House Appropriations Committee realigned its thirteen subcommittees in February 2003, changing the Transportation subcommittee into the Homeland Security Appropriations Subcommittee, chaired by Rep. Harold Rogers (R-KY).[35] The Senate followed the House's lead in March 2003, with Thad Cochran (R-MS) as chair of its subcommittee.[36] Congress appropriated $29.4 billion for FY 2004 for homeland security, and $32 billion for FY 2005. In order to make its efforts more noticeable, Congress also began treating the homeland security funds as a separate category, reporting them as a proportion of the federal budget (along with the other two discretionary categories, defense and nondefense spending).[37] So Congress has made good strides in using its budget power to manage DHS, even if critics assail the way DHS funds are spent.[38] In the face of continuing deficits due to the combination of tax cuts and higher defense spending to support the wars in Iraq and Afghanistan, Congress will face a tough time finding increasing funds for homeland security, but at least the appropriators have organized themselves in a way to ensure that Congress can focus its attention on the issue.

That is not the case with the oversight power. Despite hopeful signs early in the 108th Congress, there has been little forward progress on improving oversight of homeland security. On the House side, the Select Committee on Homeland Security still struggles to work out a plan to adjust the jurisdictions of the many House committees with responsibility for monitoring DHS components. With little demonstrated willingness to compromise from the chairs of the other oversight committees, committee chair Rep. Chris Cox will not be able to craft a workable plan that will make the select committee a permanent standing committee with full jurisdiction over the many agencies that make up DHS. And with no support from the GOP leadership to bring the other committee chairs to the table to negotiate, even a skilled and well-respected member like Rep. Cox cannot force a solution. So although there is a select committee to oversee homeland security in the House, the committee is hamstrung by shared jurisdiction with many other committees and no desire to move forward on committee realignment.[39] And the Senate has made no moves at all to address the jurisdictional challenge. The Governmental Affairs Committee's subcommittee on homeland security can provide some oversight, but it is forced to share jurisdiction with many of the other standing committees, just as the House committee must do. The Senate finds realignments of committee responsibility very difficult. As a smaller body, with more nearly equal members, the Senate has great trouble in stripping power from anyone or any committee. It is likely that the Senate will do nothing on jurisdiction until it sees the House devise a workable solution to the problem, which the Senate can then copy. Until that time, the Senate has renamed its Governmental Affairs Committee the Committee on Homeland Security and Governmental Affairs.[40]

Congress has difficulty making use of the three powers to solve policy challenges and enforce the decision on the executive branch. Congress does not use the organizing power for major shifts in the structure of the executive branch, preferring, as it did with DHS, to shift existing offices into new arrangements. Congress quickly dealt with its appropriating mechanism for homeland security by creating subcommittees to produce homeland security spending bills. Previous congressional decisions to reduce federal revenue through tax cuts and to increase defense spending put pressure on discretionary spending, which will make fully funding homeland security difficult, but Congress has the appropriations subcommittees in place to handle the work. Congressional oversight of DHS is still a mess, with the designated committees forced to share oversight with nearly the entire committee structure.

Given the three challenges that Congress sought to address with the creation of DHS (interagency coordination, improved intelligence, and emergency response), we can see that Congress can claim only limited success with its DHS legislation. DHS does promise better interagency coordination for homeland security in the future, and DHS should provide better coordination between state/local and federal responses to emergencies. But Congress did not to address the intelligence failings identified shortly after 9/11. Congress could not respond to the intelligence challenge until a joint House-Senate intelligence report and an independent commission investigated the intelligence problems and made recommendations that dealt with intelligence issues ignored in the DHS bill.[41]

Throughout the debates and political wrangling that led up to the passage of the DHS bill in November 2002, many observers and participants, including President Bush on several occasions, noted that the creation of this new department would be the largest government reorganization since the establishment of the Department of Defense in 1947.[42] Had they looked to the history of DOD's creation, they would have found a good model for successful reorganization. Since no members of either the Congress or the executive branch had been involved in that earlier round of reorganizing, a brief comparison of the two reorganization efforts will underscore how much more effectively Congress might have managed the establishment of DHS.

1947: Creating the Defense Department

The largest and most well-prepared reorganization of the federal government occurred in 1947 when Congress established the Department of Defense. Congress could look back at two decades of debate, investigation, and experience as it designed DOD. With World War II recently ended, Congress realized that modern warfare had become too technologically advanced to manage in the traditional way. Prior to 1947, Congress had separate military and naval committees to oversee the War and Navy Departments, which operated separate forces independently of each other.[43] World War I had demanded intense joint army-navy cooperation for the first time since the Civil War, and World War II intensified that trend. Realizing that the forces of the United States would be deployed worldwide for the foreseeable future and that they would need to work seamlessly together, Congress undertook to create a new, unified DOD to meet the need.[44]

Congress had worked on the question of defense unification several times throughout the 1920s and 1930s and had ample evidence from World War II, which saw 12 million Americans in uniform fighting in two major theaters at opposite ends of the globe. War and Navy Department leaders threw together ad hoc boards to coordinate joint planning, which brought army, navy, marine, and army air force leaders together to make decisions on weapons manufacturing, logistical support, and combat operations.[45] Congressional committees monitoring the war effort saw what worked and what did not. After the war, Congress reorganized its committee structure in anticipation of postwar challenges. The Legislative Reorganization Act of 1946 included the new Armed Services Committees to oversee the military services. Those two committees went to work immediately to write the bill to establish DOD. Working from its many debates in the years between the wars and from its wartime experience, Congress organized the new U.S. Air Force, and combined it with the army and navy into DOD. Congress also established the National Security Council to coordinate policymaking among the agencies responsible for foreign and defense policy.[46]

Even with its experience, Congress did not create a perfect agency at the first try. Over the next four decades Congress was forced to return to the question of defense organization, adding reforms to improve the operation of the department. The work of reform began almost immediately. In 1949, Congress made the secretary of defense the main defense official and removed the secretaries of the services from operational command.[47] In 1953, Congress and the White House clarified the role and powers of the Joint Chiefs of Staff, who advised the president on defense matters.[48] In 1958, Congress created the network of regional commands that employ U.S. forces,[49] such as U.S. Central Command, in charge of the Persian Gulf War in 1991 and the recent Afghan and Iraqi operations. In 1959, recognizing the broad consensus on the national security strategy of containment of the USSR, Congress changed its internal procedures. The Armed Services Committees began to authorize DOD spending program by program, rather than in large categories. This resulted in longer, more complicated authorization bills that limited the spending options of the appropriators—and kept the defense oversight committees powerful.[50] And in 1986, Congress made the chair of the Joint Chiefs more powerful, as well as requiring the services to provide joint-training assignments for their senior officers.[51] Even with two decades to think about the issue and a world war to provide direct experience, Congress found its three powers tricky to use successfully! Congress had to return to DOD organization over and over to get it right. In addition, Congress had to examine and adjust its own processes to ensure that they made good use of oversight, budget, and organization to keep the Pentagon in line.

Congress could have looked back to its own successful management of the DOD reorganization in 1947 to find a thoughtful model for the creation of DHS. A few points distinguish the effective DOD process from the more troubled birth of DHS. First, Congress in 1947 had a wealth of experience on hand as it designed DOD. President Harry Truman supported the creation of DOD from the start, and the army and navy both contributed ideas and advice to Congress as it devised the new Defense Department. Congress first reorganized its own oversight structure and then it created DOD, ensuring that the committees would align with the new department structure, making oversight more effective. Notably, though, Congress still had to make repeated adjustments to DOD during the course of the Cold War to make sure that the department met its responsibilities in a way that Congress could support. Despite Congress's careful preparation for the changes and its comparatively broader experience in managing a global military operation, the initial version of DOD did not work as well as hoped, and Congress had to reform it repeatedly.

Even though the process that led to the creation of DHS was not as neat or organized as the history of DOD, we might take some consolation from that history. Although several commissions and think tanks had studied the issue of homeland security after the end of the Cold War, their work did not receive wide attention, especially not in decision-making circles. The terrorist attacks of 9/11 compelled Congress to address homeland security without preparation and with little time for reflection. The fractured, busy, partisan Congress of today—albeit with more tools than Congress in 1947, but with bigger headaches too—found it hard to address homeland security head on. The majority party in the House was also not comfortable with its institutional responsibilities for addressing the nature, organization, and purpose of government; it has been very successful at achieving party goals, but it has not effectively managed Congress as an independent power base. The Republicans were overwhelmed by a politically clever White House and, blinded by their partisan (or representative) role, they moved too quickly on a difficult task, resulting in a poorly designed DHS that they will most likely need to spend a lot of time fixing in the future. And they have made next to no progress on the urgent responsibility to oversee this new department: they have not addressed the jurisdictional issues within their own ranks and show little desire to do so any time soon.

What do we learn from these two different examples of major challenges demanding use of Congress's three powers? Two lessons should stand out clearly. First, the three powers are complicated and blunt tools for enforcing policy decisions. Even when used with care and thoughtfulness, oversight, budget, and organization are difficult to combine into an effective program for controlling the executive branch. Second, political pressure can derail effective use of the three powers. Although the executive branch needs congressional support for its operations, that does not imply that the president will cooperate with Congress to address big challenges. Presidents see the world differently from Congress, and because they are responsible for managing the executive branch, presidents seek more freedom to operate than Congress is comfortable allowing. But when the White House and Capitol Hill agree on the need and the way to reorganize, as they did in 1947, then the two branches can work together to develop a practical reorganization that both sides can support. In 2002, the White House did not agree with any of the specific plans moving through the Congress so it offered its own, which combined aspects of several of the bills making their way through committee. White House political pressure on a loyal House, and the looming deadline of the midterm elections, disrupted congressional plans and made the creation of DHS less successful than it could have been. Party loyalty, in other words, can overwhelm the effectiveness of Congress's three powers. In the face of a politically skilled White House that used the upcoming elections to press Congress for rapid action, party leaders on the Hill decided they had to pursue party goals over institutional ones, and they passed a White House–approved DHS bill.

Summary

Congress has three important constitutional powers to use in shaping how the executive branch carries out the policy decisions made by Congress. Singly, each of the three powers of oversight, budget, and organization has the potential to be convincing; together, they should grant sufficient power to Congress to retain its intended dominance of Washington. But that does not necessarily happen, because each power is unwieldy in practice and very difficult to coordinate with the other powers.

Congress is not a monolith. The House and Senate operate on different principles: each uses a committee system that is fragmented and partisan, and each takes a separate approach to policymaking that serves the needs of its members. It is therefore very challenging for Congress to send executive branch officials clear signals using the three powers. In the case of DHS, we can see just how tough it is to use the three powers together—especially in the face of a White House that has other ideas. With oversight shared among eighty-eight committees and subcommittees, Congress has a difficult time setting priorities for homeland security. Congress will have an easier time making appropriations for DHS because of its realignment of the Appropriations Committees, but with the budget pressures Congress is likely to face for some time, fully funding the department will be difficult. DHS is a complicated agency with numerous missions and with many different and diverse subunits, which originated all over the executive branch. The department's leaders and Congress can expect many years of hard work before they can feel confident that the department is as well organized as it can be to meet the demands of homeland security.

Web Resources

9/11 Commission: The commission examined the 9/11 attacks and recommended a set of changes to the structure of the government, in order to prevent future attacks (www.9–11commission.gov/).

Central Intelligence Agency: The CIA is the centerpiece of the nation's intelligence community; until the creation of the position of national intelligence director in 2004, the director of the CIA was also in charge of the whole community (www.cia.gov).

Director of National Intelligence: A new position created in 2004, the DNI is intended to manage the whole intelligence community, fostering better cooperation and coordination among the nation's spy agencies (www.dni.gov).

Homeland Security Institute, ANSER: Another well-known Washington defense think tank and consulting firm, ANSER was among the first to create a clearinghouse for homeland security information, and its Web site is still among the best available (www.homelandsecurity.org/).

Homeland Security Policy Institute, GWU: Sponsored by DHS, this institute at George Washington University studies homeland security issues and provides analysis and support to the department (www.homelandsecurity.gwu.edu/hspi.htm).

Homeland Security Program, Center for Strategic and International Studies: CSIS, one of Washington's leading defense policy think tanks, also produces work on foreign policy and homeland security, including several studies assessing DHS performance on many tasks (www.csis.org/hs/index.htm).

House Committee on Homeland Security: This committee, made a standing committee of the House in 2005, oversees DHS (http://hsc.house.gov/).

House Permanent Select Committee on Intelligence: This committee oversees the intelligence community for the House (intelligence.house.gov/).

Senate Select Committee on Intelligence: The committee produced an important study that reported on the failings within the intelligence community (http://intelligence.senate.gov/).

WMD Commission: This presidential commission reported to the White House in 2005 on the intelligence failures leading up to the war in Iraq (www.wmd commission.org/).

9 • Conclusions

This Government will set out a moderate Aristocracy; it is at
present impossible to foresee whether it will, in its Operation,
produce a Monarchy, or a corrupt tyrannical Aristocracy.
—George Mason, 1787[1]

Complexity comes from simplicity, making the Framers chaos theorists two centuries early.[2] To create the complexity they sought, the Framers made a few simple choices. They created a bicameral Congress in which each chamber has to balance two jobs. Although the chambers differ in only three key traits, the nature of representation, scale, and time frame make the House of Representatives and the Senate two completely different political environments, generating endless complexity despite a fairly simple set of initial rules governing the two bodies.

The Framers' intent still guides Congress, and it still works largely as they intended it to: government is slow, balky, and challenging. No tyrant has managed to take over the U.S. government, even when one party controls all the levers of power. The differences among the institutions established by the Framers make it quite difficult to maintain party unity across the House, Senate, and executive branch. The Framers' fear of tyranny and their long experience with self-government drove them to seek complexity in government—and we can understand why they felt that complexity was so important if we ground our own understanding of U.S. political institutions correctly, in their historical context. The Founders feared that without complexity, a power-hungry American Cromwell could amass all the federal power into one position; their dark view of human nature required the creation of a complicated, power-sharing system for their new federal government.

The Framers and Change

Although the Framers' initial intent was to prevent tyranny, their plan of government has proved to be flexible and adaptable to many situations. It has stood the test of time. Their system responded well to the expansion of the country throughout the nineteenth century, allowing the House to grow quickly to reflect the growing population of the United States, while the Senate slowly expanded. In both chambers the increase did not overwhelm the original idea—the House is still majoritarian, and the Senate remains individualistic. As the nation expanded, so did the federal government, from a small and distant entity to the large and powerful institution we know today. Congress adapted to the growth of the executive branch. It developed the committee structure and leadership posts, and it learned to use the oversight, budget, and organizing powers granted by the Constitution. Even though those three tools are complex to use and difficult to coordinate, Congress is reasonably successful in keeping the federal agencies in line with legislative intent.

The one innovation that has undermined the Framers' intent has been the rise and institutionalization of the two-party system. Party loyalty introduced another variable into legislators' political calculus, and its effects can overpower the controls developed by the Founders. Particularly in the House, partisanship has taken advantage of the rules of the chamber, shifting the system away from pure majoritarianism toward majority-party–ism, which is not the same thing. This shift is not new; it has been slowly gathering over nearly the entire history of the House, particularly since the Jacksonian era. In the atmosphere of Washington since the rise of the modern conservative movement, the trend has accelerated. Republicans and Democrats in the House can barely speak to each other in the fractious partisan environment of the past two decades. And the promotion of several unabashedly conservative House alumni to the Senate injected some of the same strong partisanship into the quieter, more collegial Senate, as well. Some factors do mitigate the rise of partisanship, such as the independent power bases, financial support, and media visibility of many members of both chambers, which allow individuals a good bit of freedom from party ties. Perhaps the times we live in and the hard questions on the national agenda since the end of the Cold War have intensified the party pressures on lawmakers of both parties. One-party rule after 2001 certainly added pressure on the GOP leadership in the House and the Senate to push hard for President George W. Bush's policy proposals, and it is likely that similar pressure will continue to complicate party leaders' lives on the Hill for the foreseeable future, regardless of which party holds the White House or the houses of Congress. Partisanship will always be a part of Washington, even if civility eventually returns to national politics.

Congress Today and Into the Future

The Framers' system works. Nonetheless, Congress could do better in executing its responsibilities. Leaders in both parties, in both chambers, seem to be comfortable with the status quo, too slow to respond to tough issues, and sometimes too intent on accentuating the partisan over the substantive. It is one thing to argue differences of opinion, which is the point of legislatures after all, and another entirely to act always for purely partisan advantage. Majority leaders in the House, and leaders of both parties in the Senate, bear two responsibilities, and every choice they make to push their party's goals must be weighed against the potential impacts upon the institution's power. Party leaders must decide what balance they want to strike between what is good for their party and what is good for their chamber as a player in the political struggle in Washington. The House leaders' decision to impeach President Bill Clinton after the 1998 elections turned against the House majority was driven by party leaders' political calculations more than by any consideration of the powers of the House or the Congress. And the entirely predictable failure of the articles of impeachment in the Senate led to a drop in the House's influence in Washington and its popularity nationwide.[3] At the same time the whole mess pumped Clinton's ratings up and emboldened him in his dealings with the House for the remainder of his term.[4] Republican obstruction of Clinton's judicial nominees and Democratic obstruction of Bush's picks have done nothing for the authority of the Senate, resulting in slower federal court actions due to the many open judgeships.

Ten years into majority status, the House Republican leadership has only recently started to appreciate the difficulty of balancing its duty to pursue its party goals with its institutional responsibilities. When the Republicans were in the minority before 1994, they had no responsibilities to the chamber and could focus on purely party concerns. But with their 1994 election victories, they earned the responsibility to govern, even though they have yet to fully embrace this fact. This is not surprising, since no Republicans serving in the Congress in 1995 were there the last time their party had run the House (in 1954), so nobody knew how to run the place. The Republicans before 1994 had just been along for the ride while Democrats managed the House, operated the committees, scheduled floor action, and generally ignored GOP concerns. Now, GOP leaders seem to spend inordinate time on symbolic gestures to press party goals, such as a constitutional amendment to ban flag burning, instead of devoting House floor time to more pressing matters. Committees have been weak on oversight since 2001, as well. While House committees aggressively questioned Clinton administration officials constantly, oversight dropped significantly (in both the House and Senate) once President Bush took office.[5] Without regular oversight, the House loses some of its ability to influence executive branch activities. At the same time committees reduced their oversight work, House Republican leaders spent much of their energy working to increase GOP power, such as House majority leader Tom DeLay's

Texas redistricting maneuver and his efforts to force the major lobbying organizations (whose officers line Washington DC's K Street) to hire only Republican lobbyists to work with the House.[6] During their long years in the minority, House Republicans strongly supported Republican presidents against the Democrats in the House, and they still seem to see themselves as the president's good soldiers on the major issues of the day. While President Clinton was in the White House, the House GOP battled with him incessantly, just as House Democrats had fought Eisenhower, Nixon, Ford, Reagan, and the first Bush. But DeLay and Speaker Dennis Hastert have been forceful advocates for President Bush's key policies, such as his budget proposals, tax cuts, and Medicare drug benefit plan. Whereas previous House majority leaders have chosen to maintain some distance between themselves and whoever was in the White House, Hastert and DeLay chose to ally closely with Bush, gaining clear benefits for the Republican Party—but at the cost of freedom of action for the House, which has ceded agenda control to the White House and the Senate.

After the 2004 elections, though, House GOP leaders began to confront the dual nature of their responsibility. In their willingness to change the Appropriations Subcommittees to pay for homeland security, and in the establishment of the Homeland Security Committee, House leaders demonstrated their growing understanding of their duty to manage the House as effectively as they have served the party interests of GOP House members. But their chairs proved as independent as their Democratic predecessors, fighting any adjustment of their own committee jurisdictions in order to help the new Homeland Security committee. If the House GOP leaders can grapple with their responsibility to run the House for the good of the institution as well as their party, they will probably enjoy continued success, in policymaking and in politics. But if they choose to follow their party interests too closely, they could end up losing all their power to the executive branch and therefore not really mattering any more. House GOP support for both President Bush's tax cuts and the Iraq war has plunged Washington back into deficit spending, limiting the House's ability to expand popular programs. Should the budget issue or U.S. foreign policy drop too far in popularity, such tight devotion to White House priorities could cost the GOP its narrow House majority. A few seats changing hands could throw the chamber back to the Democrats, who will not be inclined to be pleasant in the wake of continued GOP use of its House control only for GOP purposes. Campaign finance reforms, ethics probes, and calls for implementing nonpartisan redistricting all point to the potential danger of spending too much time on party goals and not enough on institutional goals: a majority party seen as out of touch and abusive of its power is a party ripe for minority status, much as the bloated Democratic majority was in 1994.[7]

Party has also had an influence on the Senate, but the Senate's political style mitigates the impact. The Senate serves the needs of its hundred members well, and that individual focus limits the potential for partisanship. In addition, the Senate has been blessed with several senior members of both parties who are careful to protect the Senate's prerogatives. GOP senators Ted Stevens and John McCain have fought frequently with their peers, the House, and the executive branch in order to protect the power of the Senate—Stevens on spending bills and McCain on oversight of federal agencies. And Senator Robert Byrd lets nothing go by that could lessen the influence or authority of the Senate. With such jealous guardians of the Senate's place in American politics, it is unlikely that the Senate's leaders would ever simply take their marching orders from any White House. Members of both parties in the Senate are familiar with majority and minority status as well— the Senate has switched hands several times in the past two decades. Interestingly, though, the House-trained hard-right senators who moved up from the House after 1994 have never served in the minority (except for the short period from June 2001 to November 2002, following Senator James Jefford's switch from Republican to Independent, which gave the Democrats a majority of one). Without personal experience of at least one of those previous takeovers, the younger Republican senators have been more comfortable with partisanship than their older peers in both parties. Even so, most senators understand the utility of the chamber's long-standing protections afforded to the minority, which have been an even more important feature of Senate politics since 1980, since the majorities for either party have been fairly narrow. With little chance of enforcing cloture on contentious issues, majority leaders have grown accustomed to, and adept at, accommodating the concerns of the minority members.

The Senate could be a more effective part of the government, though. It serves its members' needs very well, but sometimes at the cost of good committee work or effective floor action. As in the House, Senate committees have not used oversight recently as much as they have in the past, although some senators, especially John McCain, have used their roles as committee chairs to highlight failed administration efforts, such as the 2002 air force decision to award a huge aircraft contract to Boeing without following Pentagon rules on such contracts.[8] More attention by the majority leader to working with committee chairs to perform regular oversight might make the Senate a more powerful player. Of course, the Senate waited for the House to reorganize itself to deal with homeland security before the Senate did so; it is difficult for members of the Senate to work out changes to committee practices, or jurisdictions, making it tough for the majority leader to have much impact on the issue. Senate floor debate could also benefit from reform, but with the narrow party majorities that have been the main characteristic of Senate life since the late 1970s, it has proved nearly impossible for the Senate to address divisive issues, such as tax cuts, budget bills, or confirmation of judges. The confirmation process is an especially difficult and damaging issue for the Senate. In addition to leaving many courts without judges, the fights of the past twenty years have only increased partisan feeling in the Senate. Presidents and senators need to work together to devise a more effective system of advice and consent. The Senate cannot do any better, however, if the White House continues sending unacceptably ideological judges up for confirmation, as both Presidents Clinton and Bush did. Until the Senate finds a way to control the individualism of the hundred senators, it is likely to be a very tough place to do business.

Two Centuries of Success

The Framers did an amazing thing by binding the nation together out of thirteen disparate states. They created a complicated system of government that would not allow tyranny, and it has somehow proved flexible enough to react to the changing circumstance facing the country over the past 200 years. Their partisan House of the moment and their individualistic, deliberative Senate work well to represent the people and the states, and the two chambers do a marvelous job of controlling each other's worst excesses. They can also do a good job of counterbalancing the power of the executive branch.

Optimism is the right attitude toward the future for Congress and the constitutional order. Many observers of American politics have a low opinion of Congress, as does the public. In a CBS News–*New York Times* poll in June 2005, 53 percent disapproved of how Congress handled its job, with only 33 percent approving the institution.[9] But these negative views focus on only one of Congress's two roles, which should be clear when we remember from Chapters 3 and 4 that 93 percent of House members and 80 percent of senators, on average, get reelected! Congressional policymaking is slow, disorganized, and difficult—just as the Framers intended. Public policy research and opinion journals focus on this role and give Congress poor marks for it—even when Congress operates in the intended manner.[10] In any event, we should also recall that the Framers built in a different actor to take the broad view on policy issues, and that is the presidency. Only the president has a national electoral base, and only the president has the capacity to see problems in a truly national perspective; Congress cannot do it, no matter how far-seeing, or how conscientious, individual members might be. Seen against the Framers' design, Congress can do a decent job on its particular role in policymaking. The members of Congress are supposed to come together to make policy decisions for the nation—which they manage to do, even when it is not attractive to watch.

In its second role, Congress the representative does a good job of serving the needs of the active, involved constituencies that participate in congressional decision making. Even allowing for incumbent advantages and careful redistricting to protect sitting members, reelection rates and the popularity of individual legislators make it clear that Congress does this job very well.[11] Following the 2004 elections, congressional Republicans showed signs of understanding that they run an institution as well as a party, and congressional Democrats acted like a functioning party again, which are hopeful signs that Congress can continue to balance its appointed tasks of lawmaking for the nation and representation of specific constituencies.

No people had ever built a self-governed country before the Framers wrote the Constitution. Congress is at the center of the system they built, but it does need help from the citizenry if it is to continue to work. The "relationship between the representative and the represented—and the honesty of the exchange between the two—shapes the strength of our representative democracy."[12] In the end, the tyranny that haunted the Framers cannot be kept at bay by their Congress, or by their system, alone. Without us, the people, the Framers' system cannot endure.

And that is still all Cromwell's fault!

Notes

Chapter 1

1. James Madison, in Clinton Rossiter, ed., *The Federalist Papers* (New York: Mentor Books, 1961), 322.

2. APSA Task Force on Graduate Education, *2004 Report to the Council* (Washington, DC: American Political Science Association, 2004), 1–2.

3. See Thomas Birkland, *An Introduction to the Policy Process* (Armonk, NY: M.E. Sharpe), 2001, for a discussion of the steps in the policy process, as well as competing models of the process (particularly in chapter 9).

4. Kingdon's *Agendas, Alternatives, and Public Policies* (New York: HarperCollins, 1984), is the source for this discussion of his "multiple streams" model of policymaking.

5. See Paul Sabatier and Hank Jenkins-Smith, "The Advocacy Coalition Framework: An Assessment," in *Theories of the Policy Process,* ed. Paul Sabatier (Boulder, CO: Westview Press, 1999), 117–166. See also Birkland, *Introduction to the Policy Process,* 224–227 for a short review of the model.

6. Carl Van Horn, Donald Baumer, and William Gormley lay out the domains approach in their text, *Politics and Public Policy,* 3rd ed. (Washington, DC: Congressional Quarterly, 2001).

7. Deborah Stone, *Policy Paradox: The Art of Political Decision Making,* rev. ed. (New York: W.W. Norton, 2002), 7.

8. Anthony Downs's *An Economic Theory of Democracy* (New York: HarperCollins, 1957), one of the earliest attempts to draw on the economics literature for insights into politics, remains a classic of the genre.

9. See Stone, *Policy Paradox,* for the clearest explanation of this approach. Another excellent source for exploring the impact of ideas on contemporary American politics is Marc Landy and Martin Levin, ed., *The New Politics of Public Policy* (Baltimore, MD: Johns Hopkins University Press, 1995).

10. All definitions are derived from Randall Ripley and Grace A. Franklin, *Congress, the Bureaucracy, and Public Policy,* 5th ed. (Pacific Grove, CA: Brooks/Cole, 1991), 3–5.

11. James E. Anderson, *Public Policymaking: An Introduction,* 2nd ed. (Boston, MA: Houghton Mifflin, 2000), 62–73, examines the actors in detail. He uses two broad categories to classify players: official participants, who have a statutory or legal role in the process, and unofficial participants, who do not.

12. Bruce Wolpe and Bertram Levine, *Lobbying Congress: How the System Works,* 2nd ed. (Washington, DC: Congressional Quarterly, 1996), 1–5, 13.

13. David Ricci, *The Transformation of American Politics: The New Washington and the Rise of the Think Tanks* (New Haven, CT: Yale University Press, 1993).

14. Timothy Cook, *Governing With the News: The News Media as a Political Institution* (Chicago: University of Chicago Press, 1998), 61–115.

15. Stephen Hess, *The Government/Press Connection: Press Officers and Their Offices* (Washington, DC: Brookings Institution, 1984), 111–115.

16. Richard Neustadt, *Presidential Power and the Modern Presidents* (New York: Free Press, 1990); see also Samuel Kernell, *Going Public* (Washington, DC: Congressional Quarterly, 1993), and Matthew Kerbel, *Beyond Persuasion* (Albany, NY: SUNY Press, 1991).

17. Jon Bond and Richard Fleisher, *The President in the Legislative Arena* (Chicago: University of Chicago Press, 1990).

18. John Anthony Maltese, *Spin Control: The White House Office of Communications and the Management of Presidential News,* 2nd ed. (Chapel Hill, NC: University of North Carolina Press, 1994), 1–12.

19. Morris Fiorina, *Retrospective Voting in American National Elections* (New Haven, CT: Yale University Press, 1981).

20. Sidney Verba and Norman Nie, *Participation in America* (Chicago: University of Chicago Press, 1972), 334–336.

21. R. Douglas Arnold, *The Logic of Congressional Action* (New Haven, CT: Yale University Press, 1990), 60–87.

22. Ripley and Franklin devised this classification scheme using a broad array of previous research on the subject. They do note the existence of another domestic policy type, which they call competitive regulatory policy, which involves limiting the number of providers or producers of a good or service. As an example, they mention the allocation of frequencies to radio and television stations. But since the mid-1980s, deregulation has been the norm in Washington, so they do not track this kind of policy in the rest of their analysis. See Ripley and Franklin, *Congress, the Bureaucracy, and Public Policy,* 20–21.

23. Ripley and Franklin, *Congress, the Bureaucracy, and Public Policy,* 17–20.

24. Ripley and Franklin, *Congress, the Bureaucracy, and Public Policy,* 21.

25. Ripley and Franklin, *Congress, the Bureaucracy, and Public Policy,* 21–22.

26. Randall Ripley and James M. Lindsay, eds., *Congress Resurgent: Foreign and Defense Policy on Capitol Hill* (Ann Arbor: University of Michigan Press, 1993), 19.

27. Ripley and Franklin, *Congress, the Bureaucracy, and Public Policy,* 23.

28. Ripley and Franklin, *Congress, the Bureaucracy, and Public Policy,* 24.

29. Ripley and Lindsay, *Congress Resurgent,* 19.

30. Ripley and Franklin, *Congress, the Bureaucracy, and Public Policy,* 23–24.

31. During his tenure as Chairman of the Joint Chiefs of Staff (JCS), Adm. William Crowe noted this lack of congressional strategic focus. As he states, since the president and his national security agencies formulated strategic policy, Congress had little to do on the subject. William Crowe, with David Chanoff, *The Line of Fire: From Washington to the Gulf, the Politics and Battles of the New Military* (New York: Simon and Schuster, 1993), 236–241.

32. Ripley and Franklin, *Congress, the Bureaucracy, and Public Policy,* 88–89.

33. Ripley and Franklin, *Congress, the Bureaucracy, and Public Policy,* 184.

34. Ripley and Franklin, *Congress, the Bureaucracy, and Public Policy,* 121–139.

35. Ripley and Franklin, *Congress, the Bureaucracy, and Public Policy,* 113–120.

36. Ripley and Franklin, *Congress, the Bureaucracy, and Public Policy,* 103–107.

37. Ripley and Franklin, *Congress, the Bureaucracy, and Public Policy,* 106.

38. Ripley and Franklin, *Congress, the Bureaucracy, and Public Policy,* 77. Subgovernments—the cooperating committees, agencies, and interest groups that can dominate distributive or structural policy issues—are also sometimes called "iron triangles" in recognition of their control over their respective issues.

39. Ripley and Franklin, *Congress, the Bureaucracy, and Public Policy,* 79–100.

40. Ripley and Franklin, *Congress, the Bureaucracy, and Public Policy,* 72, 76–83.

41. Ripley and Franklin, *Congress, the Bureaucracy, and Public Policy,* 187–188.

42. Ripley and Lindsay, *Congress Resurgent,* 19.

43. Ripley and Lindsay, *Congress Resurgent,* 8.

44. Ripley and Franklin, *Congress, the Bureaucracy, and Public Policy,* 181.

45. Thomas "Tip" O'Neill, with William Novak, *Man of the House: The Life and Political Memoirs of Speaker Tip O'Neill* (New York: Random House, 1987), 365–367.

46. See Carl Woodward, *The Commanders* (New York: Simon and Schuster, 1991), and Colin Powell, with Joseph Persico, *My American Journey* (New York: Random House, 1995), for detailed accounts of these two conflicts and the decision making that preceded them.

47. Ripley and Lindsay, *Congress Resurgent,* 19.

48. John Hart Ely, "Suppose Congress Wanted a War Powers Act That Worked," *Columbia Law Review* 88, no. 7 (November 1988): 1379–1431. Ely reviews the resolution's reporting requirements on p. 1380.

49. Louis Fisher and David Adler, "The War Powers Resolution: Time to Say Goodbye," *Political Science Quarterly* 113, no. 1 (Spring 1998): 1–20. Postresolution presidential actions are reviewed on pp. 10–12.

50. Louis Fisher, "Congressional Checks on Military Initiatives," *Political Science Quarterly* 109, no. 5 (Winter 1994–95): 739–762.

51. David Broder, "Harry Potter and Our Forgotten History," *Washington Post,* July 28, 2005.

Chapter 2

1. James Madison, in Clinton Rossiter, ed., *The Federalist Papers* (New York: Mentor Books, 1961), 322.

2. Dave R. Palmer, *1794: America, Its Army, and the Birth of the Nation* (Novato, CA: Presidio, 1994), 94–103.

3. *Federalist* No. 6, in Rossiter, *Federalist Papers,* 54.

4. Bernard Bailyn, *The Peopling of British North America: An Introduction* (New York: Vintage, 1988).

5. Mark Kishlansky, *A Monarchy Transformed: Britain 1603–1714* (London: Penguin, 1996), 34–40.

6. Kishlansky, *Monarchy Transformed,* 65–88. The Scottish kings were never able to use their theoretically unlimited power without careful attention to the senior nobles in the nation, whose power significantly circumscribed the king's power in reality. But even they accepted the theoretical argument about the king's prerogatives. The full clamor and intrigue of life in the Scottish court is well described in Simon Schama, *A History of Britain: At the Edge of the World, 3500 B.C.–1603 A.D.* (New York: Miramax, 2000), 349–385. Adam Nicholson offers a

sharp portrait of King James I and how he learned to navigate the difficulties of ruling Scotland in his *God's Secretaries: The Making of the King James Bible* (New York: Perennial, 2003), 1–19.

7. Kishlansky, *Monarchy Transformed,* 36, 37.

8. J.P. Somerville, *Politics and Ideology in England, 1603–1640* (London: Longman, 1986), 57–64.

9. Somerville, *Politics and Ideology,* 9–56.

10. Charles I, writing in 1629, quoted in Somerville, *Politics and Ideology,* 36.

11. Somerville, *Politics and Ideology,* 9–50.

12. Charles I's brusqueness is made clear when contrasted the tact of his father, another divine right king, James I, who addressed Parliament with these words in 1610:

> [A] king governing in a settled kingdom leaves to be a king and degenerates into a tyrant as soon as he leaves off to rule according to his laws. . . . There-fore all kings that are not tyrants or perjured will be glad to bound themselves within the limits of their laws, and they that persuade them to the contrary are vipers and pests, both against them and the commonwealth. . . . I am sure to go to my grave with that reputation and comfort, that never king was in all his time more careful to have his laws duly executed, and himself to govern there-after, than I. (quoted in Somerville, *Politics and Ideology,* 132)

13. G.E. Aylmer, *Rebellion or Revolution? England 1640–1660* (Oxford: Oxford University Press, 1986), 12–15.

14. Somerville, *Politics and Ideology,* 232.

15. From Overton's tract *A Remonstrance of Many Thousand Citizens,* quoted in A.L. Morton, ed., *Freedom in Arms: A Selection of Leveller Writings* (New York: International Publishers, 1974), 19.

16. A second round of fighting would flare up in 1648, but the main combat con-cluded by late 1646.

17. Aylmer, *Rebellion or Revolution?,* 77–84.

18. Kishlansky, *Monarchy Transformed,* 171–176.

19. Aylmer, *Rebellion or Revolution?,* 86–90.

20. Richard Clarke transcribed the first of these debates and made extensive notes of the succeeding discussions. His manuscript is available in A.S.P Woodhouse, ed., *Puritanism and Liberty: Being the Army Debates (1647–9) from the Clarke Manu-scripts with Supplementary Documents* (London: J.M. Dent, 1951).

21. Kishlansky, *Monarchy Transformed,* 174–176.

22. Christopher Hill, *The Experience of Defeat: Milton and Some Contemporaries* (London: Penguin, 1985), 30–31.

23. Woodhouse, *Puritanism and Liberty,* 35–40.

24. See the *Large Petition* of March 1647, in Morton, *Freedom in Arms,* 95–98.

25. Kishlansky, *Monarchy Transformed,* 174–175. Further instances of this feel-ing in the army and the Levellers occurred in 1648 at the end of the second round of fighting (1996, 184).

26. Morton, *Freedom in Arms,* 148. The full text of the *Agreement of the People* is available on pp. 135–149.

27. Aylmer, *Rebellion or Revolution?,* 77.

28. Kishlansky, *Monarchy Transformed,* 178, 184.

29. Aylmer, *Rebellion or Revolution?*, 131.

30. Kishlansky, *Monarchy Transformed*, 181, 184.

31. Kishlansky, *Monarchy Transformed*, 181–184; Aylmer, *Rebellion or Revolution?*, 94–99.

32. Kishlansky, *Monarchy Transformed*, 192–193; Aylmer, *Rebellion or Revolution?*, 134–160.

33. Aylmer, *Rebellion or Revolution?*, 163–165.

34. Thomas Hobbes, *Leviathan*, ed. Michael Oakeshott (New York: Collier Books, 1962), 100.

35. Hobbes, *Leviathan*, 132.

36. Aylmer, *Rebellion or Revolution*, 141; Hill, *Experience of Defeat*, 321.

37. Kishlansky, *Monarchy Transformed*, 218–219.

38. Kishlansky, *Monarchy Transformed*, 225–227.

39. Kishlansky, *Monarchy Transformed*, 265.

40. Kishlansky, *Monarchy Transformed*, 277.

41. Queen Anne took the throne in 1702, after the deaths of Mary II (1694) and William III (1702), with the intention of handing over the throne to her German cousins, rather than to her surviving Stuart relatives (Kishlansky, *Monarchy Transformed*, 310–335). When she died in 1714, George I came from Hanover to assume the throne. Stuart pretenders to the throne would continue to plague England until 1745.

42. Kishlansky, *Monarchy Transformed*, 286.

43. Kishlansky, *Monarchy Transformed*, 256–258; Bernard Bailyn, *The Ideological Origins of the American Revolution* (Cambridge, MA: Belknap, 1992), 42–43.

44. The Whigs derived their name from a slang term used to denote Scottish cattle rustlers or rebels; later, promonarchy politicians formed their own party, the Tories, and took their name from the word for Irish outlaws. Simon Schama, *A History of Britain, vol. 2, The Wars of the British, 1603–1776* (New York: Talk Miramax Books, 2001), 295.

45. Locke, *Two Treatises of Government*, ed. Peter Laslett (New York: Mentor Books, 1963). From Laslett's Introduction, 58–59.

46. Locke, *Two Treatises of Government*, 1963, 395 (emphasis in original).

47. Another key influence added to the English traditions that the colonists brought with them: their interactions with the native people living along the east coast when the first English settlements were established. From about 1632 through the French and Indian War, settlers in several colonies engaged in near-constant warfare with various tribes. The bloodiest and perhaps most important of these wars was King Philip's War, fought in Massachusetts and Connecticut in 1675. This war and its powerful impact on future relations between the natives and the English settlers are thoroughly recounted in Jill Lepore, *The Name of War: King Philip's War and the Origins of American Identity* (New York: Alfred A. Knopf, 1998).

48. Bailyn, *Ideological Origins*, 22–35.

49. Bailyn, *Ideological Origins*, 35–54.

50. Fred Anderson, *Crucible of War* (New York: Vintage, 2000), 518–528.

51. Anderson *Crucible of War*, 147–149; the lingering effects of the garrison issue are described on p. 766.

52. Anderson, *Crucible of War*, 560–603.

53. Bailyn, *Ideological Origins*, 169.

54. Bailyn, *Ideological Origins*, 169.

55. Bailyn, *Ideological Origins*, 164–169.

56. Catherine Drinker Bowen, *Miracle at Philadelphia: The Story of the Constitutional Convention, May to September 1787* (Boston, MA: Back Bay Books, 1986), 3–15.

57. For the main French writers mentioned by the Framers during the convention debates and later during ratification, see Montesquieu (Charles de Secondat, Baron de la Brède et de Montesquieu), *The Spirit of the Laws,* in *Selected Political Writings,* ed. Melvin Richter (Indianapolis, IN: Hackett, 1990), 106–242; Michel de Montaigne, *Essays,* translated by J.M. Cohen (New York: Penguin, 1958); and Jean-Jacques Rousseau, *On the Social Contract,* in *The Basic Political Writings,* translated by Donald A. Cress (Indianapolis, IN: Hackett, 1987), 141–227.

58. The leaders of the Continental Congress and the army were deeply fearful that a dictator arising out of the army could overwhelm their new country. One abortive attempt at devising a coup may have been derailed by General Washington at Newburgh in 1784; see Palmer, *1794,* 3–20. The Newburgh conspiracy is also detailed in Richard Kohn, *Eagle and Sword: The Beginnings of the Military Establishment in America* (New York: Free Press, 1985), 17–39. Kohn also describes the Framers' fear of a standing army and that fear's origin in English history (p. 3).

59. John Adams reflected this fear of Cromwell's greed for power in a letter to his son, John Quincy Adams, noting of Thomas Jefferson after he resigned as Washington's secretary of state so he could return home, "Jefferson thinks he shall by this step get a reputation of a humble modest, meek man, wholly without ambition or vanity. He may have even deceived himself into this belief. But if the prospect opens, the world will see . . . he is as ambitious as Oliver Cromwell." Quoted in David McCullough, *John Adams* (New York: Simon and Schuster, 2001), 448.

60. Brutus 10, January 24, 1788, in Ralph Ketcham, ed., *The Anti-Federalist Papers and the Constitutional Convention debates* (New York: Mentor Books, 1986), 288.

61. *Federalist* No. 51, in Rossiter, *Federalist Papers,* 322.

62. The Tenth Amendment makes this clear: "The powers not delegated to the United States by the Constitution, nor prohibited by it to the States, are reserved to the States respectively, or to the people."

63. Bailyn, *Ideological Origins,* 272–285.

64. Richard Neustadt, *Presidential Power and the Modern Presidents* (New York: Free Press, 1990), 29. Charles Jones, *Separate but Equal Branches: Congress and the Presidency* (Chatham, NJ: Chatham House, 1995), viii.

65. *Federalist* No. 51, in Rossiter, *Federalist Papers,* 322.

66. Bowen, *Miracle at Philadelphia,* 185–196.

67. Until the passage of the Sixteenth Amendment in 1913 allowed for direct election of senators, state legislatures appointed their state's senators.

68. Ronald Peters' *The American Speakership,* 2nd ed. (Baltimore, MD: Johns Hopkins Press, 1997), for instance, identifies four periods differentiated by major political issues and the role of the Speaker in each period.

69. Bowen, *Miracle at Philadelphia,* 8–11.

70. For an idea of the political impact Washington had on his contemporaries, see Joseph Ellis's excellent short biography of the first president, *His Excellency George Washington* (New York: Alfred A. Knopf, 2004).

71. One such party was the Whigs, who coalesced out of anti-Jackson politicians in the mid-1830s and would remain on the scene until the mid-1850s. Michael Holt, *The Rise and Fall of the American Whig Party: Jacksonian Politics and the Onset of the Civil War* (New York: Oxford University Press, 1999).

72. *Federalist* No. 10 is reproduced in Rossiter, *Federalist Papers,* 77–84.

73. Joseph Ellis, *Founding Brothers: The Revolutionary Generation* (New York: Alfred A. Knopf, 2000), 3–20, 162–248; Bernard Bailyn, *To Begin the World Anew: The Genius and Ambiguities of the American Founders* (New York: Alfred A. Knopf, 2003), 100–125.

74. Peters, *American Speakership,* chapter 1.

75. Stephen Skowronek, *Building a New American State: The Expansion of National Administrative Capacities, 1877–1920* (Cambridge: Cambridge University Press, 1982).

76. Skowronek, *Building a New American State,* 19–35.

77. Randall Ripley, *Power in the Senate* (New York: St. Martin's Press, 1969), 21–26.

78. Jack Knott and Gary Miller, *Reforming Bureaucracy: The Politics of Institutional Choice* (Englewood Cliffs, NJ: Prentice-Hall, 1987), 15–54.

79. Peters, *American Speakership,* chapters 2 and 3.

80. Barbara Sinclair, "House Majority Leadership in the 1980s," in Lawrence Dodd and Bruce Oppenheimer, *Congress Reconsidered,* 4th ed., (Washington, DC: Congressional Quarterly, 1989), 307–330.

81. The two most powerful Speakers were Thomas Reed and Joseph Cannon. Sinclair, "House Majority," 309, points out that both leaders centralized power in the House in their own hands and did not share it with other party leaders or committee chairs.

82. See Sinclair, "House Majority," for a review of the 1910 reforms.

83. Ripley, *Power in the Senate,* 26–29.

84. Peters, *American Speakership,* chapter 4.

85. John Judis, *The Paradox of American Democracy* (New York: Routledge, 2000).

Chapter 3

1. James Madison, in Clinton Rossiter, ed. *The Federalist Papers* (New York: Mentor Books, 1961), 32–37.

2. The sponsors were Reps. Christopher Shays (R-CT) and Martin Meehan (D-MA).

3. House leaders offered a substitute bill that was defeated during the debate. They were also allowed under the rule to offer up to ten amendments, but they were unable to derail passage of the bill, which passed the Senate later that year and was signed into law by the president. See the THOMAS Web site for the history and text of the rule, H. Res. 344, available at http://thomas.loc.gov/cgi-bin/query/D?c107:2:./temp/~c107ESVClP::.

4. See especially *Federalist* Nos. 47 and 48 (Rossiter, *Federalist Papers,* 300–312) on the challenges the Framers faced in crafting a workable separation of powers that would make it difficult for Congress to take on too much power, and Nos. 52 and 53 (325–335) on the rationale behind the electoral reasoning that guided the convention's thinking about the House.

5. Richard Hall, *Participation in Congress* (New Haven, CT: Yale University Press, 1996).

6. This overview of the schools of thought is drawn from Jack Knott and Gary

Miller, *Reforming Bureaucracy: The Politics of Institutional Choice* (Englewood Cliffs, NJ: Prentice-Hall, 1987), 6–8.

7. Robert Rycroft, "Innovation Networks and Complex Technologies: Policy Implications of the Unknown, and the Unknowable," Occasional Paper Series # CSGOP-03-24, George Washington Center for the Study of Globalization, George Washington University, October 24, 2003, www.gwu.edu/~cistp/PAGES/Innovation Networks_RWR_10.24.03.pdf.

8. See Barbara Sinclair, "The New World of U.S. Senators," in *Congress Reconsidered,* 7th ed., ed. Lawrence Dodd and Bruce Oppenheimer (Washington, DC: Congressional Quarterly, 2001), 1–20.

9. For a fine set of examples of historical research, see *Party, Process, and Political Change in Congress,* ed. David Brady and Mathew McCubbins (Stanford, CT: Stanford University Press, 2002).

10. Steven Kull and I.M. Destler, *Misreading the Public: The Myth of a New Isolationism* (Washington, DC: Brookings Institution, 1999).

11. Charles Ragin, *The Comparative Method: Moving Beyond Qualitative and Quantitative Strategies* (Berkeley: University of California, 1989), 34–52. Chapter 8 will rely on the case study method to examine Congress's response to the 9/11 terrorist attacks.

12. See Giovanni Sartori's *The Theory of Democracy Revisited,* I: *The Contemporary Debate,* and *The Theory of Democracy Revisited,* II: *The Classical Issues* (Chatham, NJ: Chatham House, 1987).

13. Five nonvoting members of the House join the members representing the 435 congressional districts. American Samoa, Puerto Rico, the U.S. Virgin Islands, Guam, and the District of Columbia all have delegates in Congress, who serve on committees and participate in all other House activities, other than voting on the floor of the House.

14. Susan Webb Hammond, "Congressional Caucuses in the 104th Congress," in *Congress Reconsidered,* 6th ed., ed. Lawrence Dodd and Bruce Oppenheimer (Washington, DC: Congressional Quarterly, 1997), 274–292.

15. David Mayhew, *Congress: The Electoral Connection* (New Haven, CT: Yale University Press, 1974); David Rohde, *Parties and Leaders in the Post-Reform House* (Chicago: University of Chicago Press, 1991), 28–29.

16. Thomas Kazee, "The Emergence of Congressional Candidates," in *Who Runs for Congress?,* ed. Thomas Kazee (Washington, DC: Congressional Quarterly, 1994), 1–22.

17. David Price, *The Congressional Experience: Transforming American Politics,* 3rd ed. (Boulder, CO: Westview, 2004), 9–62; Sherrod Brown, *Congress from the Inside: Observations from the Majority and the Minority* (Ohio: Kent State University Press, 1999), 3–21.

18. Morris Fiorina, *Congress: Keystone of the Washington Establishment,* 2nd ed. (New Haven, CT: Yale University Press, 1989), 43.

19. Not all the staffers are fresh out of college, although most of them are. Most offices also have an older staffer as administrative assistant or legislative director, Hill veterans who play a key role in teaching the young staffers how the House works.

20. Betsy Wright Hawkings, ed., *Setting Course: A Congressional Management Guide* (Washington, DC: Congressional Management Foundation, 1996).

21. Price, *Congressional Experience,* 77–94.

22. Figure 3.1 is adapted from the schedules of several serving members of Congress and is similar to the weekly schedule depicted in Price, *Congressonal Experi-*

ence, 71; see also the daily schedule listed in Michael Koempel and Judy Schneider, *Congressional Desk Book 2003–2004* (Washington, DC: Capitol.Net, 2003), 14.

23. Richard Forgette, *Congress, Parties, and Puzzles: Politics as a Team Sport* (New York: Peter Lang), 2004.

24. Gary Cox and Mathew McCubbins, *Legislative Leviathan: Party Government in the House* (Berkeley: University of California Press), 1993.

25. Figure 3.3 is replicated from Keith Poole, "NOMINATE: A Short Intellectual History," http://voteview.com/nominate/nominate.htm.

26. Keith Poole and Howard Rosenthal, "A Spatial Model for Legislative Roll Call Analysis," *American Journal of Political Science* 29, no. 2 (May 1985): 357–384; Kenneth Koford, "Dimensions in Congressional Voting," *American Political Science Review* 83, no. 3, (September 1989): 949–962; Jeff Gill and Jason Gainous, "Why Does Voting Get So Complicated? A Review of Theories for Analyzing Democratic Participation," *Statistical Science* 17, no. 4 (2002): 383–404.

27. Clerk of the U.S. House of Representatives, *Party Divisions, 1789 to Present,* http://clerk,.house.gov/histHigh/Congressonal_History/partyDiv.html, 2005.

28. House of Commons Information Office, Factsheet G3, General Series, *A Brief Chronology of the House of Commons,* Revised January 2004, 4, www.parliament.uk/documents/upload/g03.pdf.

29. Campaign funds reported on *Open Secrets* Web site, www.opensecrets.org/parties/index.asp.

30. House Rules Committee Minority Office, *Broken Promises: The Death of Deliberative Democracy; A Congressional Report on the Unprecedented Erosion of the Democratic Process in the 108th Congress,* House of Representatives, 109th Cong., 1st sess., 2005.

31. DCCC spending total reported on *Open Secrets* Web site (see note 29).

32. Lewis Deschler reviews the history of each committee in *Deschler's Precedents, Including References to Provisions of the Constitution and Laws, and to Decisions of the Courts,* House of Representatives, 94th Cong., 2nd sess., 1976, H. Doc. 94–661, Ch. 17, Sections 26, 30–51.

33. Steven Smith and Christopher Deering, *Committees in Congress,* 2nd ed. (Washington, DC: Congressional Quarterly, 1990), 45–56.

34. Smith and Deering, *Committees in Congress,* 2.

35. David King, *Turf Wars: How Congressional Committees Claim Jurisdiction* (Chicago: University of Chicago Press, 1997).

36. King, *Turf Wars,* 105–120. See also Bryan Jones, Frank Baumgartner, and Jeffrey Talbert, "The Destruction of Issue Monopolies in Congress," *American Political Science Review* 87 (1993): 657–671, for an excellent discussion of jurisdictional change in Congress. Jones et al. argue that committees can break down other committees' monopolies on certain issues by carefully redefining a political issue. In 1993, for example, Rep. Henry Waxman (D-CA) challenged the Agriculture Committee's monopoly on tobacco issues by framing the issue of smoking as a health concern, rather than as a farm issue.

37. See Congressional Fellowship Program, www.apsanet.org/section_165.cfm.

38. See THOMAS Web site for information on bills introduced into the House of Representatives, http://thomas.loc.gov/home/c107query.html and http://thomas.loc.gov/home/c108query.html.

39. Robert Peabody, *Leadership in Congress: Stability, Succession and Change* (Boston: Little, Brown, 1976), 5, 8.

40. Garry Wills, *Certain Trumpets: The Call of Leaders* (New York: Simon and Schuster, 1994), 17.

41. House leadership has long been a subject of research. For strategic or institutional leadership in the House, see Cox and McCubbins, *Legislative Leviathan.* Rohde, *Parties and Leaders,* details both institutional and programmatic leadership concerns, and R. Douglas Arnold, *The Logic of Congressional Action* (New Haven, CT: Yale University Press, 1990), explores tactical leadership. I adapt the three-level conception of leadership from military leadership doctrine and apply it to the political challenges of House leadership.

42. Barbara Sinclair, *Unorthodox Lawmaking* (Washington, DC: Congressional Quarterly, 1995), 8.

43. Smith and Deering, *Committees in Congress,* 174–175.

44. Mark Leibovich, "The Convict's Campaign Staff: Jim Traficant May Be in Jail, But Supporters Still Work for His Reelection, *Washington Post,* October 27, 2002. For broader explanations of congressional response to these kinds of issues, see Cox and McCubbins, *Legislative Leviathan;* Peabody, *Leadership in Congress.*

45. Bob Cusack and Klaus Marre, "Vets Fight to Save Rep. Chris Smith from Hastert's Ax," *The Hill,* January 5, 2005.

46. Sinclair, *Unorthodox Lawmaking.*

47. Rohde, *Parties and Leaders,* and Barbara Sinclair, *Majority Leadership in the U.S. House* (Baltimore, MD: Johns Hopkins University Press, 1983), 127–172.

48. Arnold *Logic of Congressional Action,* 108–115.

49. Christopher Deering, "Congress, the President, and Automatic Government: The Case of Military Base Closures," in *Rivals for Power,* ed. James Thurber (Washington, DC: Congressional Quarterly, 1996), 153–169.

50. Keith Krehbiel, *Information and Legislative Organization* (Ann Arbor: University of Michigan Press, 1991).

51. See Krehbiel, *Information and Legislative Organization,* and Richard L. Hall and Bernard Grofman, "The Committee Assignment Process and the Conditional Nature of Committee Bias," *American Political Science Review* 84 (1990): 1149–1166.

52. Krehbiel, *Information and Legislative Organization,* 61.

53. Hall and Grofman, "Committee Assignment," 1163.

54. Roger Davidson and Waller J. Oleszek, *Congress and Its Members,* 9th ed. (Washington, DC: 2004), 221–224.

55. Richard L. Hall and Frank W. Wayman, "Buying Time: Moneyed Interests and the Mobilization of Bias in Congressional Committees," *American Political Science Review* 84 (1990): 797–820.

56. Forrest Maltzman, *Competing Principals: Committees, Parties, and the Organization of Congress* (Ann Arbor: University of Michigan Press, 1997).

57. Walter J. Oleszek, *Congressional Procedures and the Policy Press,* 3rd ed. (Washington, DC: Congressional Quarterly, 1989), 95.

58. Steven Smith, *Call to Order: Floor Politics in the House and Senate* (Washington, DC: Brookings Institution, 1989).

59. Oleszek, *Congressional Procedures,* 114–116.

60. Rules only very rarely fail. With the Rules Committee overwhelmingly in the hands of majority party loyalists, the committee usually produces acceptable rules. Since he took over the House in 1999, Speaker Dennis Hastert (R-IL) has lost only three rules votes (Davidson and Oleszek, *Congress and Its Members,* 246).

61. See Oleszek, *Congressional Procedures,* for an exhaustive description of the House's floor procedure.

62. Oleszek, *Congressional Procedures,* 239–261.

63. See THOMAS Web site for final tally of public laws passed in the 108th Congress, http://thomas.loc.gov/bss/d108/d108laws.html.

64. E.E. Schattschneider, *The Semisovereign People* (Fort Worth, TX: Harcourt Brace Jovanovich, 1988), 135.

65. Price, *Congressional Experience,* 44–45.

66. The states that use a commission for redistricting are Iowa, Maryland, North Carolina, Idaho, Hawaii, Maine, Montana, New Jersey, and Washington. Connecticut and Indiana use a combined commission/legislature method; see Michael P. McDonald, "A Comparative Analysis of Redistricting Institutions in the United States, 2001–02," *State Politics and Policy Quarterly,* 4, no. 4 (Winter 2004): 371–395.

67. In 2002, only four incumbents lost House races. Fred Hiatt, "Time to Draw the Line," *Washington Post,* May 3, 2004.

68. Mike Allen, "House GOP Leaders Name Loyalist to Replace Ethics Chief," *Washington Post,* February 3, 2005.

Chapter 4

1. James Madison, in *The Federalist Papers,* ed. Clinton Rossiter (New York: Mentor Books, 1961), 378.

2. Helen Dewar, "Senate GOP and Democrats Agree on Power-Sharing Deal," *Washington Post,* January 7, 2001.

3. C. Lawrence Evans, *Leadership in Committee: A Comparative Analysis of Leadership Behavior in the U.S. Senate* (Ann Arbor: University of Michigan, 2001).

4. All data reported in Gregory Giroux, "A Touch of Gray on Capitol Hill," *CQ Weekly Report,* January 31, 2005, 240–243. Also reported in tables and graphic form in "109th Congress: Statistically Speaking," *CQ Today,* November 4, 2004, 62.

5. Center for Responsive Politics, *Reelection Rates over the Years,* www.opensecrets.org/bigpicture/reelect.asp?Cycle=2002&chamb=S.

6. Paul Herrnson, *Congressional Elections,* 2nd ed. (Washington, DC: Congressional Quarterly, 1998), 56–57.

7. Betsy Wright Hawkings, ed., *Setting Course: A Congressional Management Guide* (Washington, DC: Congressional Management Foundation, 1996), 177–194.

8. For an early report on McCain's efforts, see Dan Balz, "Analysts Predict No End to Bush-McCain Rivalry; Fight Over Campaign Reform Seen as Just a Round," *Washington Post,* March 29, 2001.

9. Walter Oleszek, *Congressional Procedures and the Policy Process,* 3rd ed. (Washington, DC: Congressional Quarterly, 1989), 90–106.

10. Evans, *Leadership.*

11. Randall Ripley, *Power in the Senate* (New York: St. Martin's Press, 1969), uses *individualistic, decentralized,* and *centralized* power as three potential ways to consider Senate operations.

12. For a detailed study of how the individualistic Senate has become more partisan and how it manages the tension between its tradition of equality and this increased partisanship, see Barbara Sinclair, "The New World of Senators," in *Congress Reconsidered,* 7th ed., ed. Lawrence Dodd and Bruce Oppenheimer (Washington, DC: Congressional Quarterly, 2001), 1–20.

13. David McCullough, *John Adams* (New York: Simon and Schuster, 2001), 389–460.

14. Floyd Riddick, *Riddick's Senate Procedure: Precedents and Practices,* rev. and ed. Alan Frumin. 101st Cong., 2nd sess., 1992. S. Doc. 101–128.

15. Cloture failed on S.J. Res. 40 on July 12, 2004, by a 48–50 vote; U.S. Senate, *Cloture Motion,* 108th Cong., 2nd sess., November 19, 2004, 2, www.senate.gov/reference/resources/pdf/Cloture/c1108–2.pdf. For a detailed explanation of the political benefits of winning by losing, see Deborah Stone, *Policy Paradox: The Art of Political Decision Making,* rev. ed. (New York: W.W. Norton, 2002).

16. Roger Davidson, "The Senate: If Everybody Leads, Who Follows?" in *Congress Reconsidered,* 4th ed., in ed. Lawrence Dodd and Bruce Oppenheimer (Washington, DC: Congressional Quarterly, 1989), 275–306.

17. This is the same bill discussed in Chapter 2. Kathleen Day, "Senate Passes Bill to Restrict Bankruptcy; Credit Card Business Backed Measure to Collect More Debt," *Washington Post,* March 11, 2005.

18. Evans, *Leadership,* 127–154.

19. Shailagh Murray, "Stevens Wages His Best Shot to Open Arctic Refuge," *Washington Post,* March 14, 2005.

20. Senator John McCain rails against pork and other add-ons to bills nearly every time the Senate debates a major spending bill; John McCain, "Statement of Senator John McCain on the Fiscal Year 2005 Omnibus Appropriations Bill," Press Release, 108th Cong., 2nd sess., November 20, 2004. See also Helen Dewar, "Senate Partisanship Worst in Memory; Key Legislation Languishes as Democrats and Republicans Jockey for Power," *Washington Post,* May 2, 2004; Jonathan Weisman, "Voinovich Now Backs Pay-as-You-Go Budget; Amendment Aims to Finance Future Tax Cuts," *Washington Post,* March 15, 2005.

21. Steven Smith, *Call to Order: Floor Politics in the House and Senate* (Washington, DC: Brookings Institution, 1989), 86.

22. Smith, *Call to Order,* 86–129.

23. Smith, *Call to Order,* 113, describes the famous "Metzenbaum Rule."

24. Smith, *Call to Order,* notes that as many as three-quarters of all bills debated by the Senate came to the floor in the six Congresses he studied; see table on p. 114.

25. Evans, *Leadership,* 129.

26. Richard Beth and Stanley Bach, *Filibusters and Cloture in the Senate,* Report for Congress (Washington, DC: Congressional Research Service, 2003), 10.

27. Smith, *Call to Order,* 86–92.

28. Roger Davidson and Walter Oleszek, *Congress and Its Members,* 9th ed. (Washington, DC: Congressional Quarterly, 2004), 256.

29. Davidson and Oleszek, *Congress and Its Members,* 259.

30. Smith, *Call to Order,* 197.

31. Smith, *Call to Order,* 203.

32. Madison, *Federalist* No. 62, in Rossiter, *Federalist Papers,* 376.

33. Helen Dewar, "Senate Approves Chemical Arms Pact After Clinton Pledge," *Washington Post,* April 25, 1997.

34. David Silverberg, "Nasty, Brutish and Short: The CTBT Debate," *The Hill,* December 8, 1999, 16.

35. Davidson and Oleszek, *Congress and Its Members,* 432–435.

36. Committee on Government Reform, U.S. House of Representatives, *Policy and Supporting Positions,* 108th Cong., 2nd sess., 2004, 3.

37. Davidson and Oleszek, *Congress and Its Members,* 357.

38. See Davidson and Oleszek, *Congress and Its Members,* 356–364, for a discussion of judicial nomination battles. For a wrap-up report on the Gonzales nomination, see Charles Babington and Dan Eggen, "Senate Confirms Gonzales, 60 to 36; Vote Reflects Concern Over Detainee Policy," *Washington Post,* February 4, 2005.

39. "Senate Unanimously Confirms Chao as Secretary of Labor," *Washington Post,* January 30, 2001.

40. Dan Balz, "Management of Crisis Reveals Clinton's Style; Quick Action on Baird Limited Political Toll," *Washington Post,* January 23, 1993.

41. Helen Dewar, "Daschle Warns GOP on Judicial Confirmations," *Washington Post,* May 3, 2001.

42. The filibuster fight continued throughout President Bush's first term and into his second term. Senate majority leader Bill Frist (R-TN) threatened to force a rules change in 2005 if the practice did not cease; see Charles Babington, "Senate Work May Come to Halt If GOP Bars Judicial Filibusters," *Washington Post,* March 16, 2005.

43. Figures reported in table in Frances Lee and Bruce Oppenheimer, *Sizing Up the Senate: The Unequal Consequences of Equal Representation* (Chicago: University of Chicago Press, 1999), 162.

44. Lee and Oppenheimer, *Sizing Up the Senate,* 12, also mention that some researchers think that the Constitution requires unanimous approval for any amendment that would modify representation in the Senate.

45. Kevin Merida, "Party of One: In the Middle of the Aisle, Sen. Jim Jeffords Is Both Hero and Outcast," *Washington Post,* June 27, 2001.

Chapter 5

1. *Centinel* No. 1, October 5, 1787, in *The Anti-Federalist Papers and the Constitutional Convention Debates,* ed. Ralph Ketcham (New York: Mentor Books, 1986), 232.

2. Richard Clarke, "Testimony of Richard A. Clarke Before the National Commission on Terrorist Attacks Upon the United States," Transcript, Public Hearing 8, March 24, 2004, www.9–11commission.gov/hearings/hearing8/clarke_statement.pdf.

3. James Anderson, *Public Policymaking,* 4th ed. (New York: Houghton Mifflin, 2000), 272.

4. Frederick Kaiser reviews the origins of the oversight power and court cases recognizing Congress's authority to conduct oversight in *Congressional Oversight, CRS Report for Congress,* 97–936, GOV, Library of Congress, January 2, 2001.

5. Kaiser, *Congressional Oversight,* 3–4.

6. David Rosenbloom, "'Whose Bureaucracy Is This, Anyway?'" Congress' 1946 Answer," *PS: Political Science & Politics,* December 2001, 773–775.

7. John Huber and Charles Shipan, *Deliberate Discretion? The Institutional Foundations of Bureaucratic Autonomy* (Cambridge: Cambridge University Press, 2002), 216–224.

8. Cornelius Kerwin, *Rulemaking* (Washington, DC: Congressional Quarterly, 1994), 250–267.

9. James Q. Wilson, *Bureaucracy: What Government Agencies Do and Why They Do It* (New York: Basic Books, 1989), 279–282.

10. Charles Shipan, *Designing Judicial Review* (Ann Arbor: University of Michigan, 1997).

11. Anderson, *Public Policymaking,* 272.

12. We will consider the budget process in more detail in the next chapter, when we examine the activities of the money committees of Congress. Randall Ripley and Grace Franklin, *Congress, the Bureaucracy, and Public Policy,* 5th ed. (Pacific Grove, CA: Brooks/Cole, 1991), 189–190, argue that the money committees, particularly the Appropriations Committees, also do a great deal of oversight when they examine the budgets of the federal agencies every year.

13. Chapter 7 explores organizational issues in detail, noting that congressional committees frequently study small reorganizations within their jurisdictions. Whenever agency performance does not meet congressional expectations, the question of organization comes up, even if it not always acted upon by the relevant oversight committees.

14. Ripley and Franklin, *Congress, the Bureaucracy, and Public Policy,* 14.

15. Ripley and Franklin, *Congress, the Bureaucracy, and Public Policy,* 14.

16. Ripley and Franklin, *Congress, the Bureaucracy, and Public Policy,* 190.

17. Ripley and Franklin, *Congress, the Bureaucracy, and Public Policy,* 193.

18. Ripley and Franklin, *Congress, the Bureaucracy, and Public Policy,* 192, 195.

19. Ripley and Franklin, *Congress, the Bureaucracy, and Public Policy,* 190; John Johannes, "Individual Outputs: Legislators and Constituency Service," in *Congressional Politics,* ed. Chris Deering (Homewood, IL: Dorsey Press, 1989), 90–110, 102.

20. Ripley and Franklin, *Congress, the Bureaucracy, and Public Policy,* 195.

21. Ripley and Franklin, *Congress, the Bureaucracy, and Public Policy,* 189–193.

22. Morris Fiorina, *Congress: Keystone of the Washington Establishment,* 2nd ed. (New York: Yale University Press, 1989), 40–42.

23. Fiorina, *Congress,* 40–41.

24. For a good review of the theory described here, see James True, Bryan Jones, and Frank Baumgartner, "Punctuated Equilibrium Theory: Explaining Stability and Change in American Policymaking," in *Theories of the Policy Process,* ed. Paul Sabatier (Boulder, CO: Westview Press, 1999), 97–116.

25. Ripley and Franklin, *Congress, the Bureaucracy, and Public Policy,* 196.

26. John Kingdon, *Agendas, Alternatives, and Public Policies* (New York: HarperCollins, 1984), lays out this explanation of the policymaking process, called the "garbage can" model.

27. Fiorina, *Congress,* 40–42.

28. Deborah Stone, *Policy Paradox: The Art of Political Decision Making,* rev. ed. (New York: W.W. Norton, 2002).

29. Anderson, *Public Policymaking,* 272–273.

30. David Kessler, *A Question of Intent: A Great American Battle With a Deadly Industry* (New York: PublicAffairs, 2001), 45–47.

31. Walter J. Oleszek, *Congressional Procedures and the Policy Process,* 3rd ed., (Washington, DC: Congressional Quarterly, 1989), 266.

32. Carl Van Horn, Donald Baumer, and William Gormley, *Politics and Public Policy,* 3rd ed. (Washington, DC: Congressional Quarterly, 2001), 150.

33. Van Horn, et al., *Politics and Public Policy,* 90–91.

34. Oleszek, *Congressional Procedures,* 269–270.

35. Wilson, *Bureaucracy,* 251.

36. Oleszek, *Congressional Procedures,* 272–273.

37. Oleszek, *Congressional Procedures,* 266.

38. Louis Fisher, *The Politics of Shared Power,* 4th ed. (College Station: Texas A&M University, 1998), 73–74.

39. Subcommittee on Health, Committee on Veterans' Affairs, House of Representatives, "Cleanliness and Management Practices at the Kansas City VAMC," Field Hearing, Kansas City, MO, June 17, 2002, Serial No. 107–34, 107th Cong., 2nd sess.

40. Oleszek, *Congressional Procedures,* 268.

41. Article I, Section 7, Clause 9 of the Constitution requires all money spent by the federal government to be *appropriated* by Congress first; the rules of the House and Senate specify a separate first step, in which the oversight committee must first pass a bill *authorizing* the expenditure.

42. Committee on Transportation and Infrastructure, House of Representatives, "House Approves One Month Extension For Federal Highway & Transit Funding; 42 Provisions Approved By House-Senate Conference Committee," Press Release, House of Representatives, June 23, 2004; see also "House Approves Extension For Federal Highway & Transit Funding," Press Release, July 23, 2004.

43. Committee on Armed Services, House of Representatives, "House Approves Fiscal Year 2005 National Defense Authorization Act: Includes More than $2 Billion for Protecting Our Troops; Supports Military Personnel and Their Families; Increases Survivor Benefit Plan Payments by Eliminating the 'Widow's Tax,'" Press Release, May 20, 2004.

44. Wilson, *Bureaucracy,* 244, notes the example of 1986, at the height of the Reagan defense buildup, when the bill took thirteen days to clear the House and faced 148 floor amendments. This trend has been controlled in recent years; for instance, the House considered HR 1588, the Fiscal 2004 Defense Authorization Act, for two days and allowed thirteen amendments; the Senate allowed a further six on its version, which it debated for one day. See legislative history of HR 1588, http://thomas.loc.gov/cgi-bin/bdquery/z?d108:h.r.01588.

45. Anderson, *Public Policymaking,* 272.

46. Olezsek, *Congressional Procedures,* 269, 270.

47. Wilson, *Bureaucracy,* 244.

48. Oleszek, *Congressional Procedures,* 273–274.

49. Helen Dewar, "Senate Democrats Block 3 More Bush Judicial Nominees," *Washington Post,* July 23, 2004.

50. Michael Oreskes, "Senate Rejects Tower, 53–47; First Cabinet Veto Since '59; Bush Confers on New Choice," *New York Times,* March 10, 1989; Ed Magnuson, Michael Duffy, and Hays Gorey, "Collapse of a Confirmation," *Time,* March 6, 1989, 24–25; Pat Towell, "Senate Spurns Bush's Choice in a Partisan Tug of War," *Congressional Quarterly Weekly Report,* March 11, 1989, 530–534; "Bush, Cheney Meet the Press: Discuss Views, Concerns," *Congressional Quarterly Weekly Report,* March 18, 1989, 610–612.

51. The decision, *Immigration and Naturalization Service v. Chadha,* 103 Sup. Ct. 2764 (1983), found that previous uses of the legislative veto violated the Constitution because the veto methods did not allow both full chambers to vote on the legislative veto. As a result, now the vetoes are designed as joint resolutions, which meet this test. See Wilson, *Bureaucracy,* 243; Oleszek, *Congressional Procedures,* 266–268.

52. Van Horn, et al., *Politics and Public Policy,* 112–113.

53. GAO, *Executive Guide: Effectively Implementing the Government Performance and Results Act,* GAO/GGD-96–118ds (Washington, DC: GAO, 2001); see also GAO,

Results-Oriented Government: GPRA Has Established a Solid Foundation for Achieving Greater Results (Washington, DC: GAO-04–38, GAO, 2004).

54. Jeffrey Trandahl, *Rules of the House of Representatives, 108th Congress,* Clerk of the House of Representatives (Washington, DC: House of Representatives, 2003), 7; Committee on Governmental Affairs, U.S. Senate, *Standing Rules of the Senate* (Washington, DC: U.S. Senate, 2003), 31.

55. *History of the Senate Governmental Affairs Committee,* http://hsgac.senate.gov/index.cfm?Fuseaction=About.History.

56. Van Horn, et al., *Politics and Public Policy,* 129. See also Anderson, *Public Policymaking,* 273–275.

57. "History of the CRS," www.loc.gov/crsinfo/whatscrs.html#hismiss.

58. GAO Human Capital Reform Act of 2004, Public Law 108–271, 108th Cong., 2nd sess., 2004.

59. Anderson, *Public Policymaking,* 273–275.

60. "GAO at a Glance" summary statistics for fiscal 2003, www.gao.gov/about/gglance.html.

61. The CBO's mission statement and history are described on the CBO Web site, www.cbo.gov/Mission.cfm, accessed 9 March 2005.

62. "Technology Assessment and the Work of Congress," available on *The OTA Legacy,* a Web site of official OTA records maintained by the Woodrow Wilson School of Public and international affairs, Princeton University, www.wws.princeton.edu/~ota/ns20/cong_f.html.

63. Anderson, *Public Policymaking,* 275; Ripley and Franklin, *Congress, the Bureaucracy, and Public Politics,* 191. Each chamber does have a few permanent select committees, particularly the intelligence committees, but they are exceptions, carefully defined in the House and Senate rules assigning committee jurisdiction.

64. See the Cox Committee's findings, Select Committee on U.S. National Security and Military/Commercial Concerns with the People's Republic of China, House of Representatives, *Report of the House of Representatives Select Committee on U.S. National Security and Military/Commercial Concerns with the People's Republic of China,* 1999. For a critical assessment of the report, see Anjal Bhattacharjee, *Politics and Proliferation: Analysis and Summary of the Cox Committee Report and the Allegations of Chinese Nuclear Espionage* (Washington, DC: British American Security Information Committee, 1999).

65. National Missile Defense Act of 1999, Public Law 105–39, 106th Cong., 1st sess., 1999; Commission to Assess the Ballistic Missile Threat to the United States, *Report of the Commission to Assess the Ballistic Missile Threat to the United States* (Washington: DC: Government Printing Office, 1998).

66. Commission on National Security/21st Century, *New World Coming: American Security in the 21st Century,* Phase I Report (Washington, DC: Government Printing Office, 1999); *Seeking a National Strategy: A Concert for Preserving Security and Promoting Freedom,* Phase II Report (Washington, DC: Government Printing Office, 2000); and *Roadmap for National Security: Imperative for Change,* Phase III Report (Washington, DC: Government Printing Office, 2001). We will examine the recommendations of this commission in more detail in chapters 6 and 7.

67. National Commission on Terrorist Attacks Upon the United States, *Report of the National Commission on Terrorist Attacks Upon the United States* (Washington, DC: Government Printing Office, 2004); Senate Select Committee on Intelligence and House Permanent Select Committee on Intelligence, *Joint Inquiry into Intelli-*

gence Community Activities Before and After the Terrorist Attacks of September 11, 2001, 107th Cong., 2nd sess., 2002. S. Rept. 107–351 and H. Rept. 107–792. In late fall 2004, Congress passed a bill to create a national director for intelligence, broadly in line with the commission's proposals.

68. Matthew McCubbins and Thomas Schwartz, "Congressional Oversight Overlooked: Police Patrols Versus Fire Alarms," *American Journal of Political Science* 28, no. 1 (February 1984): 165–179; see also Oleszek, *Congressional Procedures,* 277, who uses the idea of fire alarms and police patrols in his assessment of oversight, as well.

69. Oleszek, *Congressional Procedures,* 278–283.

70. Ripley and Franklin, *Congress, the Bureaucracy,* 199.

71. Geoff Earle, "Dems Did Oversight Better, Says Grassley; Lawmakers Lament Lack of Scrutiny," *The Hill,* May 13, 2004, www.hillnews.com/news/051304/oversight.aspx, accessed May 13, 2004; Carl Hulse, "Congressional Memo: Even Some in G.O.P. Call for More Oversight of Bush," *New York Times,* May 31, 2004.

72. William Gormley and Steven Balla, *Bureaucracy and Democracy: Accountability and Performance* (Washington, DC: Congressional Quarterly, 2004), 69.

73. Dan Eggen and Walter Pincus, "Rice Defends Pre-9/11 Anti-Terrorism Efforts; U.S. 'Was Not on War Footing,' She Says," *Washington Post,* April 9, 2004.

Chapter 6

1. Philip Kurland and Ralph Lerner, ed., *The Founders' Constitution,* Vol. 2, Document 15 (Chicago: University of Chicago Press, 1986). Excerpted from ed. Jonathan Elliot, *The Debates in the Several State Conventions on the Adoption of the Federal Constitution as Recommended by the General Convention at Philadelphia in 1787,* 5 vols. 2nd ed., 1888, ed. Reprint (New York: Burt Franklin, n.d.), http://press-pubs.uchicago.edu/founders/documents/a1_8_1s15.html.

2. David Maraniss and Michael Weisskopf, *"Tell Newt to Shut Up!" Prizewinning* Washington Post *Journalists Reveal How Reality Gagged the Gingrich Revolution* (New York: Simon and Schuster Touchstone Books, 1996), 146–177.

3. Aaron Wildavsky, *The New Politics of the Budgetary Process* (Upper Saddle River, NJ: Scott, Foresman, 1988), 1–12.

4. Article I, Section 9, Clause 7: "No money shall be drawn from the treasury, but in consequence of appropriations made by law; and a regular statement and account of receipts and expenditures of all public money shall be published from time to time."

5. Lewis Deschler, *Deschler's Precedents, Including References to Provisions of the Constitution and Laws, and to Decisions of the Courts,* chapter 17, "Committees," section 31: Committee on Appropriations, 94th Cong., 2nd sess., 1976, H. Doc. 94–661, 2799–2821.

6. In February 2005, the House Appropriations Committee announced a reorganization, from thirteen subcommittees to ten, but the Senate chose to reorganize into twelve subcommittees, making House and Senate appropriations work different from each other; this is explained in more detail below, p. 219.

7. Deschler, *Deschler's Precedents,* chapter 17, "Committees," section 32: Committee on Armed Services, 2821–2834.

8. Richard Parker offers a readable, nontechnical explanation of economic policy recommendations in the twentieth century in his *John Kenneth Galbraith: His Life, His Politics, His Economics* (New York: Farrar Strauss and Giroux, 2005).

9. David A. Stockman, *The Triumph of Politics* (New York: Harper and Row, 1986).

10. John M. Berry, "Budget Success Depends on Economy; White House Betting Against Recession and on Lower Oil Prices," *Washington Post,* October 2, 1990.

11. For specific impact of the Iraq and Afghanistan operations, see Congressional Budget Office, "Estimated Costs of Continuing Operations in Iraq and Other Operations of the Global War on Terrorism," Letter to the Honorable Kent Conrad, U.S. Senator, June 25, 2004, www.cbo.gov/iraq.cfm.

12. Office of Management and Budget, White House, Historical Tables, *Budget of the United States Government, Fiscal Year 2006* (Washington, DC: Government Printing Office, 2005). Figure 6.1 draws on Table 7.1, "Federal Debt at the End of the Fiscal Year: 1940–2010," 118–119, and Figure 6.2 draws on Table 1.4, "Receipts, Outlays, and Surpluses or Deficits (–) by Fund Group: 1934–2010," 27–28.

13. House Budget Committee, "The Federal Government Dollar, Fiscal Year 2004," www.house.gov/budget/spendingpie.pdf.

14. Office of Management and Budget, Summary Tables, *Budget of the United States Government,* 360.

15. Percentages reported in House Budget Committee, "Federal Government Dollar, 2004." Budget dollar figures reported by Senate Budget Committee, *President Bush's 2006 Budget: A Brief Overview,* February 7, 2005, Table 2, 10.

16. Wildavsky, *New Politics,* 268–273. Wildavsky also notes elsewhere, however, that some entitlements stay stable over time, some rise, and some shrink (see his "Politics of the Entitlement Process," in *The New Politics of Public Policy,* ed. Marc Landy and Martin Levin [Baltimore, MD: Johns Hopkins University Press, 1995], 143–179). As he notes in *New Politics of the Budgetary Process,* 268, it is difficult to say much that covers all entitlements, since they are products of political or historical evolution.

17. Wildavsky, *New Politics,* 273–274; 346–347. Theda Skocpol's *The Missing Middle: Working Families and the Future of American Social Policy* (New York: W.W. Norton, 2000) describes the politics of entitlements and the decline of support in Washington for new programs.

18. Since its inception, major changes to the Social Security program are fraught with danger for politicians who support them. When President George W. Bush announced his goal of partially privatizing the program during his State of the Union message in January 2005, he faced a storm of protest from Hill Democrats and tepid support from his own party supporters in Congress. See Jim VandeHei and Mike Allen, "Bush Shops Social Security Plan; Seeking Support, President Visits States of Vulnerable Democratic Senators," *Washington Post,* February 4, 2005; see also Joseph Curl and Amy Fagan, "Social Security Details Left to Congress," *Washington Times,* February 4, 2005; and Jeffrey H. Birnbaum and Ben White, "Social Security Tactics Escalate: Unions, Business Groups Seek to Influence Debate," *Washington Post,* February 23, 2005.

19. See the section on the House Appropriations Committee, below, for an extended discussion of a reorganization of the committee into ten subcommittees, from the thirteen that have been in use for decades.

20. House Budget Committee, "Basics of the Budget Process," www.house.gov/budget/budgcalendar.pdf.

21. Walter Oleszek, *Congressional Procedures and the Policy Process,* 3rd ed., (Washington, DC: Congressional Quarterly, 1989), 74–75.

22. Versions of the bankruptcy bill have been introduced since 1997 without passing both chambers; the House has passed its version in each Congress, but the bill has failed to pass in the Senate in every Congress. In 1998 (HR 833/S 3186), 2000 (S 420/ HR 333), and 2002 (S 1920/HR 975), the Senate agreed to consider the bill but failed to pass it before adjourning to campaign, and in February 2004, the Senate refused to go to conference on the bill (HR 685/S 256). See THOMAS Web site for details, http://thomas.loc.gov/home/search.html. For an opinion of the bill and its prospects, see "Morally Bankrupt," *The New Republic Online,* February 25, 2005, www.tnr.com/doc.mhtml?i=20050307&s=editoria1030705.

23. James Anderson, *Public Policymaking: An Introduction,* 4th ed. (Boston: Houghton Mifflin, 2000), 174–175. For a broader discussion of incrementalism in American politics, see Martin Shapiro, "Of Interests and Values: The New Politics and the New Political Science," in *The New Politics of Public Policy,* ed. Marc Landy and Martin Levin (Baltimore, MD: Johns Hopkins Press University, 1994), 12.

24. For an excellent overview of JCT responsibilities, see Joint Committee on Taxation, *Background Information Relating to the Joint Committee on Taxation,* JCX-2–05, 2005.

25. This process is called the "crosswalk" and is described in Oleszek, *Congressional Procedures,* 62–63.

26. Although current law requires the House and Senate to agree to a budget resolution, in 2004 the two Budget Committees could not reach an agreement, and no resolution for fiscal 2005 was ever passed; the two chambers resolved their budget differences during the completion of the appropriations bills. This failure to pass the resolution earned GOP leaders in Congress a stinging rebuke from the *Washington Times* editorial board, "Watching the U.S. Wallet," November 17, 2004.

27. Anderson, *Public Policymaking,* 182.

28. See Wildavsky, *New Politics,* 210–211 for a discussion of the difference in enforcement mechanisms between the House and Senate.

29. In a six-year period (1999–2004), Congress has only managed to pass all thirteen appropriations bills once, in 2001 (for FY 2002), and it required eight continuing resolutions after the fiscal year started before it could pass all the bills. In 1999, Congress passed five of the FY 2000 bills, but had to combine the rest into a year-ending omnibus appropriations bill. In 2000, Congress passed ten of its FY 2001 bills, but required twenty-one CRs before it could combine the remaining three into a final omnibus bill. In 2002, Congress passed only two of the FY 2003 bills before resorting to twelve CRs in order to combine the remaining eleven bills into an omnibus. In 2003, Congress passed six of the thirteen bills for FY 2004 before using seven CRs to finish an omnibus bill. And in 2004, Congress approved four of the FY 2005 bills before requiring three CRs to complete a final omnibus. Final year-end appropriations status is available at the THOMAS Web site, http://thomas.loc.gov/home/approp/app05.html and http://thomas.loc.gov/home/approp/approplink.html.

30. Committee on Appropriations, "Chairman Cochran Announces New Structure for Senate Appropriations Committee," Press Release, U.S. Senate, March 2, 2005.

31. Oleszek, *Congressional Procedures,* 54–55.

32. Oleszek, *Congressional Procedures,* 51.

33. The HAC announced its organizational changes for the 109th Congress in a press release, "Chairman Lewis Announces Major Reorganization of the House Appropriations Committee and Slate of Subcommittee Chairmen," U.S. House of Representatives, February 9, 2005.

34. Susan Milligan of the *Boston Globe* investigated trends in Congress in a series of special reports in October 2004. She found that GOP leaders and committee chairs had attached 3,407 of these pork barrel projects in conference committee hearings on FY 2005 appropriations bills passed in 2004. In contrast, she noted that the last Democratically controlled (103rd) Congress had approved forty-seven pork programs in conference committee in 1994. Susan Milligan, "Back-room Dealing a Capitol Trend; GOP Flexing Its Majority Power," *Boston Globe,* October 3, 2004.

35. See Wildavsky, *New Politics,* 397–406, for a discussion of budget norms and, in his analysis, their complete collapse after 1960.

36. CBO's budget outlook in February 2001 predicted that the government would be able to pay off all federal debt by 2006 (CBO, *Budget Options* [Washington, DC: Government Printing Office, 2001], 13). By August 2001, the CBO's revised figures indicated a small deficit for the year, with pay-off year moved out to 2010 (CBO, *The Budget and Economic Outlook: An Update* [Washington, DC: Government Printing Office, 2001], ix). By January 2002, however, CBO predicted that the federal budget would produce deficits until 2010 (CBO, *The Budget and Economic Outlook: Fiscal Years 2003–2012* [Washington, DC: Government Printing Office, 2002], xiii-xiv).

37. For exact deficit figures by year, see CBO, Summary Table 1: CBO's Baseline Budget Outlook, *The Budget and Economic Outlook: An Update* (Washington, DC: Government Printing Office, September 2004), x.

38. Both House and Senate leasers ignored authorization and budget limits in the rush to complete the FY 2005 legislation in time for the 2004 election cycle. See Dan Morgan and Helen Dewar, "Hill Spending Limits Tested; Bills for Domestic Programs and Disaster Relief Get Support," *Washington Post,* September 15, 2004.

39. This does not always work. A civilian army official was fired in 2002 for trying to drum up congressional support for the Crusader artillery system, canceled in May 2002 by Secretary of Defense Donald Rumsfeld. Despite the army's effort to rally supporters on the Hill, both the House and Senate eventually supported the Pentagon decision to kill the weapons program. Ellen Nakashima, "Crusader Claims an Army Official; Liaison Staffer Resigns as Report Finds He Faxed Weapon's 'Talking Points' to Hill," *Washington Post,* May 11, 2002.

40. Roger Davidson and Walter Oleszek, *Congress and Its Members,* 9th ed., (Washington, DC: Congressional Quarterly, 2004), 401–404.

41. Maraniss and Weisskopf, *"Tell Newt to Shut Up!"* 203–206.

Chapter 7

1. Melancton Smith, speech to the New York ratifying convention, June 25, 1788, in *The Anti-Federalist Papers and the Constitutional Convention Debates,* ed. Ralph Ketcham (New York: Mentor Books, 1986), 353.

2. U.S. Special Operations Command, *Special Operations Forces Posture Statement* (Washington, DC: Government Printing Office, 2003), 8.

3. Jack Knott and Gary Miller make this case in their book, *Reforming Bureaucracy: The Politics of Institutional Choice* (Englewood Cliffs, NJ: Prentice-Hall, 1987).

4. Richard Stillman, *Preface to Public Administration: A Search for Themes and Direction* (New York: St. Martin's Press, 1991), 219–220; see also James Q. Wilson, *Bureaucracy: What Government Agencies Do and How They Do it* (New York: Basic Books, 1989), 377–378.

5. Knott and Miller, *Reforming Bureaucracy,* 10.

6. Stephen Skowronek, *Building a New American State: The Expansion of Na-*

tional Administrative Capacities, 1877–1920 (Cambridge: Cambridge University Press, 1982), 16, 45–46.

7. Skowronek, *Building a New American State,* 16.

8. Charles Lindblom, "The Science of 'Muddling Through,'" *Public Administration Review* 19, no. 2 (1959): 79–88.

9. Stillman, *Preface,* chapter 1.

10. Knott and Miller, *Reforming Bureaucracy,* 34.

11. See Skowronek, *Building a New American State,* for a description of the partisan nature of federal executive officeholders.

12. Stillman, *Preface,* 57–58.

13. Stillman *Preface,* 45–72, 84–102.

14. Knott and Miller, *Reforming Bureaucracy.*

15. Knott and Miller, *Reforming Bureaucracy,* 75–93.

16. Pauly Hammond, *Organizing for Defense: The American Military Establishment in the Twentieth Century* (Princeton, NY: Princeton University, 1961).

17. U.S. Environmental Protection Agency, *The Guardian: Origins of the EPA,* EPA Historical Publication 1, Spring 1992, www.epa.gov/history/publications/print/origins.htm.

18. Terrence Fehner and Jack Holl, *Department of Energy, 1977–1994: A Summary History,* U.S. Department of Energy History Series, 1994, http://ma.mbe.doe.gov/me70/history/Summary_History.pdf.

19. U.S. Department of Education, *Overview: The Federal Role in Education,* 2004, available at www.ed.gov/about/overview/fed/role.html?src=sm.

20. Skowronek, *Building a New American State,* 19–36; Knott and Miller, *Reforming Bureaucracy,* 15–32.

21. Skowronek, *Building a New American State,* 37–84.

22. Knott and Miller, *Reforming Bureaucracy,* 34.

23. Knott and Miller, *Reforming Bureaucracy,* 34–35.

24. Knott and Miller, *Reforming Bureaucracy,* 35–36.

25. Knott and Miller, *Reforming Bureaucracy,* 36–37.

26. Knott and Miller, *Reforming Bureaucracy,* 37–38.

27. Knott and Miller, *Reforming Bureaucracy,* 38.

28. Knott and Miller, *Reforming Bureaucracy,* 39.

29. Knott and Miller, *Reforming Bureaucracy,* 41.

30. Knott and Miller, *Reforming Bureaucracy,* 41–42.

31. Knott and Miller, *Reforming Bureaucracy,* 42.

32. Knott and Miller, *Reforming Bureaucracy,* 42.

33. Knott and Miller, *Reforming Bureaucracy,* 77–100.

34. Stillman, *Preface,* 42–74, 104–140.

35. David Osborne and Ted Gaebler, *Reinventing Government* (New York: Plume, 1993). Ronald Moe adds that a number of scholars interested in public administration question the legitimacy of market measures for government operations in his *Administrative Renewal: Reorganization Commissions in the 20th Century* (Lanham, MD: University Press of America, 2003), 21–24.

36. David Rosenbloom, *Building a Legislative-Centered Public Administration* (Tuscaloosa: University of Alabama Press, 2000), 23–59, suggests that the Administrative Procedures Act was a mechanism for Congress to turn the agencies into extensions of the legislature.

37. See, for example, "Futures Initiative," a comprehensive internal review by the Centers for Disease Control to restructure its offices in order to prepare for emerging public health issues; U.S. Centers for Disease Control, "CDC Announces New Goals

204 NOTES TO PAGES 146–153

and Organizational Design," Press Release, May 13, 2004, www.cdc.gov/od/oc/media/
pressrel/r040513.htm.

38. Moe, *Administrative Renewal,* 114–117.

39. Office of the US Trade Representative, *History of the United States Trade
Representative,* www.ustr.gov/Who_We_Are/History_of_the_United_States_
Trade_Representative.html.

40. Bruce James, Public Printer of the United States, "The Transformation of the
U.S. Government Printing Office to Meet the Demands of the 21st Century," prepared
statement before the Committee on Administration, U.S. House of Representatives,
April 28, 2004, www.gpoaccess.gov/cr/testimony/oversight.pdf.

41. Foreign Affairs Reform and Restructuring Act of 1998 (included as part of the
Omnibus Appropriations bill FY99), 105th Cong., 2nd sess., 1998, Public Law 105–277.

42. National Commission on the Public Service, *Urgent Business for America: Revi-
talizing the Federal Government* (Washington, DC: Government Printing Office, 2003).

43. Committee on Governmental Affairs, U.S. Senate, "Reorganizing America's
Intelligence Community: A View from the Inside," hearing, July 16, 2004.

44. Senate Select Committee to Study Governmental Operations With Respect to
Intelligence Activities, *Final Report of the Select Committee to Study Governmental
Operations With Respect to Intelligence Activities,* S. Rep. 94–755 (Washington, DC:
Government Printing Office, 1976), 471.

45. Moe, *Administrative Renewal,* 58–74.

46. Moe, *Administrative Renewal,* 75–84. See also Department of Defense Reorganization Act of 1958, 85th Cong., 2nd sess, 1958, Public Law 85–599.

47. Commission to Assess United States National Security Space Management
and Organization, *Report of the Commission to Assess United States National Secu-
rity Space Management and Organization* (Washington, DC: Government Printing
Office, 2001). See also Department of Defense, "Secretary Rumsfeld Announces Major
National Security Space Management and Organizational Initiative," Press Release
No. 201–01, Department of Defense, May 8, 2001.

48. After the failure of his White House bid, Smith returned to the GOP fold, but
he was opposed in his 2002 reelection campaign by John Sununu, whose candidacy
earned the support of Senate GOP leaders. Sununu won the primary, ending Smith's
congressional career. CNN AllPolitics, "Reno Trails McBride; Sununu Beats Smith,"
September 10, 2002, www.cnn.com/2002/ALLPOLITICS/09/10/primary.wrap/.

49. John Kingdon, *Agendas, Alternatives, and Public Policies* (New York:
HarperCollins, 1984), 122–151.

50. Skowronek, *Building a New American State,* explains the challenge facing
reformers and recognizes that incrementalism is usually the preferred first step in any
reform effort. He calls these first steps at major reform "patchwork."

51. Wilson, *Bureaucracy,* 235–236.

52. Deborah Barfield Berry, "House OKs Security Panel," New York *Newsday,*
January 5, 2005.

53. Skowronek, *Building a New American State,* argues that the major reform takes
place in a second wave of reorganization, which he calls "reconstitution." After a
series of patchwork reforms sets the stage for a major reform, Skowronek argues,
Congress and internal reformers within the agency gain sufficient leverage to shift to
a new structure that can sweep away the old way of doing things and replace it with a
new system, designed to meet Congress's intent for the agency.

54. Nuclear Regulatory Commission, *Our Organization,* www.nrc.gov/who-we-
are/organization.html.

55. U.S. Central Command, *The Global War on Terrorism: The First 100 Days* (Baghdad, Iraq: Coalition Information Center, 2001), 11–12. See also Barton Gellman and Dafna Linzer, "Afghanistan, Iraq: Two Wars Collide," *Washington Post,* October 22, 2004.

Chapter 8

1. "Brutus," number XI, January 31, 1788. Excerpted in *The Anti-Federalist Papers and the Constitutional Convention Debates,* ed. Ralph Ketcham (New York: Mentor Books, 1986), 296.

2. White House, *A National Security Strategy of Engagement and Enlargement* (Washington, DC: Government Printing Office), 1996.

3. Commission on National Security in the 21st Century, *New World Coming: American Security in the 21st Century.* (Washington, DC: Government Printing Office, 1999).

4. U.S. Commission on National Security/21 Century, *Seeking a National Strategy: A Concert for Preserving Security and Promoting Freedom* (Washington, DC: Government Printing Office, 2000).

5. U.S. Commission on National Security/21 Century, *Road Map for National Security: Imperative for Change* (Washington, DC: Government Printing Office, 2001).

6. White House, *National Strategy for Homeland Security* (Washington, DC: Government Printing Office, 2002), 2.

7. For an example of the challenges facing the NSC and other federal agencies, see David A. Vise and Dan Eggen, "FBI Warns of Cyber-Attack Threat; U.S. 'Very Concerned' About Vulnerability of Infrastructure," *Washington Post,* March 21, 2001.

8. One example of an interagency working group is the Federal Interagency Working Group on Brownfields, which brings together officials from seventeen federal agencies to deal with redevelopment issues on lands that were formerly toxic waste sites. See Environmental Protection Agency, *Federal Interagency Working Group on Brownfields—Fact Sheet,* www.epa.gov/cgi-bin/epaprintonly.cgi.

9. Sherry Sontag, Christopher Drew, and Annette Lawrence Drew, *Blind Man's Bluff: The Untold Story of American Submarine Espionage* (New York: PublicAffairs, 1998).

10. Some of the challenges confronting the CIA in the region are detailed in National Commission on Terrorist Attacks Upon the United States, *Intelligence Policy: Staff Statement No. 7* and *The Performance of the Intelligence Community: Staff Statement No. 11,* www.9–11commission.gov/staff_statements/index.htm. For further reports on intelligence issues in the region, see Walter Pincus, "An Intelligence Gap Hinders U.S. in Iraq," *Washington Post,* December 24, 2004; Josh White and Barton Gellman, "Defense Espionage Unit to Work With CIA," *Washington Post,* January 25, 2005; Anthony H. Cordesman, with the assistance of Patrick Baetjer and Stephen Lanier, *Strengthening Iraqi Military and Security Forces,* Working Draft update. (Washington, DC: Center for Strategic and International Studies, February 17, 2005).

11. National Commission on Terrorist Attacks Upon the United States, *The 9/11 Commission Report* (Washington, DC: Government Printing Office, 2004), 407–418.

12. National Commission on Terrorist Attacks Upon the United States, *9/11 Commission Report,* 418–419; see also Drew Ladner and Daniel B. Prieto, "Technology Upgrade Urgency," *Washington Times,* February 6, 2005; Dan Eggen, "Computer Woes Hinder FBI's Work, Report Says; Mueller Disputes Watchdog's Findings,"

Washington Post, February 4, 2005; "FBI Accountability," *Washington Post,* January 24, 2005.

13. Christopher Cavas, "Pace Urges Homeland Security Council," *Defense News,* September 13, 2004, 36; Jim Garamone, "Discussion Needed to Change Interagency Process, Pace Says," American Forces Press Service press release, September 17, 2005, www.dod.gov/news/Sep2004/n09172004_2004091704.html.

14. White House, Executive Order Establishing the Office of Homeland Security and the Homeland Security Council, Office of the Press Secretary, October 8, 2001.

15. Donald Kettl, *The Department of Homeland Security's First Year: A Report Card* (New York: Century Foundation, 2004), 20–21.

16. Eric Pianin and Bradley Graham, "Ridge: Goal Isn't to Create Bureaucracy; Head of Homeland Office Says Role Is to Coordinate Agencies, Streamline Security," *Washington Post,* October 4, 2001.

17. August Gribbin, "Anti-terrorism Agency Faces Turf Wars, Critics Say," *Washington Times,* November 25, 2001.

18. Mike Allen and Bill Miller, "Bush Seeks Security Department: Cabinet-Level Agency Would Coordinate Anti-Terrorism Effort," *Washington Post,* June 7, 2002.

19. Amy Schatz, "Homeland Security Bill Was Bush's Political Juggernaut," Cox News Service, November 22, 2002.

20. Aviation and Transportation Security Act, 107th Cong., 1st sess., 2001. Public Law 107–71.

21. Nicole Duran, "Select Homeland Security Committee Faces Hurdles," *Roll Call,* May 5, 2003.

22. Committee on Homeland Security, U.S. House of Representatives, *Calendar,* http://hsc.house.gov/schedule.cfm?get_archive=yes#.

23. See, for example, Secretary Ridge's testimony concerning the FY 2005 budget request, Committee on Homeland Security and Governmental Affairs, *Statement of Secretary Tom Ridge before the United States Senate Committee on Governmental Affairs, February 9, 2004,* U.S. Senate, 2004.

24. Christopher Lee and David Von Drehle, "Homeland Defense Funding Blasted; White House Accused of Shortchanging Effort," *Washington Post,* December 19, 2002.

25. Senator Charles Schumer, *Three Years Later: Is the Federal Government Doing Enough to Protect New York?* (Washington, DC: U.S. Senate, 2004), 14.

26. Mike Allen and John Mintz, "Homeland Department May Take a Year to Take Shape; Bush to Nominate Ridge as Secretary; Nightmares Seen in Blending 22 Agencies' Cultures and Workforces," *Washington Post,* November 21, 2002; John Mintz and Mike Allen, "Ridge Leaving Cabinet; Homeland Security Changes Predicted," *Washington Post,* December 1, 2004.

27. Stephen Dinan, "Byrd Presses Senate for Caution in Debate on Homeland Agency," *Washington Times,* July 31, 2002.

28. Stephen Skowronek, *Building a New American State: The Expansion of National Administrative Capacities, 1877–1920* (Cambridge: Cambridge University Press, 1982).

29. Tom Teepen, "Commentary: Homeland Security or Homeland Politics?" Cox News Service, November 21, 2002.

30. Walter Pincus, Juliet Eilperin, and Bill Miller, "Details of Homeland Plan Assailed; House Panels Vote to Block Transfers of Some Agencies," *Washington Post,* July 11, 2002.

31. Library of Congress, *HR 5005, An Act to Establish the Department of Home-*

land Security, and for Other Purposes, Legislative History, 107th Congress, http://thomas.loc.gov/cgi-bin/bdquery/z?d107:HR05005:@@@X.

32. Many of these concerns are summarized IN Government Accountability Office, *Status of Key Recommendations GAO Has Made to DHS and Its Legacy Agencies,* GAO-04–865R, 2004.

33. David M. Walker, *9/11 Commission Report: Reorganization, Transformation, and Information Sharing,* Statement of the Honorable David M. Walker, Comptroller General of the United States; Testimony Before the Committee on Government Reform, House of Representatives, Government Accountability Office, 2004.

34. Government Accountability Office, *Financial Management: Department of Homeland Security Faces Significant Financial Management Challenges,* GAO-04–774, 2004. See also House Select Committee on Homeland Security, *An Analysis of First Responder Grant Funding,* Staff Report, 2004.

35. Committee on Appropriations, U.S. House of Representatives, "Chairman Young Announces Homeland Security Reorganization," Press Release, January 29, 2003.

36. Committee on Appropriations, U.S. Senate, "Appropriations Committee Sets Subcommittee Assignments," Press Release, March 4, 2003. The Senate established a new subcommittee for homeland security issues by merging its Transportation and Treasury/General Government Subcommittees.

37. Office of Management and Budget, *Budget of the United States, Fiscal Year 2006, Summary Tables,* Table S-2 (Washington, DC: Government Printing Office, 2005), 244.

38. Veronique de Rugy, *What Does Homeland Security Spending Buy?* AEI Working Paper #107 (Washington, DC: American Enterprise Institute, 2004). See also Lee and Von Drehle, "Homeland Defense Funding Blasted."

39. "Work in Progress," *Washington Post,* April 11, 2004.

40. Committee on Homeland Security and Governmental Affairs, "Senator Collins Re-elected as Chairman of Senate Homeland Security and Governmental Affairs Committee," Press Release, U.S. Senate, January 5, 2005.

41. National Commission on Terrorist Attacks, *9/11 Commission Report;* Intelligence Reform and Terrorism Prevention Act of 2004, 108th Cong., 2nd sess., 2004. Public Law 108–458. ˙

42. Office of the Press Secretary, White House, "President to Propose Department of Homeland Security," Press Release, June 6, 2002.

43. Paul Y. Hammond, *Organizing for Defense: The American Military Establishment in the Twentieth Century* (Princeton, NJ: Princeton University Press, 1961).

44. Russell Weigley, *The American Way of War: A History of United States Military Strategy and Policy* (Bloomington, IN: Indiana University Press, 1977), 366.

45. Hammond, *Organizing for Defense,* 107–185.

46. National Security Act of 1947, Public Law 80–253, 1947, and Committee on Armed Services, House of Representatives, *Conference Report,* H. Rep. 1051, 80th Cong., 1st sess., 1947.

47. National Security Amendments of 1949, Public Law 81–216, 1949, and Committee on Armed Services, House of Representatives, *Conference Report,* H. Rep. 1142, 81st Cong., 1st sess., 1949.

48. Committee on Government Operations, House of Representatives, 83rd Cong., 1st sess., 1953. H. Rep. 633; Committee on Government Operations, House of Representatives, *Message From the President of the United States Transmit-*

ting Reorganization Plan No. 6 of 1953, Defense Department, 83rd Cong., 1st sess., 1953. H. Doc. 136.

49. Department of Defense Reorganization Act of 1958, Public Law 85–599, 1958, and Committee on Armed Services, House of Representatives, *Conference Report,* 85th Cong., 2nd sess., 1958. H. Rep. 2261.

50. Raymond Dawson, "Congressional Innovation and Intervention in Defense Policy: Legislative Authorization of Weapons Systems," *American Political Science Review* 56, no. 1 (March 1962): 42–57.

51. Goldwater-Nichols Defense Reorganization Act of 1986, Public Law 99–433, 1986, and Committee on Armed Services, House of Representatives, *Conference Report,* 99th Cong., 2nd sess., 1986. H. Rep. 824.

Chapter 9

1. *Objections to This Constitution of Government,* memorandum presented to the Constitutional Convention, September 15, 1787. Excerpted in *The Anti-Federalist Papers and the Constitutional Convention Debates,* ed. Ralph Ketcham (New York: Mentor Books, 1986), quotation on page 175.

2. James Gleick, *Chaos: Making a New Science* (New York: Penguin, 1987); see also Jack Cohen and Ian Stewart, *The Collapse of Chaos: Discovering Simplicity in a Complex World* (New York: Viking, 1994).

3. Guy Gugliotta, "Partisanship Carries the Day; For Polar Opposites, Common Ground Nowhere to Be Found," *Washington Post,* December 13, 1998; Ian Christopher McCaleb, "Clinton's Impeachment: One Year Later, a Defining Moment Fades from the National Consciousness," CNN.com news analysis, December 17, 1999, http://archives.cnn.com/1999/ALLPOLITICS/stories/12/17/impeachment/index.html#THOSE.

4. Jennifer Harper, "If Nothing Else, Scandal Jarred an Indifferent Nation; Clinton's Acclaim Rose as Reputation Fell," *Washington Times,* February 13, 1999.

5. For instance, see Geoff Earle, "Dems Did Oversight Better, Says Grassley: Lawmakers Lament Lack of Scrutiny," *The Hill,* May 13, 2004, 1; Stephen Dinan, "Congress Urged to Take More Power," *Washington Times,* August 4, 2004; Rep. Henry A. Waxman, "Free Pass from Congress," (editorial), *Washington Post,* July 6, 2004; Victoria Toensing, "Oversee? More Like Overlook," *Washington Post,* June 13, 2004; Dan Morgan, "GOP Lawmakers Reclaim Purse Strings; Days of Little Oversight on Administration Spending Could Be Over," *Washington Post,* June 13, 2004.

6. Geoff Earle, "Dems Fear Lobbying Blacklist," *The Hill,* November 16, 2004, 1.

7. Bruce Oppenheimer makes the point that GOP leaders have surrendered much power to the executive with their style; this could cause electoral difficulties if the White House plans go awry. See "Abdicating Congressional Power: The Paradox of Republican Control," in *Congress Reconsidered,* 6th ed., ed. Lawrence Dodd and Bruce Oppenheimer (Washington, DC: Congressional Quarterly, 1997), 371–389.

8. Megan Scully, "Pentagon Investigations Stir the Pot on Capitol Hill," *The Hill,* February 16, 2005, 16.

9. Poll conducted June 10–15, 2005. Findings reported on *Congress: Overall Job Ratings,* www.pollingreport.com/job.htm.

10. For instance, see Joseph Cooper, ed., *Congress and the Decline of Public Trust* (Boulder, CO: Westview, 1999). Kenneth Mayer and David Cannon argue that the members' behavior helps them but hurts the institution in *The Dysfunctional Congress: The Individual Roots of an Institutional Dilemma* (Boulder, CO: Westview, 1999).

11. Roger Davidson and Walter Oleszek, *Congress and Its Members,* 9th ed. (Washington, DC: Congressional Quarterly, 2004), 456.

12. Lee Hamilton (D-IN), quoted in Davidson and Oleszek, *Congress and Its Members,* 463.

Selected Bibliography

"109th Congress: Statistically Speaking." *CQ Today,* November 4, 2004, 62.

Abramson, Paul, and John Aldrich. "The Decline of Electoral Participation in America." *American Political Science Review,* 76 (1982): 502–521.

Adams, Gordon. *The Iron Triangle: The Politics of Defense Contracting.* New York: Council on Economic Priorities, 1981.

Anderson, Fred. *Crucible of War.* New York: Vintage, 2000.

Anderson, James E. *Public Policymaking: An Introduction.* 25th ed. Boston, MA: Houghton Mifflin, 1994.

Arnold, R. Douglas. *Congress and the Bureaucracy.* New Haven, CT: Yale University Press, 1979.

———. *The Logic of Congressional Action.* New Haven, CT: Yale University Press, 1990.

Aviation and Transportation Security Act. 107th Cong., 1st sess., 2001. Public Law 107–171.

Aylmer, G.E. *Rebellion or Revolution? England 1640–1660.* Oxford: Oxford University Press, 1986.

Bailyn, Bernard. *The Peopling of British North America: An Introduction.* New York: Vintage, 1988.

———. *The Ideological Origins of the American Revolution.* Boston, MA: Belknap Press, 1992.

———. *To Begin the World Anew: The Genius and Ambiguities of the American Founders.* New York: Alfred A. Knopf, 2003.

Beth, Richard, and Stanley Bach. *Filibusters and Cloture in the Senate.* Report for Congress. Washington, DC: Congressional Research Service, 2003.

Bhattacharjee, Anjal. *Politics and Proliferation: Analysis and Summary of the Cox Committee Report and the Allegations of Chinese Nuclear Espionage.* Washington, DC: British American Security Information Committee, 1999.

Birkland, Thomas. *An Introduction to the Policy Process.* Armonk, NY: M.E. Sharpe, 2001.

Bond, Jon, and Richard Fleisher. *The President in the Legislative Arena.* Chicago: University of Chicago Press, 1990.

Bowen, Catherine Drinker. *Miracle at Philadelphia: The Story of the Constitutional Convention, May to September 1787.* Boston, MA: Back Bay Books, 1986.

Brown, Sherrod. *Congress from the Inside: Observations from the Majority and the Minority.* Ohio: Kent State University, 1999.

Cohen, Jack, and Ian Stewart. *The Collapse of Chaos: Discovering Simplicity in a Complex World.* New York: Viking, 1994.

Commission on National Security in the 21st Century. *New World Coming: American Security in the 21st Century.* Phase I Report. Washington, DC: Government Printing Office, 1999.

———. *Seeking a National Strategy: A Concert for Preserving Security and Promoting Freedom.* Phase II Report. Washington, DC: Government Printing Office, 2000.

———. *Roadmap for National Security: Imperative for Change.* Phase III Report. Washington, DC: Government Printing Office, 2001.

Commission to Assess the Ballistic Missile Threat to the United States. *Report of the Commission to Assess the Ballistic Missile Threat to the United States.* Washington, DC: Government Printing Office, 1998.

Committee on Armed Services, U.S. House of Representatives. *Conference Report,* 80th Cong., 1st sess., 1947. H. Rep. 1051.

———. *Conference Report,* 81st Cong., 1st sess., 1949. H. Rep. 1142.

———. *Conference Report,* 85th Cong., 2nd sess., 1958. H. Rep. 2261.

———. *Conference Report,* 99th Cong., 2nd sess., 1986. H. Rep. 99–700.

———. *Conference Report,* 99th Cong., 2nd sess., 1986. H. Rep. 824.

———. *Reserve Officer Personnel Management Act.* 102nd Cong., 2nd sess., 1992. H. Rep. 102–897.

Committee on Armed Services, U.S. Senate. *Defense Organization: The Need for Change.* 99th Cong., 1st sess., 1985. S. Rep. 99–86.

Committee on Government Operations, U.S. House of Representatives. 83rd Cong., 1st sess., 1953. H. Rep. 633.

———. *Message from the President of the United States Transmitting Reorganization Plan No. 6 of 1953, Defense Department.* 83rd Cong., 1st sess., 1953. H. Doc. 136.

Conover, Pamela, and Stanley Feldman. "How People Organize the Political World." *American Journal of Political Science* 28 (1984): 95–126.

Converse, Philip. "The Nature of Belief Systems in Mass Publics." In *Ideology and Discontent,* ed. David Apter, 206–261. New York: Free Press, 1964.

Cook, Timothy. *Governing with the News: The News Media as a Political Institution.* Chicago: University of Chicago Press, 1998.

Cooper, Joseph, ed. *Congress and the Decline of Public Trust.* Boulder, CO: Westview, 1999.

Cooper, Joseph, and David W. Brady. "Institutional Context and Leadership Style: The House from Cannon to Rayburn." *American Political Science Review* 75 (1981): 411–425.

Cordesman, Anthony, with the assistance of Patrick Baetjer and Stephen Lanier. *Strengthening Iraqi Military and Security Forces.* Working Draft update. Washington, DC: Center for Strategic and International Studies, February 17, 2005.

Cox, Gary, and Mathew McCubbins. *Legislative Leviathan: Party Government in the House.* Berkeley: University of California Press, 1993.

Crowe, William, with David Chanoff. *The Line of Fire: From Washington to the Gulf, the Politics and Battles of the New Military.* New York: Simon and Schuster, 1993.

Davidson, Roger. "The Senate: If Everybody Leads, Who Follows?" In *Congress Reconsidered,* ed. Lawrence Dodd and Bruce Oppenheimer, 4th ed., 275–306. Washington, DC: Congressional Quarterly, 1989.

Davidson, Roger, and Walter Oleszek. *Congress and Its Members.* 9th ed. Washington, DC: Congressional Quarterly, 2004.

Dawson, Raymond. Congressional Innovation and Intervention in Defense Policy: Legislative Authorization of Weapons Systems. *American Political Science Review* 56, 1 (March 1962): 42–57.

Deering, Christopher, ed. Decision Making in the Armed Services Committees. In *Congress Resurgent: Foreign and Defense Policy on Capitol Hill,* ed. Randall Ripley and James M. Lindsay. Ann Arbor: University of Michigan, 1993.

———. "Congress, the President, and Automatic Government: The Case of Military Base Closures." In *Rivals for Power,* ed. James Thurber, 153–169. Washington, DC: Congressional Quarterly, 1996.

———. *Congressional Politics.* Homewood, IL: Dorsey Press, 1998.

Department of Defense Reorganization Act of 1958. Public Law 85–599. 85th Cong., 2nd sess.

Deschler, Lewis. *Deschler's Precedents Including References to Provisions of the Constitution and Laws, and to Decisions of the Courts.* 94th Cong., 2nd sess., 1976. H. Doc. 94–661.

Downs, Anthony. *An Economic Theory of Democracy.* New York: HarperCollins, 1957.

Edwards, George, and Stephen Wayne. *Presidential Leadership: Politics and Policy Making.* 2nd ed. New York: St. Martin's Press, 1990.

Ellis, Joseph. *Founding Brothers: The Revolutionary Generation.* New York: Alfred A. Knopf, 2000.

———. *His Excellency George Washington.* New York: Alfred A. Knopf, 2004.

Ely, John Hart. "Suppose Congress Wanted a War Powers Act That Worked." *Columbia Law Review* 88, no. 7 (November 1988): 1379–1431.

Evans, C. Lawrence. *Leadership in Committee: A Comparative Analysis of Leadership Behavior in the U.S. Senate.* Ann Arbor: University of Michigan, 2001.

Fallows, James. *Breaking the News: How the Media Undermine American Democracy.* New York: Vintage, 1997.

Farnham, Barbara, special ed. *Political Psychology.* Special Issue: Prospect Theory and Political Psychology 13, no. 2 (June 1992).

Feldman, Stanley. "Structure and Consistency in Public Opinion: The Role of Core Beliefs and Values." *American Journal of Political Science* 32 (1988): 416–440.

Fenno, Richard. *Congressmen in Committees.* Boston, MA: Little, Brown, 1973.

Fiorina, Morris. *Retrospective Voting in American National Elections.* New Haven, CT: Yale University Press, 1981.

———. *Congress: Keystone of the Washington Establishment.* 2nd ed. New Haven, CT: Yale University Press, 1989.

Fisher, Louis. "Congressional Checks on Military Initiatives." *Political Science Quarterly* 109, no. 5 (Winter 1994–95): 739–762.

———. *The Politics of Shared Power.* 4th ed. College Station: Texas A & M University, 1998.

Fisher, Louis, and David Adler. "The War Powers Resolution: Time to Say Goodbye." *Political Science Quarterly* 113, no. 1 (Spring 1998): 1–20.

Foreign Affairs Reform and Restructuring Act of 1998. Included as part of the Omnibus Appropriations Act, FY99. 105th Cong., 2nd sess., Public Law 105–277.

Forgette, Richard. *Congress, Parties, and Puzzles: Politics as a Team Sport.* New York: Peter Lang, 2004.

Galbraith, James. *Created Unequal.* Chicago: University of Chicago, 2000.

Gill, Jeff and Jason Gainous. "Why Does Voting Get so Complicated? A Review of Theories for Analyzing Democratic Participation." *Statistical Science* 17, no. 4 (2002): 383–404.

Giroux, Gregory. "A Touch of Gray on Capitol Hill." *CQ Weekly Report,* January 31, 2005, 240–243.

Gleick, James. *Chaos: Making a New Science.* New York: Penguin, 1987.

Goldwater-Nichols Defense Reorganization Act of 1986. 99th Cong., 2nd sess. Public Law 99–433.

Gormley, William, and Steven Balla. *Bureaucracy and Democracy: Accountability and Performance.* Washington, DC: Congressional Quarterly, 2004.

Green, Donald, and Ian Shapiro. *Pathologies of Rational Choice Theory.* New Haven, CT: Yale University Press, 1994.

Haig, Alexander, with Charles McCarry. *Inner Circle: How America Changed the World.* New York: Warner Books, 1992.

Hall, Richard L. *Participation in Congress.* New Haven, CT: Yale University Press, 1996.

Hall, Richard L., and Bernard Grofman. "The Committee Assignment Process and the Conditional Nature of Committee Bias." *American Political Science Review* 84 (1990): 1149–1166.

Hall, Richard L., and Frank W. Wayman. "Buying Time: Moneyed Interests and the Mobilization of Bias in Congressional Committees. *American Political Science Review,* 84 (1990): 797–820.

Halperin, Morton. *Bureaucratic Politics and Foreign Policy.* Washington, DC: Brookings Institution, 1974.

Hammond, Paul Y. *Organizing for Defense.* Princeton, NJ: Princeton University Press, 1961.

Hammond, Susan Webb. "Congressional Caucuses in the 104th Congress." In *Congress Reconsidered,* ed. Lawrence Dodd and Bruce Oppenheimer, 6th ed., 274–292. Washington, DC: Congressional Quarterly, 1997.

Hawkings, Betsy Wright, ed. *Setting Course: A Congressional Management Guide.* Washington, DC: Congressional Management Foundation, 1996.

Heineman, Robert, William Bluhm, Steven Peterson, and Edward Kearny. *The World of the Policy Analyst.* Chatham, NJ: Chatham House, 1990.

Herrnson, Paul. *Congressional Elections.* 2nd ed. Washington, DC: Congressional Quarterly, 1998.

Hess, Stephen. *The Government/Press Connection: Press Officers and Their Offices.* Washington, DC: Brookings Institution, 1984.

Hill, Christopher. *The Experience of Defeat: Milton and Some Contemporaries.* London: Penguin, 1985.

Hobbes, Thomas. *Leviathan,* ed. Michael Oakeshott. New York: Collier Books, 1962.

Holt, Michael. *The Rise and Fall of the American Whig Party: Jacksonian Politics and the Onset of the Civil War.* Oxford: Oxford, 1999.

House of Representatives. Conference Report. 99th Cong., 2nd sess., 1986. H. Rep. 99–824.

———. *Message from the President Transmitting His Views on the Future Strength and Organization of Our Defense Establishment.* 99th Cong., 2nd sess., 1986. H. Doc. 209.

Huber, John, and Charles Shipan. *Deliberate Discretion? The Institutional Foundations of Bureaucratic Autonomy.* Cambridge: Cambridge University Press, 2002.

Iyengar, Shanto, and Donald Kinder. *News That Matters.* Chicago: University of Chicago Press, 1987.

Iyengar, Shanto, Mark Peters, and Donald Kinder. "Experimental Demonstrations of the 'Not-So-Minimal' Consequences of Television News Programs." *American Political Science Review* 76 (1982): 848–858.

Janos, Andrew. *Politics and Paradigms: Changing Theories of Change in Social Science.* Stanford, CA: Stanford University Press, 1986.

Johnson, Dennis. *Congress Online.* New York: Routledge, 2004.

Jones, Bryan, Frank Baumgartner, and Jeffrey Talbert. "The Destruction of Issue Monopolies in Congress." *American Political Science Review* 87 (1993): 657–671.

Jones, Charles O. *Separate but Equal Branches: Congress and the Presidency.* Chatham, NJ: Chatham House, 1995.

Judis, John. *The Paradox of American Democracy.* New York: Routledge, 2000.

Kahneman, Daniel, and Amos Tversky. "Choices, Values, and Frames." *American Psychologist* 39 (1984): 341–350.

Kaiser, Frederick. *Congressional Oversight.* CRS Report for Congress. Washington, DC: Library of Congress, January 2, 2001. 97–936 GOV.

Kauffman, Stuart. *At Home in the Universe: The Search for the Laws of Self-Organization and Complexity.* Oxford: Oxford University Press, 1995.

Kazee, Thomas, ed. *Who Runs for Congress?* Washington, DC: Congressional Quarterly, 1994.

Kernell, Samuel. *Going Public.* Washington, DC: Congressional Quarterly, 1993.

Kerwin, Cornelius. *Rulemaking.* Washington, DC: Congressional Quarterly, 1994.

Kessler, David. *A Question of Intent: A Great American Battle with a Deadly Industry.* New York: PublicAffairs, 2001.

Ketcham, Ralph, ed. *The Anti-Federalist Papers and the Constitutional Convention Debates.* New York: Mentor Books, 1986.

Kettl, Donald. *The Department of Homeland Security's First Year: A Report Card.* New York: Century Foundation, 2004.

Kiewiet, D. Roderick, and Mathew McCubbins. *The Logic of Delegation.* Chicago: University of Chicago Press, 1991.

King, David. *Turf Wars: How Congressional Committees Claim Jurisdiction.* Chicago: University of Chicago Press, 1997.

Kingdon, John. *Agendas, Alternatives, and Public Policies.* New York: HarperCollins, 1984.

———. *Congressmen's Voting Decisions.* 3rd ed. Ann Arbor: University of Michigan, 1989.

Kishlansky, Mark. *A Monarchy Transformed: Britain 1603–1714.* London: Penguin, 1996.

Knott, Jack H., and Gary J. Miller. *Reforming Bureaucracy: The Politics of Institutional Choice.* Englewood Cliffs, NJ: Prentice-Hall, 1987.

Koempel, Michael, and Judy Schneider. *Congressional Desk Book 2003–2004.* Washington, DC: Capitol.Net, 2003.

Koford, Kenneth. "Dimensions in Congressional Voting." *American Political Science Review* 83, no. 3 (September 1989): 949–962.

Kohn, Richard. *Eagle and Sword: The Beginnings of the Military Establishment in America.* New York: Free Press, 1985.

Kosko, Bart. *Fuzzy Thinking: The New Science of Fuzzy Logic.* New York: Hyperion, 1993.

Krehbiel, Keith. *Information and Legislative Organization.* Ann Arbor: University of Michigan Press, 1991.

Krueger, Anne, et al. "Report of the Commission on Graduate Education in Economics." *Journal of Economic Literature* 29, no. 3 (September 1991): 1035–1053.

Kull, Steven, and I.M. Destler. *Misreading the Public: The Myth of a New Isolationism.* Washington, DC: Brookings Institution, 1999.

Kurland, Philip B., and Ralph Lerner, eds. *The Founders' Constitution.* Vol. 2, Document 15. Chicago: University of Chicago Press, 1986. Excerpted from Jonathan Elliot, ed., *The Debates in the Several State Conventions on the Adoption of the Federal Constitution as Recommended by the General Convention at Philadelphia in 1787.* 5 vols. 2nd ed. 1888. Reprint. New York: Burt Franklin, n.d., http://press-pubs.uchicago.edu/founders/documents/a1_8_1s15.html.

Laitin, David. "The Civic Culture at 30." Book review. *American Political Science Review* 89 (1995): 168–173.

Landy, Marc, and Martin Levin, eds. *The New Politics of Public Policy.* Baltimore, MD: Johns Hopkins University Press, 1994.

Lee, Frances, and Bruce Oppenheimer. *Sizing up the Senate: The Unequal Consequences of Equal Representation.* Chicago: University of Chicago Press, 1999.

Lepore, Jill. *The Name of War: King Philip's War and the Origins of American Identity.* New York: Alfred A. Knopf, 1998.

Levy, Jack S. "Prospect Theory and International Relations: Theoretical Applications and Analytical Problems." *Political Psychology* 13 (1992): 283–311.

Light, Paul C. *The President's Agenda.* Rev. ed. Baltimore, MD: Johns Hopkins University Press, 1991.

Lindblom, Charles. "The Science of 'Muddling Through.'" *Public Administration Review* 19, no. 2 (1959): 79–88.

Locke, John. *Two Treatises of Government,* ed. Peter Laslett. New York: Mentor Books, 1963.

MacKuen, Michael, Robert Erikson, and James Stimson. "Macropartisanship." *American Political Science Review* 83 (1989): 1125–1142.

Maltese, John Anthony. *Spin Control: The White House Office of Communications and the Management of Presidential News.* 2nd ed. Chapel Hill: University of North Carolina Press, 1994.

Maltzman, Forrest. *Competing Principals: Committees, Parties, and the Organization of Congress.* Ann Arbor: University of Michigan Press, 1997.

Maraniss, David, and Michael Weisskopf. *"Tell Newt to Shut Up!"* Prizewinning Washington Post *Journalists Reveal How Reality Gagged the Gingrich Revolution.* New York: Simon and Schuster Touchstone Books, 1996.

Mayer, Kenneth, and David Cannon. *The Dysfunctional Congress: The Individual Roots of an Institutional Dilemma.* Boulder, CO: Westview, 1999.

Mayhew, David. *Congress: The Electoral Connection.* New Haven, CT: Yale University Press, 1974.

———. *Divided We Govern.* New Haven, CT: Yale University Press, 1991.

McCubbins, Matthew, and Thomas Schwartz. Congressional Oversight Overlooked: Police Patrols Versus Fire Alarms. *American Journal of Political Science* 28, no. 1 (February 1984): 165–179.

McCullough, David. *John Adams.* New York: Simon and Schuster, 2001.

McDonald, Michael P. "A Comparative Analysis of Redistricting Institutions in the

United States, 2001–02." *State Politics and Policy Quarterly* 4, no. 4 (Winter 2004): 371–395.

Milligan, Susan. "Back-room Dealing a Capitol Trend; GOP Flexing Its Majority Power." *Boston Globe,* October 3, 2004.

Moe, Ronald. *Administrative Renewal: Reorganization Commissions in the 20th Century.* Lanham, MD: University Press of America, 2003.

de Montaigne, Michel. *Essays.* Translated by J.M. Cohen. New York: Penguin, 1958.

Montesquieu (Charles de Secondat, Baron de la Brède et de Montesquieu). *The Spirit of the Laws.* In *Selected Political Writings,* ed. Melvin Richter. Indianapolis, IN: Hackett, 1990.

Morton, A.L, ed. *Freedom in Arms: A Selection of Leveller Writings.* New York: International Publishers, 1974.

National Commission on Terrorist Attacks Upon the United States. *Report of the National Commission on Terrorist Attacks Upon the United States.* Washington, DC: Government Printing Office, 2004.

National Missile Defense Act of 1999. 106th Cong., 1st sess. Public Law 105–39.

National Security Act of 1947. 80th Cong., 1st sess. Public Law 80–253.

National Security Amendments of 1949. 81st Cong., 2nd sess. Public Law 81–216.

Neustadt, Richard E. *Presidential Power and the Modern Presidents.* New York: Free Press, 1990.

Nicholson, Adam. *God's Secretaries: The Making of the King James Bible.* New York: Perennial, 2003.

Office of Management and Budget. *Budget of the United States Government, Fiscal Year 2006.* Washington, DC: Government Printing Office, 2005.

O'Neill, Thomas "Tip", with William Novak. 1987. *Man of the House: The Life and Political Memoirs of Speaker Tip O'Neill.* New York: Random House, 1987.

Oleszek, Walter J. *Congressional Procedures and the Policy Process.* 3rd ed. Washington, DC: Congressional Quarterly, 1989.

Osborne, David, and Ted Gaebler. *Reinventing Government.* New York: Plume, 1993.

Palmer, Dave R. *1794: America, Its Army, and the Birth of the Nation.* Novato, CA: Presidio, 1994.

Parker, Richard. *John Kenneth Galbraith: His Life, His Politics, His Economics.* New York: Farrar, Straus and Giroux, 2005.

Paulos, John Allen. *A Mathematician Reads the Newspaper.* New York: Basic Books, 1995.

Peabody, Robert. *Leadership in Congress: Stability, Succession and Change.* Boston, MA: Little, Brown, 1976.

Peters, Ronald. *The American Speakership: The Office in Historical Perspective.* 2nd ed. Baltimore, MD: Johns Hopkins University Press, 1997.

Pfeiffer, Andrew, ed. *Television News Index and Abstracts.* Nashville, TN: Vanderbilt Television News Archive, 1989–1992.

Poole, Keith, and Howard Rosenthal. "A Spatial Model for Legislative Roll Call Analysis." *American Journal of Political Science* 29, no. 2 (May 1985): 357–384.

Powell, Colin, with Joseph Persico. *My American Journey.* New York: Random House, 1995.

Price, David E. *Bringing Back the Parties.* Washington, DC: Congressional Quarterly, 1984.

———. *The Congressional Experience: Transforming American Politics.* 3rd ed. Boulder, CO: Westview, 2004.

Quattrone, George, and Amos Tversky. "Contrasting Rational and Psychological Analyses of Political Choice." *American Political Science Review* 82 (1988): 719–736.

Ragin, Charles. *The Comparative Method: Moving Beyond Qualitative and Quantitative Strategies.* Berkeley: University of California Press, 1989.

Ricci, David. *The Transformation of American Politics: The New Washington and the Rise of the Think Tanks.* New Haven, CT: Yale University Press, 1993.

Riddick, Floyd. 1992. *Riddick's Senate Procedure: Precedents and Practices,* rev. and ed. Alan Frumin. 101st Cong., 2nd sess., 1992. S. Doc. 101–128.

Ripley, Randall. 1969. *Power in the Senate.* New York: St. Martin's Press, 1969.

Ripley, Randall, and Grace A. Franklin. *Congress, the Bureaucracy, and Public Policy.* 5th ed. Pacific Grove, CA: Brooks/Cole, 1991.

Ripley, Randall, and James M. Lindsay, ed. *Congress Resurgent: Foreign and Defense Policy on Capitol Hill.* Ann Arbor: University of Michigan Press, 1993.

Rohde, David. *Parties and Leaders in the Post-Reform House.* Chicago: University of Chicago Press, 1991.

Rosenbloom, David. *Building a Legislative-Centered Public Administration.* Tuscaloosa: University of Alabama Press, 2000.

———. "'Whose Bureaucracy Is This, Anyway?' Congress' 1946 Answer." *PS: Political Science & Politics* 34, no. 4 (December 2001): 773–775.

Rossiter, Clinton, ed. *The Federalist Papers.* New York: Mentor Books, 1961.

Rousseau, Jean-Jacques. *On the Social Contract.* In *The Basic Political Writings,* trans. Donald A. Cress, 141–227. Indianapolis, IN: Hackett, 1987.

de Rugy, Veronique. *What Does Homeland Security Spending Buy?* AEI Working Paper #107. Washington, DC: American Enterprise Institute, 2004.

Sabatier, Paul, ed. *Theories of the Policy Process.* Boulder, CO: Westview, 1999.

Sanjian, Gregory. "Fuzzy Set Theory and U.S. Arms Transfers: Modeling the Decision-Making Process." *American Journal of Political Science* 32 (1988): 1018–1046.

Sartori, Giovanni. *The Theory of Democracy Revisited, I: The Contemporary Debate.* Chatham, NJ: Chatham House, 1987.

———. *The Theory of Democracy Revisited, II: The Classical Issues.* Chatham, NJ: Chatham House, 1987.

Schama, Simon. *A History of Britain: At the Edge of the World, 3500 B.C.–1603 A.D.* New York: Miramax, 2000.

———. *A History of Britain. Vol. II, The Wars of the British, 1603–1776.* New York: Talk Miramax Books, 2001.

Schattschneider, E.E. *The Semisovereign People.* Fort Worth, TX: Harcourt Brace Jovanovich, 1988.

Select Committee on U.S. National Security and Military/Commercial Concerns with the People's Republic of China, U.S. House of Representatives. *Report of the House of Representatives Select Committee on U.S. National Security and Military/Commercial Concerns with the People's Republic of China.* 106th Cong., 1st sess., 1999.

Senate Select Committee on Intelligence and House Permanent Select Committee on Intelligence. *Joint Inquiry into Intelligence Community Activities Before and After the Terrorist Attacks of September 11, 2001.* 107th Cong., 2nd sess., 2002. S. Rep. 107–351 and H. Rep. 107–792.

Senate Select Committee to Study Governmental Operations with Respect to Intelligence Activities (Church Commission). *Final Report of the Select Committee to*

Study Governmental Operations With Respect to Intelligence Activities. 94th Cong., 2nd sess., 1976. S. Rep. 94–755.

Shepsle, Kenneth, and Barry Weingast. "Structure-Induced Equilibrium and Legislative Choice." *Public Choice* 37 (1981): 503–521.

Shipan, Charles. *Designing Judicial Review.* Ann Arbor: University of Michigan Press, 1997.

Shively, W. Phillips. *The Craft of Political Research.* 3rd ed. Englewood Cliffs, NJ: Prentice Hall, 1990.

Sinclair, Barbara. *Majority Leadership in the U.S. House.* Baltimore, MD: Johns Hopkins University Press, 1983.

———. "House Majority Leadership in the 1980s." In *Congress Reconsidered,* ed. Lawrence Dodd and Bruce Oppenheimer, 4th ed., 307–330. Washington, DC: Congressional Quarterly, 1989.

———. *Legislators, Leaders, and Lawmaking.* Baltimore, MD: Johns Hopkins University Press, 1995.

———. *Unorthodox Lawmaking.* Washington, DC: Congressional Quarterly, 1995.

Skocpol, Theda. *The Missing Middle: Working Families and the Future of American Social Policy.* New York: W.W. Norton, 2000.

Skowronek, Stephen. *Building a New American State: The Expansion of National Administrative Capacities, 1877–1920.* Cambridge: Cambridge University Press, 1982.

Smith, Steven. *Call to Order: Floor Politics in the House and Senate.* Washington, DC: Brookings Institution, 1989.

Smith, Steven, and Christopher Deering. *Committees in Congress.* 2nd ed. Washington, DC: Congressional Quarterly, 1990.

Somerville, J.P. *Politics and Ideology in England, 1603–1640.* London: Longman, 1986.

Sontag, Sherry, Christopher Drew, and Annette Lawrence Drew. *Blind Man's Bluff: The Untold Story of American Submarine Espionage.* New York: PublicAffairs, 1998.

Stewart, Ian. *Nature's Numbers: The Unreal Reality of Mathematics.* New York: Basic Books, 1995.

Stillman, Richard. *Preface to Public Administration: A Search for Themes and Direction.* New York: St. Martin's Press, 1991.

Stone, Deborah. *Policy Paradox: The Art of Political Decision Making.* Rev. ed. New York: W.W. Norton, 2002.

Sullivan, Terry. "Headcounts, Expectations, and Presidential Coalitions in Congress." *American Journal of Political Science* 32 (1988): 567–589.

Sundquist, James. *The Decline and Resurgence of Congress.* Washington, DC: Brookings Institution, 1981.

Swift, Elaine. "The Electoral Connection Meets the Past, 1789–1899." *Political Science Quarterly,* 102 (Winter 1988): 625–645.

———. "Reconstitutive Chance in the U.S. Congress: The Early Senate, 1789–1841." *Legislative Studies Quarterly* 14 (May 1989): 175–203.

Tversky, Amos, and Daniel Kahneman. "The Framing of Decisions and the Psychology of Choice." *Science* 211 (1981): 453–458.

VanDoren, Peter. "Can We Learn the Causes of Congressional Decisions from Roll-Call Data?" *Legislative Studies Quarterly* 15 (1990): 311–340.

Van Horn, Carl, Donald Baumer, and William Gormley. *Politics and Public Policy.* 3rd ed. Washington, DC: Congressional Quarterly, 2001.

Verba, Sidney, and Norman Nie. *Participation in America.* Chicago: University of Chicago Press, 1972.

Waldman, Sidney. "How Congress Does the Difficult." *PS: Political Science and Politics* 33, no. 4 (December 2000): 803–808.

Waldrop, M. Mitchell. *Complexity: The Emerging Science at the Edge of Order and Chaos.* New York: Touchstone Books, 1992.

Weatherford, J. McIver. *Tribes on the Hill: The US Congress—Rituals and Reality.* Westport, CT: Bergin and Garvey, 1985.

Weigley, Russell. *The American Way of War: A History of United States Military Strategy and Policy.* Bloomington: Indiana University Press, 1977.

Weingast, Barry, and William Marshall. "The Industrial Organization of Congress: Or Why Legislatures, Like Firms, Are Not Organized as Markets." *Journal of Political Economy* 96 (1988): 132–163.

White House. *A National Security Strategy of Engagement and Enlargement.* Washington, DC: Government Printing Office, 1996.

———. *National Strategy for Homeland Security.* Washington, DC: Government Printing Office, 2002.

Wildavsky, Aaron. *The Politics of the Budgetary Process.* 4th ed. Boston, MA: Little, Brown, 1984.

———. *The New Politics of the Budgetary Process.* Upper Saddle River, NJ: Scott, Foresman, 1988.

Wills, Garry. *Certain Trumpets: The Call of Leaders.* New York: Simon and Schuster, 1994.

Wilson, James Q. *Bureaucracy: What Government Agencies Do and Why They Do It.* New York: Basic Books, 1989.

Wolpe, Bruce, and Bertram Levine. *Lobbying Congress: How the System Works.* 2nd ed. Washington, DC: Congressional Quarterly, 1996.

Woodhouse, A.S.P. ed. *Puritanism and Liberty: Being the Army Debates (1647–9) from the Clarke Manuscripts with Supplementary Documents.* London: J.M. Dent, 1951.

Woodward, Carl. *The Commanders.* New York: Simon and Schuster, 1991.

Index

Office of Technology Assessment (OTA),
108–9
Office of U.S. Trade Representative, 146
O'Neill, Thomas P., 16
Organization/organizing power, 5, 155
assessment of, 151–53, 173–74
challenge of reorganization, 145–51
major reorganizations, 148–51
within jurisdictions, 146–48
historical overview of, 141–45
importance of, 138–39
organization as policy, 139–45
Oversight committees, 99, 101–7, 110
Oversight power, 5, 14–16, 19, 97–99,
155
assessment of, 112–13, 173–74
beyond regular oversight, 110–12
committee oversight, 99, 101–7, 110
congressional agency oversight, 107–10
courts and other influences, 99
defined, 99–101
individual/committee oversight, 101–2
select committee/independent
investigation, 110
techniques for, 103
use of, 101
Overton, Richard, 25

P

Panama invasion, 16
Paper tax, 32
"Parent's Advisory" stickers, 78
Parliamentary rule, 24–27
Parochialism, 5
Partisanship, 5, 39–40, 68–69, 81, 92–93,
177–79
Party leaders, 62, 81
Patton Boggs, 9
Peace of Paris (1784), 34
Pendleton Act (1883), 141
Persian Gulf War, 16, 172
Policy actors/domains, 6–7
Policy patterns, 13–19
committee-driven patterns, 13
cooperative patterns, 13

Policy patterns *(continued)*
nonparticipatory patterns, 13
oversight power and, 104
summary of, 18
top-down pattern, 13
"Policy stages" model, 6
Policy types, 11–13
crisis policies, 12
defense and foreign policies, 12
distributive policies, 12
domestic policies, 12
redistributive policies, 12
regulatory policies, 12
strategic policies, 12
structural policies, 12
Political corruption, 32
Political parties, 38–39, 81–84, 180
Politics
partisanship and, 39–40, 177–79
values-based approach, 8
Pork barrel politics, 15
President, 7, 9, 11
President-centered budgeting, 119
Press secretary, 52
Price, David, 3
Private sector, 9
Progressive Era, 39–40, 118, 141–45, 153
Public administration, depoliticizing of,
144
Public-interest groups, 9–10, 96
Public opinion, 7
Public policymaking
agenda setting, 6
Congress and, 4–5, 9
congressional committees, 9
evaluation of, 6
key participants in, 9
Kingdon's model of, 6–7
nonofficial players in, 9–11
outside/inside groups, 7–11
policy patterns, 13–19
policy types, 11–13
private sector and, 9
public and, 11
rational choice in, 8
selecting policy option to pursue, 6

About the Author

Charles B. Cushman Jr. is associate professor and director of the Master of Arts in Legislative Affairs program in the Graduate School of Political Management at The George Washington University. His research focuses on Congress's roles in national security policymaking. He did his graduate training at the University of North Carolina at Chapel Hill and is a graduate of West Point. Before joining the faculty at GW, he was an army officer, a defense consultant and a lobbyist working to advance peace in the Middle East, and a legislative assistant to Rep. David Price (D-NC) in the 105th Congress.